IMAGES
of America

RICHMOND

ON THE COVER: This 1933 photograph depicts an early Black and White Days dairy cattle show. Known as the largest cattle show west of the Mississippi, for years Black and White Days has been attracting proud dairy farmers eager to show off their finest animals. This image was taken from the east, looking west over what are now softball and soccer fields. Notice the old Richmond Park School, which was demolished in the 1990s.

IMAGES
of America

RICHMOND

Cheri Housley, Marie Lundgreen,
and Kathy Jones

ARCADIA
PUBLISHING

ISBN 978-0-7385-8478-2

Published by Arcadia Publishing
Charleston, South Carolina

Printed in the United States of America

Library of Congress Control Number: 2011929764

For all general information, please contact Arcadia Publishing:
Telephone 843-853-2070
Fax 843-853-0044
E-mail sales@arcadiapublishing.com
For customer service and orders:
Toll-Free 1-888-313-2665

Visit us on the Internet at www.arcadiapublishing.com

To the residents of Richmond, past, present, and future,
who make this little town something special

Contents

ACKNOWLEDGMENTS

We would like to thank all those who have contributed to this work through their sharing of family photographs, histories, and stories. The foundation of the collection began in 1907 with the establishment of the Richmond Camp of the Daughters of Utah Pioneers. The collection is housed in the current James and Drusilla Hendricks Camp Relic Hall. We realize not all of the early families are represented. To ensure a more complete collection for future generations, we will continue to collect, preserve, and house any and all relevant items and artifacts pertaining to the history of Richmond.

We would especially like to extend a big thank you to Holly Broome-Hyer for the countless hours she quietly donated to the making of this book. Also, thank you to the many families who dug deep to provide us with treasured family photographs and stories.

All photographs in this book are courtesy of the James and Drusilla Hendricks Camp Relic Hall, unless otherwise noted.

INTRODUCTION

In 1855, a group of men, including John Bair, journeyed from their homes in Salt Lake and Box Elder Counties to see what was on the other side of the mountain. When they arrived in Cache Valley, they were impressed with its beauty, its abundance of water and grass, and its seemingly favorable climate. They determined that when the time came, they would stake claims in the valley and make it their home.

Four years later, in July 1859, John Bair made the move. The area around Smithfield was his original destination, but on arrival he discovered that others had already claimed that land. He and his party moved on a little farther north. There they found that a man named Agrippa Cooper had already staked a claim and was residing there with his family. The group settled nearby, close to a natural spring that would later to be known as Brower Spring, which is on the west side of the current highway about midway through town. They erected some temporary shelters, cut and stacked wild hay, and then returned home to retrieve their families. They returned in October, when it was too late to plant crops, and had to make do with very little that first winter. Those first arrivals included the families of John Bair, Moroni Cole, Isaac Shepherd, Justin Shepherd, William Aller, Joseph Biddlecomb, William H. Lewis, Margaret Petty, Thomas Petty, Hyrum Bair, Enoch Daly, Alvin F. Stewart, Henry Gibson, Gilbert Bright, Sally Petty, the widow Petty and her children, the widow Gool, and the Crandall family. There was also a man called Hell-fire Jack, whose true name was never recorded. They lived in their wagon boxes and dugouts that first winter, subsisting on boiled wheat and whatever they could hunt. The town's first baby, Rebecca Lewis, was born in November in a wagon box near City Creek.

The next spring heralded an influx of settlers, and Richmond was born. Most agree that the town was named after the Church of Jesus Christ of Latter-day Saints apostle Charles C. Rich, but there are those who believe it was named after the rich soil in the area. Still others contend that it was named in honor of the hometown in England of some of the settlers. The Church of Jesus Christ of Latter-Day Saints President Brigham Young visited the settlement and advised that a new fort be built a little to the northeast, an area better suited to warding off Indian attacks. Two rows of log cabins were built along each side of the current Main Street. The southwest corner of the fort can be located today, as a stone monument has been placed there by the Daughters of Utah Pioneers, just off the highway in what is now the city park.

Being located at the geographic center of Cache Valley, the town flourished, becoming a center of business and industry. Among the first industries was a shingle mill, which was built northeast of the settlement by W.D. Hendricks, who also built a gristmill in the same area. He partnered with W.T. Van Noy to open a horse-powered sawmill. His ambition and work ethic led to him being elected Richmond's first mayor. The first permanent building, erected in the town in 1860, was a combination meeting hall and school. It was built of adobe bricks and was located approximately where the current fire station stands today.

Richmond thrived, with the population eventually reaching nearly 5,000 people, almost double what it is today. Main Street contained a wide variety of shops, including Monson Lumber, furniture stores, confectioneries, cafés, millinery shops, a barbershop, markets, and saloons. It was home to an early J.C. Penney and Zion's Cooperative Mercantile Institution (ZCMI). Over time, people began to drift south toward Logan, which had become a good-sized city, and the population and business base of Richmond began to shrink. Still, it remained an important town because it had the largest condensed-milk plant in the west. A dairy cow show, later known as Black and White Days, was organized in 1913 and is today the largest and longest-running dairy cow show west of the Mississippi River.

The Church of Jesus Christ of Latter-day Saints has always maintained a strong presence and influence on the town. Church apostle Marriner W. Merrill made his home there and is buried in the local cemetery next to several of his wives. There was at one time a large population of Presbyterians, who contributed greatly to the growth and quality of the area. For a time in the early 1900s, the town was home to several members of the Reorganized Church, but their presence faded almost as quickly as it came. Today, Richmond is predominantly Church of Jesus Christ of Latter-day Saints, but members of other faiths find it a most tolerant and pleasant place to settle, as the people are open-minded and neighborly.

Because of its location on the main highway, Richmond has been home to many of the north county schools. It has had several elementary schools, including Richmond High School, Park Elementary, North Cache High School, North Cache Junior High, North Cache Middle School, and White Pine Middle School. Today, it is home to one elementary school and two middle schools. Richmond has come a long way since the opening in 1860 of its first one-room school, where schoolmasters Henry Standage and David P. Rainey presided. Education has always been an important issue in Richmond. This is one reason the town qualified for a Carnegie Library, which is still in use today. Helen Keller made a stop in town once, giving a very well-attended lecture at the old opera house.

Over the years, people and businesses have come and gone, each leaving their mark on this little northern Utah town. This book covers only some of the events from Richmond's first 100 years. Many of the early families of Richmond have had much written about them in various publications, and their names are familiar. Others have not been recognized as often, but they nevertheless played an important part in the evolution of the town. A history book is never finished, as new history is written daily. Nor is it possible to include everyone and everything in a single book. With that in mind, the authors hope that readers will find some interest and enjoyment in the photographs and stories included here. If ever in northern Utah, slow down, get off the highway, and take a closer look at Richmond. We welcome you.

One

Every Face Tells a Story

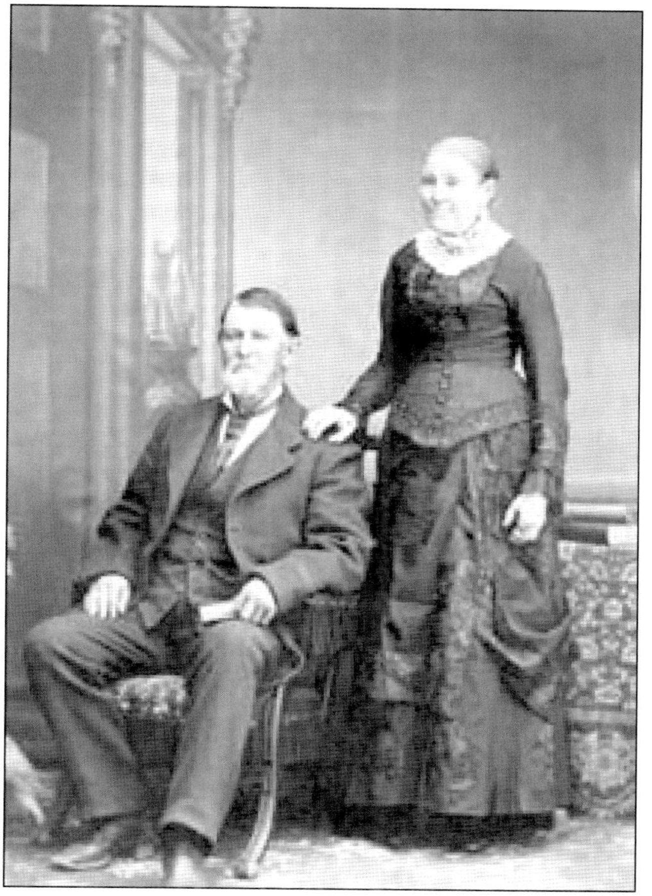

Ariah Coats Brower is pictured with his third wife, Mary Jane Humphreys Brower. Born in 1817 in New York, Ariah arrived in Richmond in 1859. He settled near a natural spring, which came to be known as Brower Springs, on the west side of the current highway. He eventually built a home there for his plural wives. The home still stands today. It is owned and occupied by Helen Robinson.

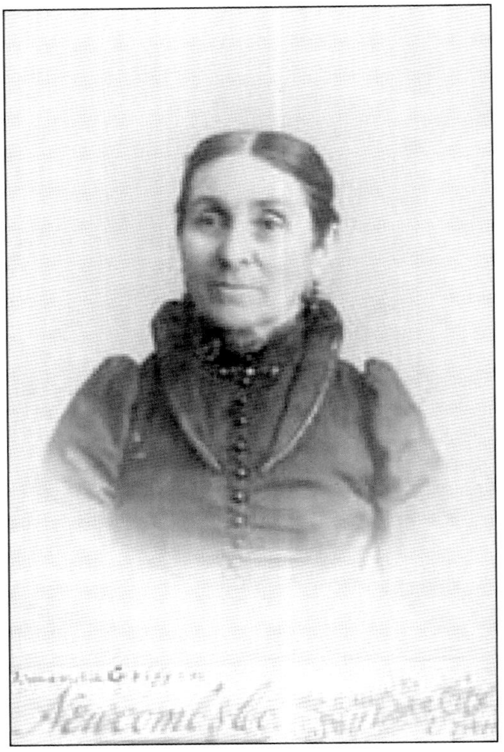

Amanda Ellen Perkins Griffin came to Utah in 1850. She married Thomas Griffin in 1856. They moved to Richmond in 1860, where they raised their family. She was the daughter of Ute and Anna Perkins, who also settled in Richmond. Many of the family's artifacts can be found at the Richmond Relic Hall.

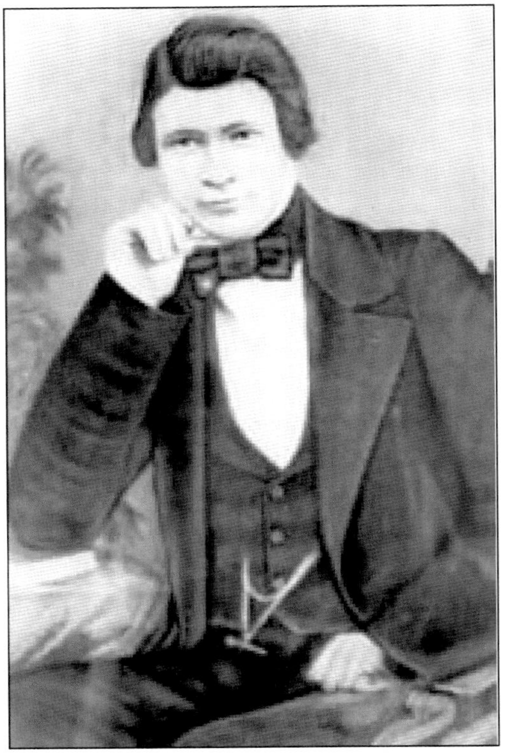

Thomas Griffin was born in Birmingham, England, in 1828. He settled in Richmond in 1860, where he would own a machine and blacksmith shop. Griffin built a working scale model of a steam engine and was awarded the silver medal for it at the Deseret Agriculture and Manufacturing Fair in 1856. He led the Richmond Brass Band, brought the first pump organ to Cache Valley, and served six terms as mayor of Richmond before his death in 1912.

Henrietta Rogers Standage was born in 1832 in Shalersville, Ohio. She became a plural wife to Henry Standage in 1851 in Salt Lake City, Utah. She received her endowments in the Nauvoo Temple at the age of 13. She was the mother of 10 children. She resided in Richmond most of her married life, later moving to Mesa, Arizona, with her husband and his first wife. She died there in 1898.

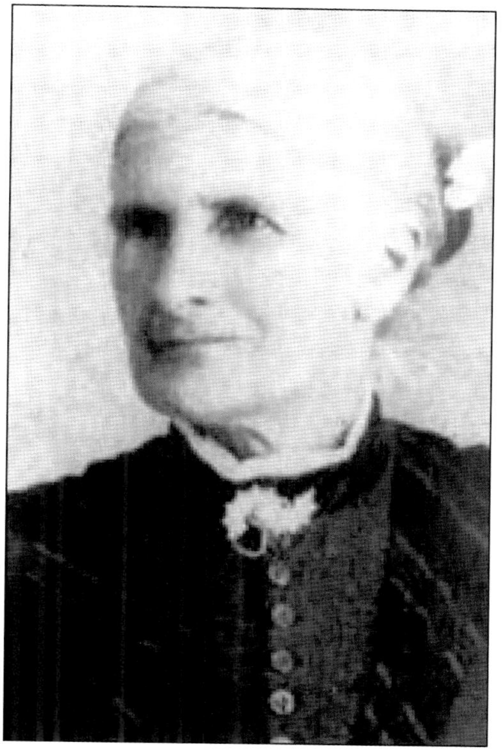

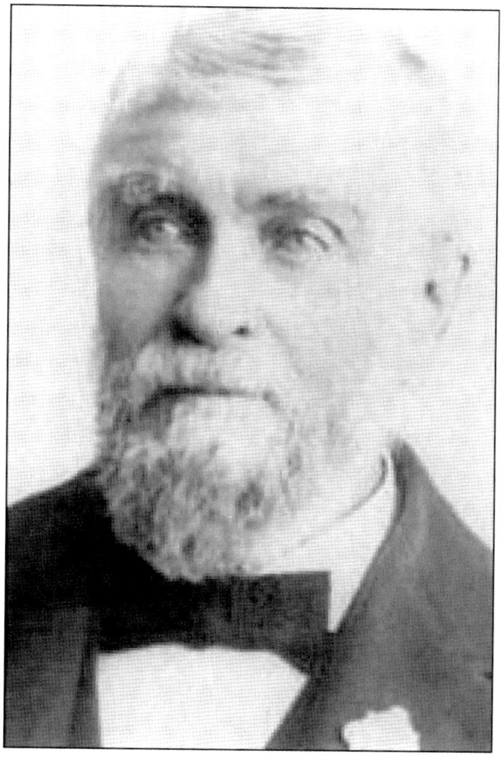

Henry Standage was born in 1818 in London, England. He was an early Richmond settler with two wives, Sophronia and Henrietta. He served in Company E of the Mormon Battalion. Henry drew up the first plot map of the Richmond Fort. His original map can be found in the Relic Hall. Henry became the first postmaster in Richmond.

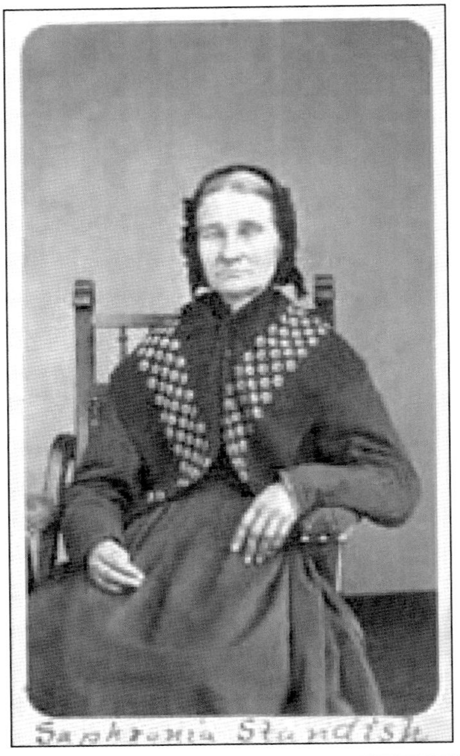

Sophronia Armenia Scott Reeves Standage was born in London, England, in 1821. She married Henry Standage in 1839. The couple had no children; however, Henry had 10 with a plural wife. Sophronia helped to raise these children. The trio helped in the settling of Richmond and remained there for several years. They eventually migrated to Mesa, Arizona, where they lived the remainder of their lives.

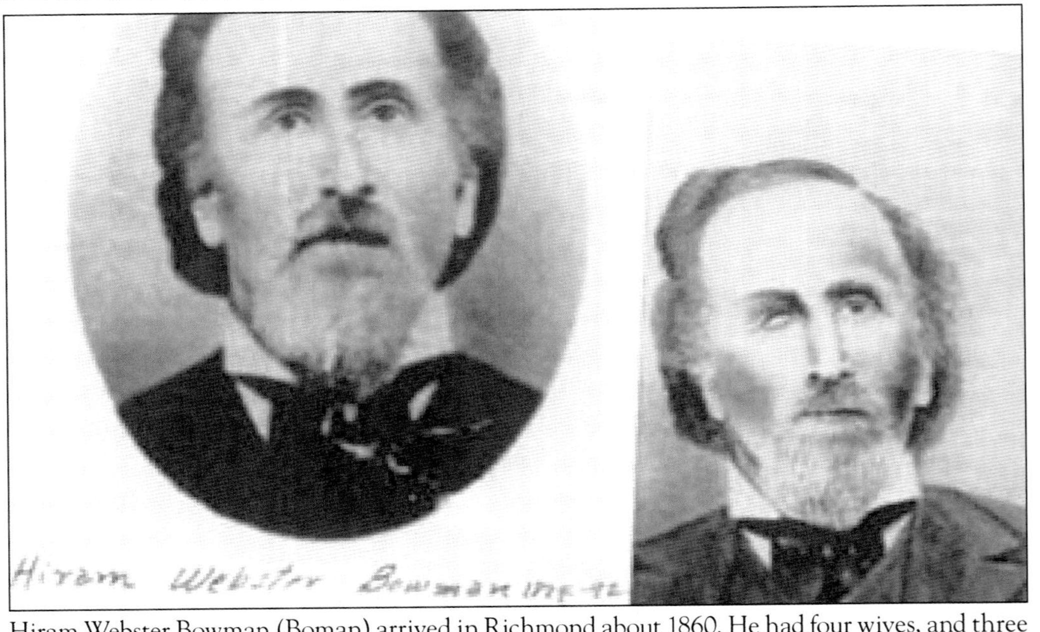

Hiram Webster Bowman (Boman) arrived in Richmond about 1860. He had four wives, and three of them lived in Richmond. He had 24 children, for whom he provided well. These images are of him in 1874 (left) and 1892. During that time, he suffered the loss of his left eye and several of the fingers from his left hand when a rifle backfired. He died in Hyde Park, Utah, in April 1892, and was buried in Richmond. (Courtesy of Delores Buttars.)

Ernest Ephraim Monson and his younger sister Eliza Victoria Monson are pictured taking a spin around their hometown of Richmond in the new family automobile, a Hupmobile. The thin tires and candle-powered headlights suggest that the photograph was taken around 1910, when Ernest and Eliza were in their early 20s.

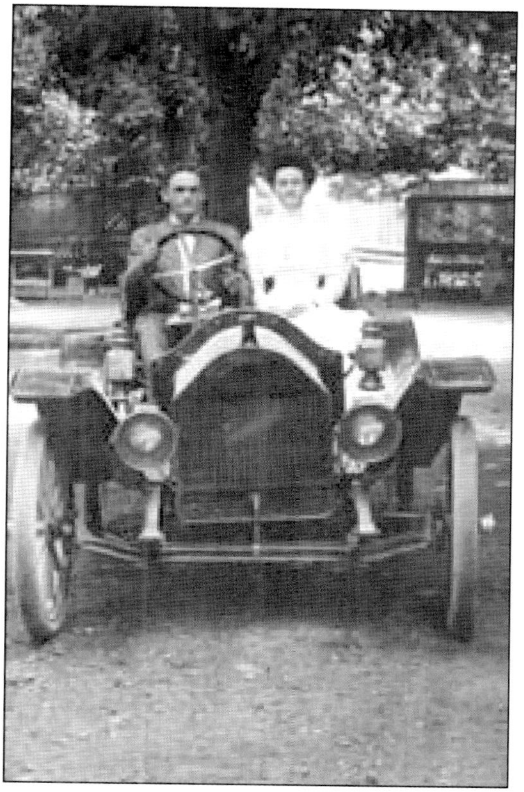

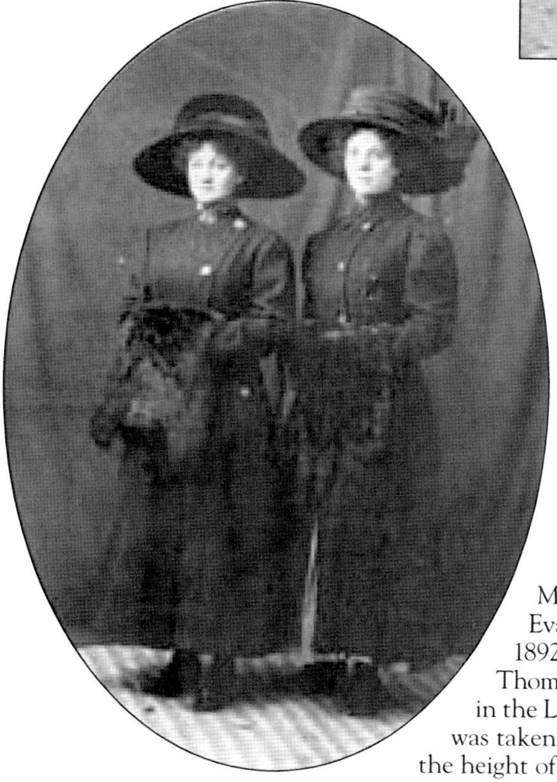

Millie Thomson (left) is pictured with her friend Eva Anderson. Millie was born in Richmond in 1892 to George Moss and Eva Cleantha Shepard Thomson. Millie married Peter Bertrand Van Orden in the Logan Temple in June 1914. This photograph was taken around 1910. Millie and Eva are dressed in the height of fashion.

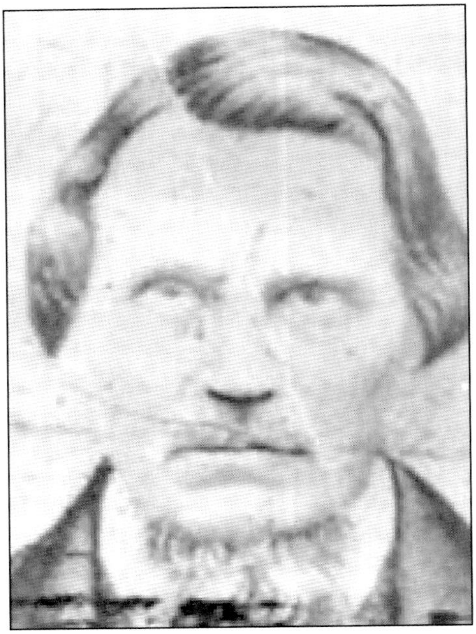

Johan Peter Johansen was born in Denmark on February 6, 1815. He immigrated to the United States in 1862 and settled in Richmond in 1863. He died there on November 30, 1875. Names were often Americanized, and Johan Peter Johansen was changed posthumously to John Peter Johnson. His family changed his headstone for ease of genealogy, and the original is on display at the Richmond Relic Hall.

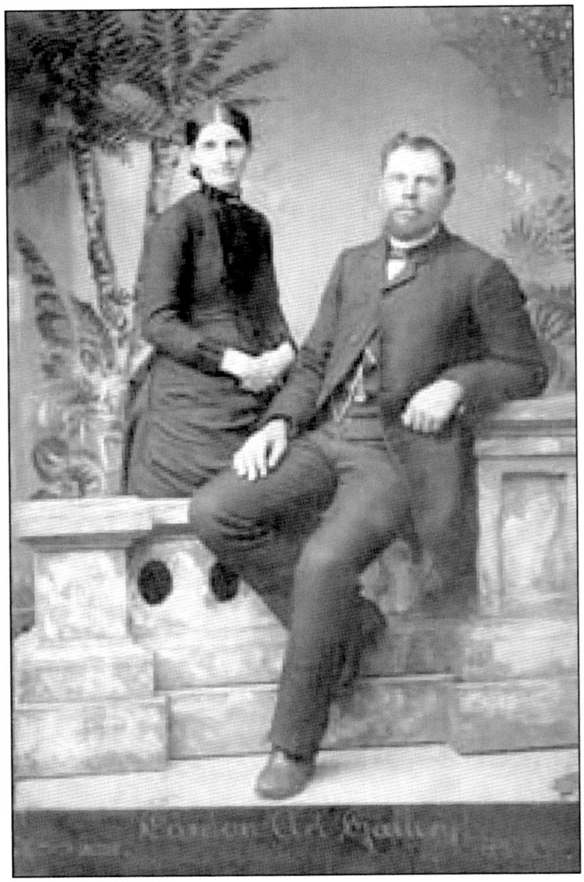

Rebecca Alvira Lewis Rawlins and her husband, Harvey McGalyard Rawlins, are pictured here. She was born November 1, 1859, in a wagon on the bank of City Creek, a few rods west of current Highway 91, to William Hendricks and Martha Petty Lewis Hendricks. Rebecca was the first white child born in Richmond.

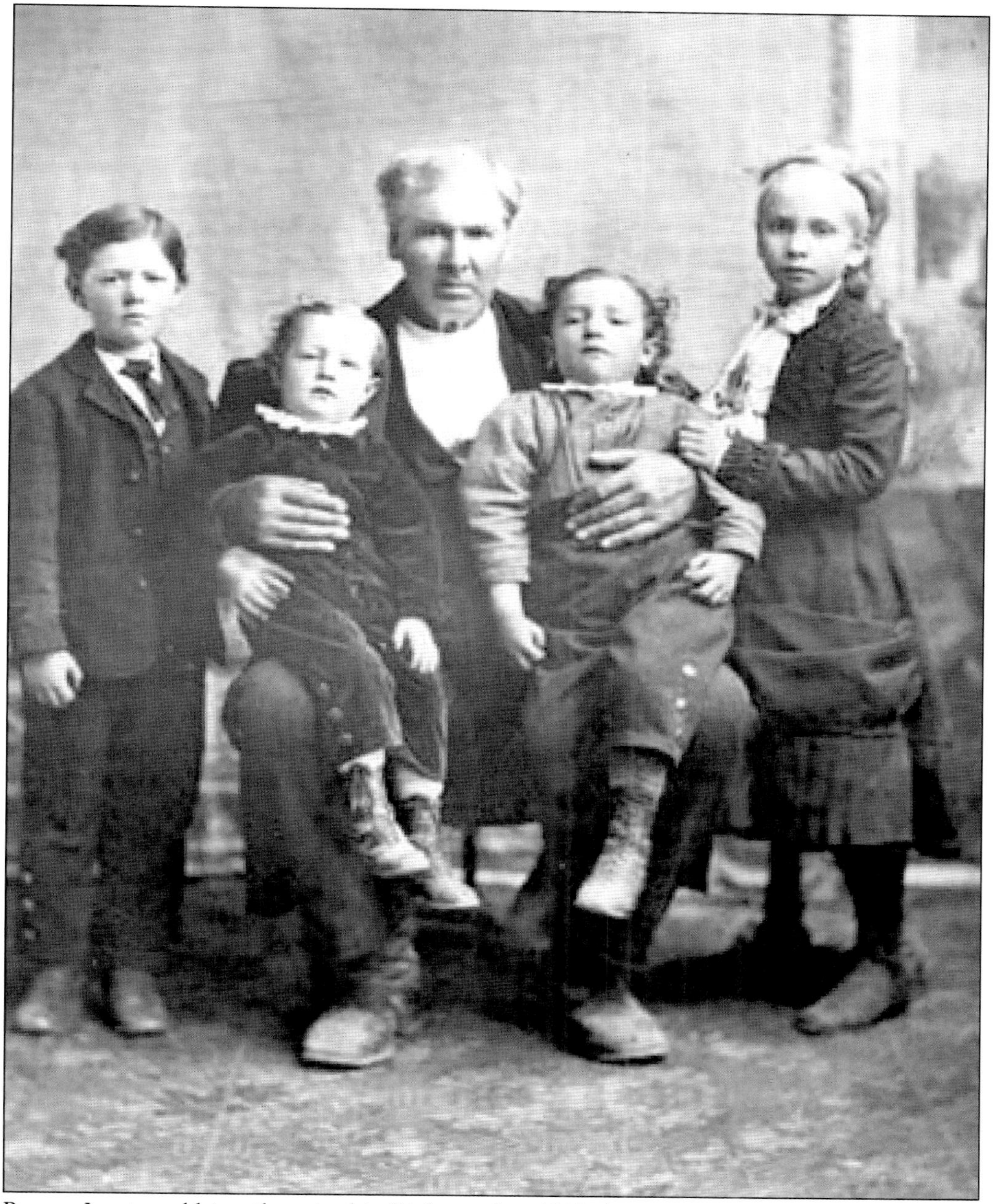

Beason Lewis and his wife arrived in Richmond in 1860. A non-Mormon who later joined the church, Beason had promised his brother, who was killed at Haun's Mill, that he would take the brother's children to Utah. Beason eventually married two more wives but never had any biological children. Well loved and respected by all, he and his wives took in and raised at least 14 orphans or children whose parents were unable to provide for them. He was very tenderhearted and hated to think of any child having to walk to school in the snow. He would hitch up his team to his sleigh, attach the town's only set of sleigh bells, and drive around picking up the children and taking them to school. He is pictured here with the children of Myra Merrill. Alveretta Merrill is on the far right.

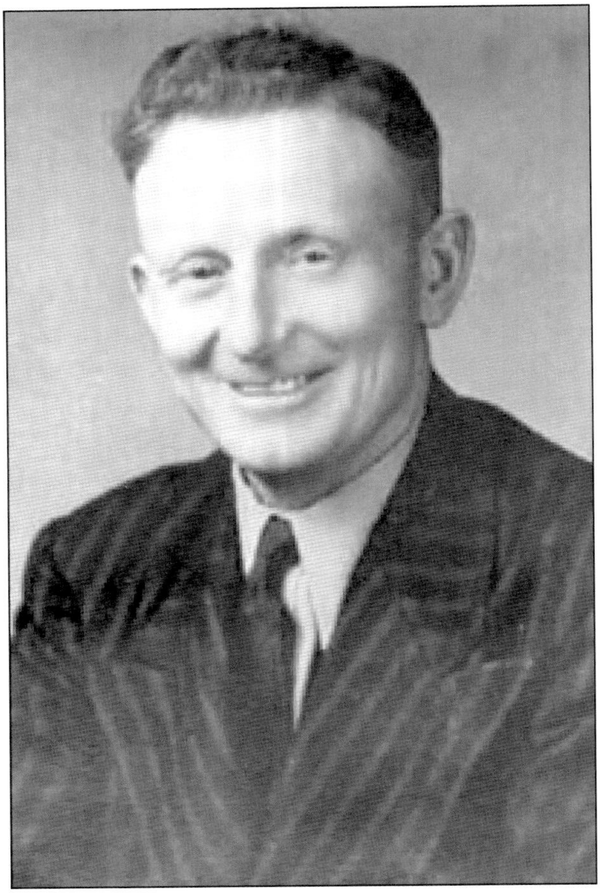

Ulyess Lewis, known commonly as "Ute," was born in Richmond in 1897. He married Rebecca Roskelley. They made their home on the northeast corner of 100 South 100 West, where they opened and operated Ute's Dairy for many years. He was known as a good storyteller, a trait he passed on to his children. (Courtesy of Lex Lewis.)

This 1932 Chevrolet convertible was owned by Ulyess Lewis. His son Jed is in the driver's seat and his younger son Lex is in the rumble seat with their dog Bird. Ute's Dairy and the family home were located across the street from Park School, which can be seen in the background. (Courtesy of Lex Lewis.)

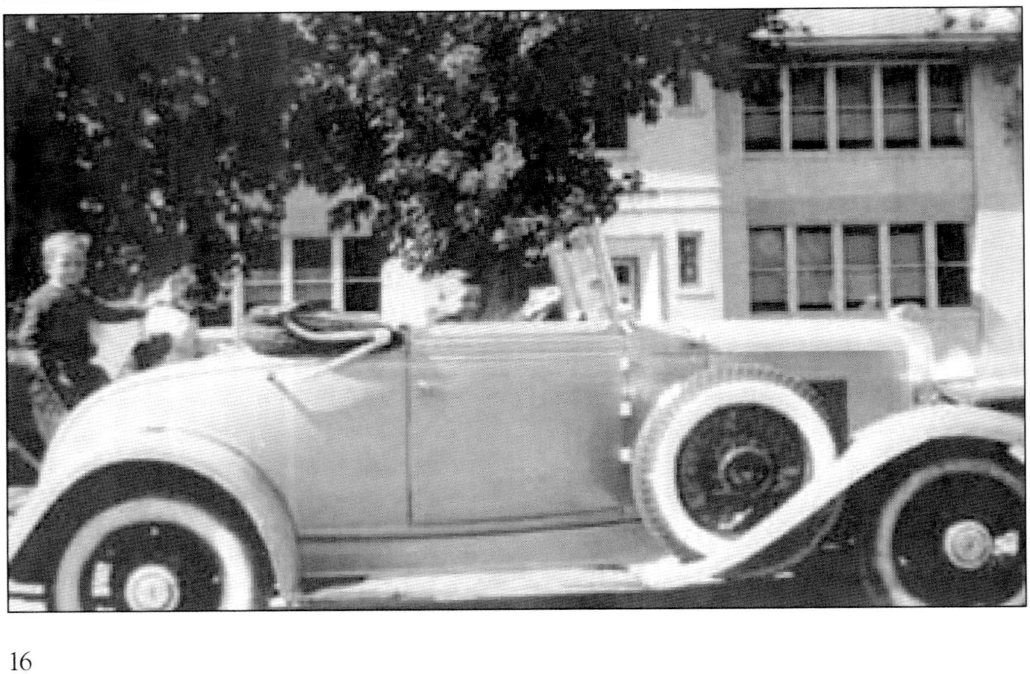

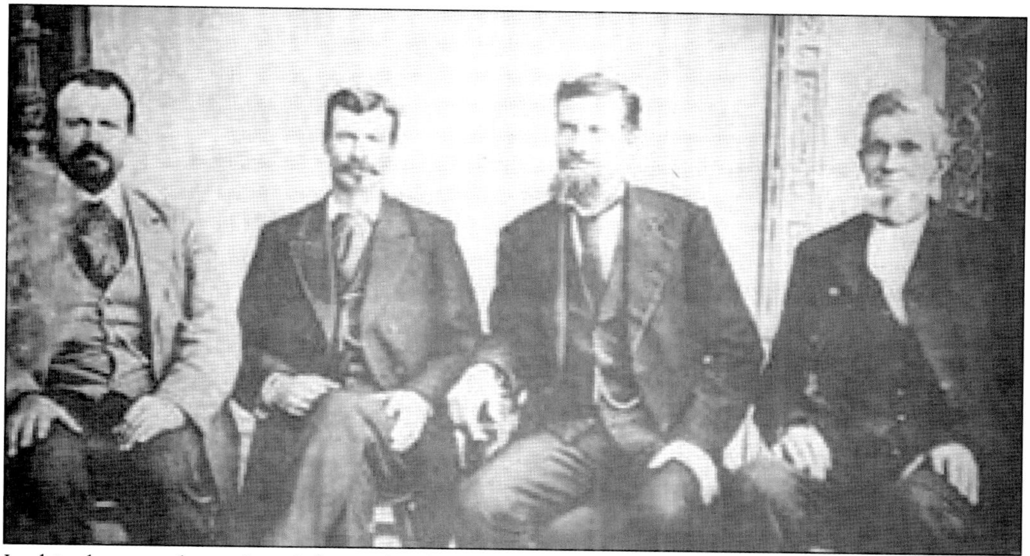

In this photograph are, from left to right, the following: Neriah Robert Lewis, appointed first marshal of Richmond, born March 10, 1843, in Carlinville, Illinois; Benjamin Marion Lewis, born March 20, 1841, in Carlinville, Illinois; William Hendricks Lewis, born October 14, 1837, in Carlinville, Illinois; and Neriah Lewis, father of the first three men, born April 29, 1816, in Simpson County, Kentucky. Neriah was the brother of Beason Lewis, one of Richmond's kindest residents.

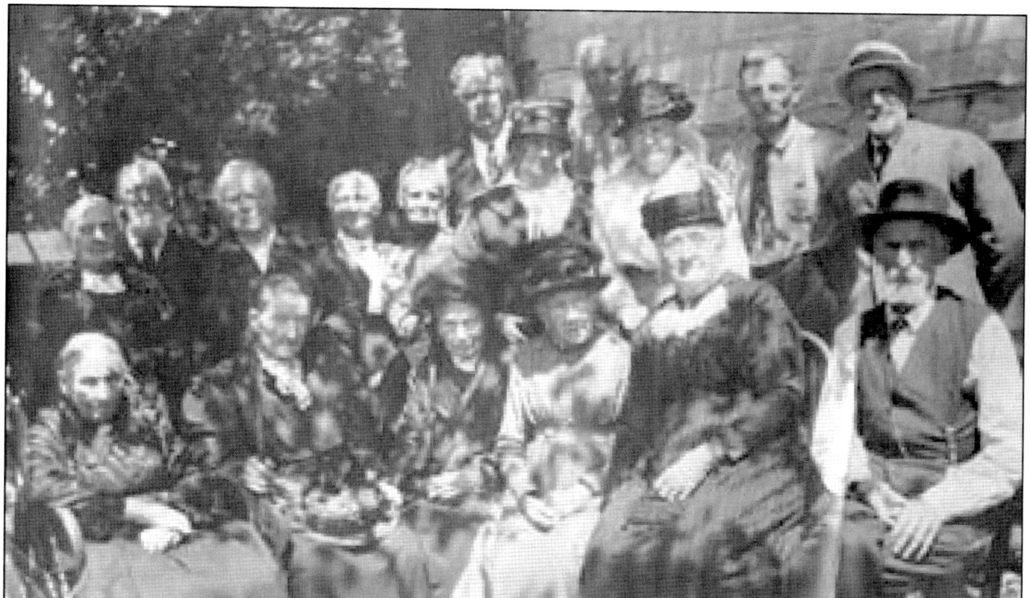

This photograph was taken about 1920 in Richmond of the surviving pioneers. Included in the image are, from left to right, (first row) Mary Jane Humphreys Brower, Lucy Ann Maria Cole Bair, Malinda Funk, Mrs. Nelson, Amanda Andrus Egan, and Simon Webb; (second row) unidentified, William Lobark Skidmore, unidentified, Harriet Fisher, Ann Dobson, Melissa McCarrey, and Elizabeth Smith Hill; (third row) Hyrum Bair, Frank Bair, William Lewis, and Eli Webb.

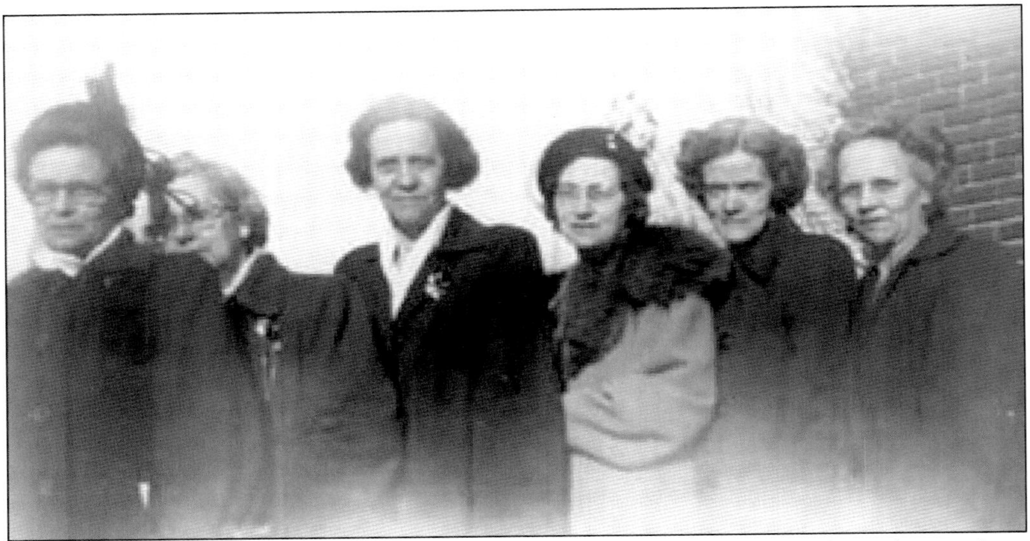

Pictured outside of the Richmond South Ward meetinghouse in 1936 are members of an auxiliary board. Included in this image are, from left to right, Agnes Bair, Lucille Hillyard, Lillian Bell, Mary Smith, Clarissa Lovenia Knapp Dobson, and Dora Hendricks. Lovenia "Lovey" Dobson's high school graduation dress is on display in the Richmond Relic Hall.

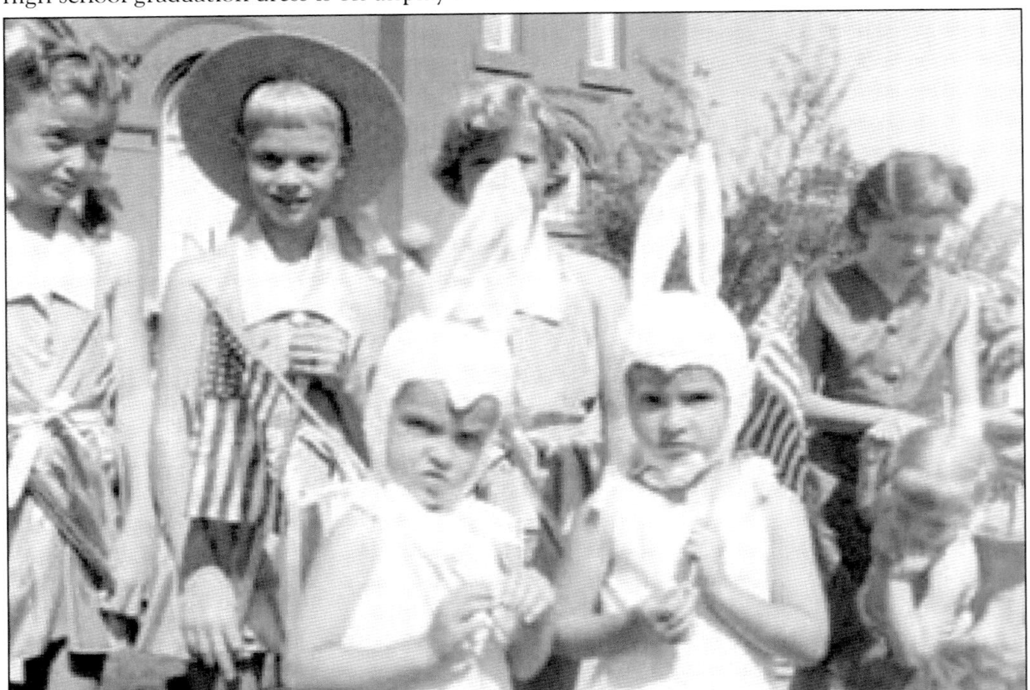

The two cute little bunnies are twin sisters Faye and Fern Housley. The photograph was taken in 1959 in front of the Benson Stake Tabernacle in Richmond. It was a tradition in Richmond for many years to have a Primary Parade each summer in which all the children would dress up, decorate their bikes or wagons, and parade around the block. (Courtesy of Ariel Benson.)

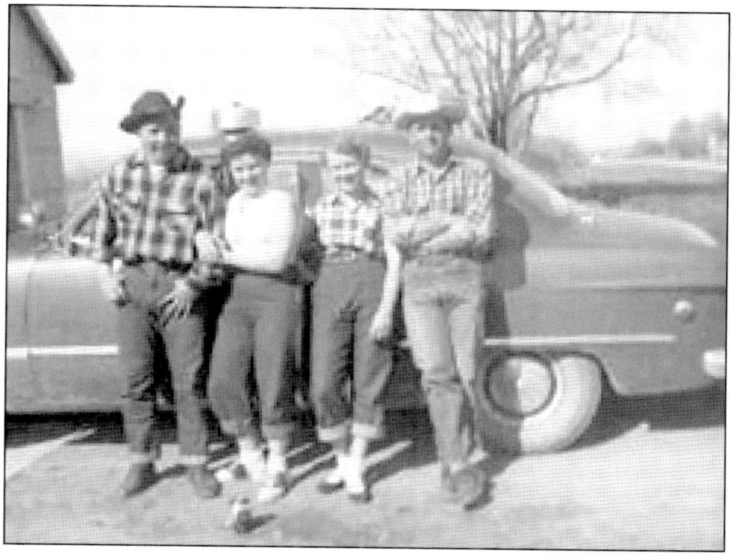

Standing in front of a 1949 Ford are, from left to right, Dale Andrus, Janice Jorgensen, Marva Dawn Spackman, and Gail Alvey. They had just returned from a double date to Idaho, where they spent the day picnicking and fishing in the summer of 1951. The photograph was taken on the corner of 100 South and 200 West, looking west. About a year later, both couples were married. (Courtesy of Cheri Housley.)

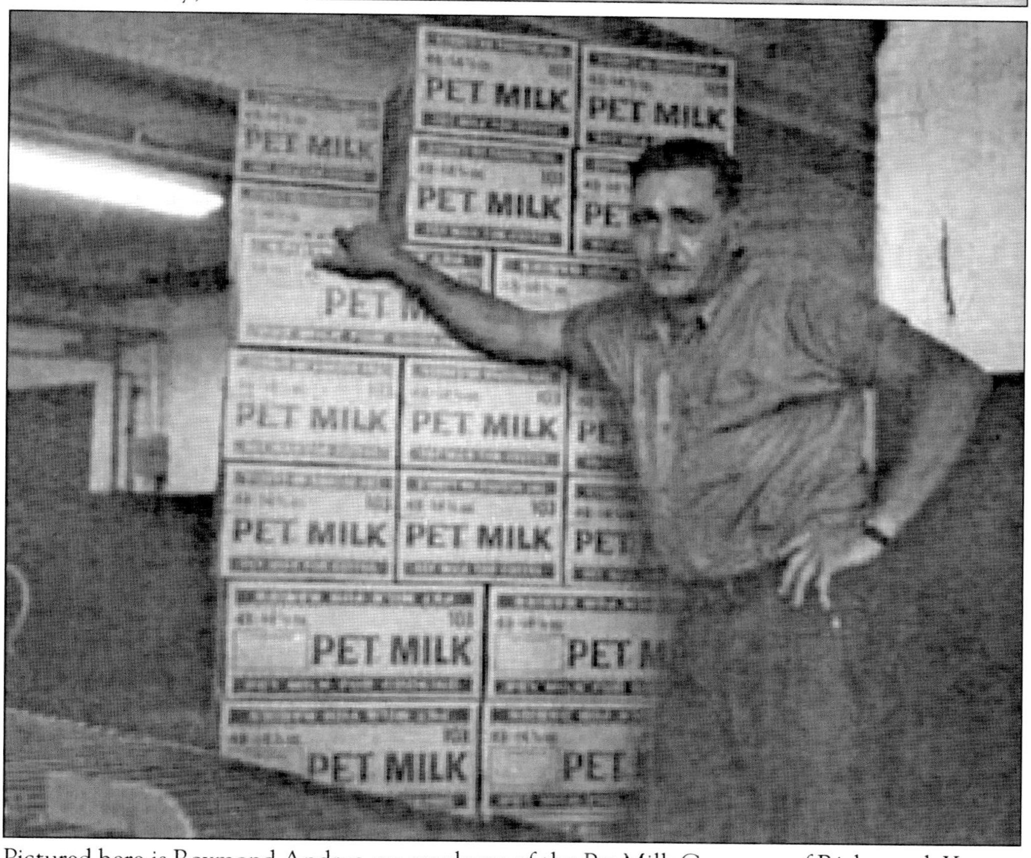

Pictured here is Raymond Andrus, an employee of the Pet Milk Company of Richmond. Known as the "Black Ace," Ray is shown standing behind the conveyor belt that helped move boxes of canned milk through the plant, later to be loaded onto a train for shipping throughout the western states. Pet Milk provided solid employment to many of the town's residents.

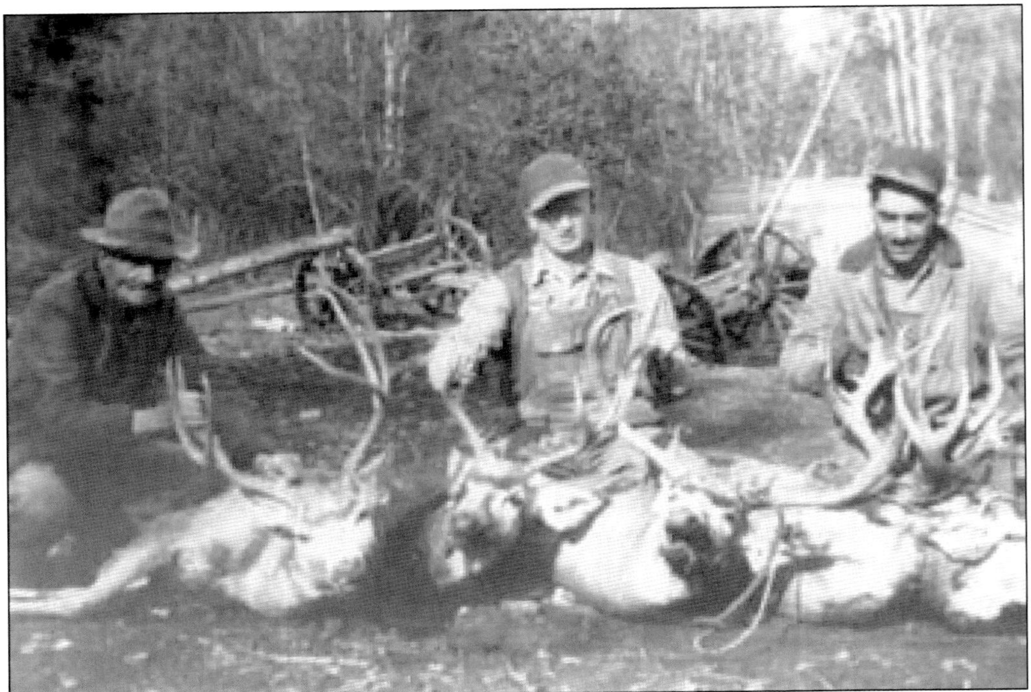

This photograph is assumed to have been taken sometime in the 1940s in one of the canyons above Richmond. Depicted from left to right are John Harrison Andrus, Doane Smith, and Joseph Daley Andrus. In days gone by, wild game such as elk and deer were plentiful in the hills above Richmond. Hunting was more than a sport, though. It was a means to feed a family. (Courtesy of Marie Lundgreen.)

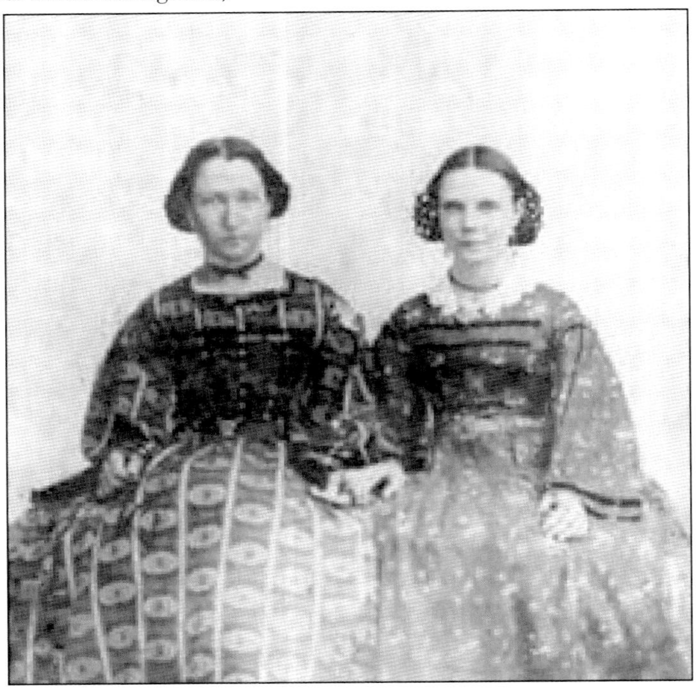

Sisters-in-law Amanda Andrus Egan (left) and Caroline Weatherbee Andrus are shown here in their younger years. Amanda was married to Howard Ransom Egan, and Caroline was married to Amanda's brother John Daley Andrus. These women were among the early settlers of Richmond. Along with their husbands, they worked long and hard to establish their homes and community.

Howard Ransom Egan was the son of Maj. Howard Egan. He is pictured as both a young man (below) and as an older man with his wife, Amanda Andrus Egan, and son Horace (right). Howard was a pony express rider from April 3, 1860, until October 1861. A full 183 men rode for the pony express, which ran day and night, summer and winter. Qualifications were that riders be "young, skinny, wiry fellows" who were "willing to risk death." Most riders were around 20 years old, with one as young as 11 and the oldest in his mid-40s. They weighed in the range of 120 pounds and were paid $100 per month. Amanda Andrus came west with her mother and four siblings from Winter Quarters, Nebraska, in the Heber C. Kimball Wagon Train Company in 1848. Her father did not accompany the family, as he had been called to serve a mission in England. A younger wife accompanied him.

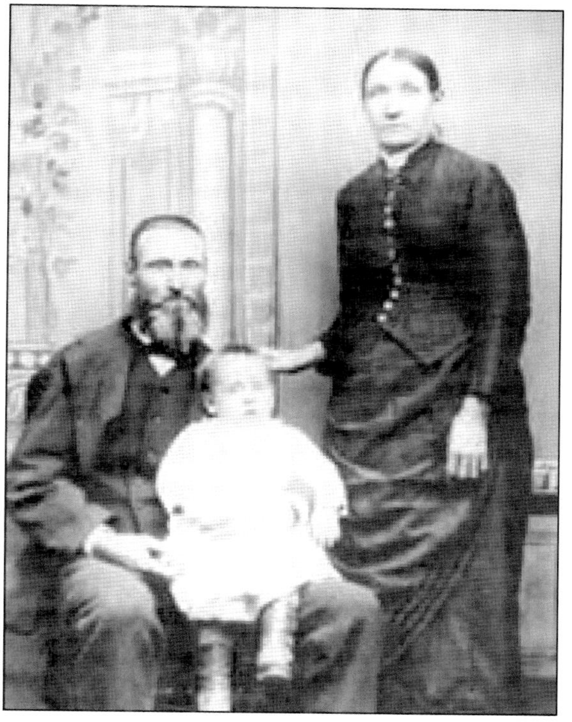

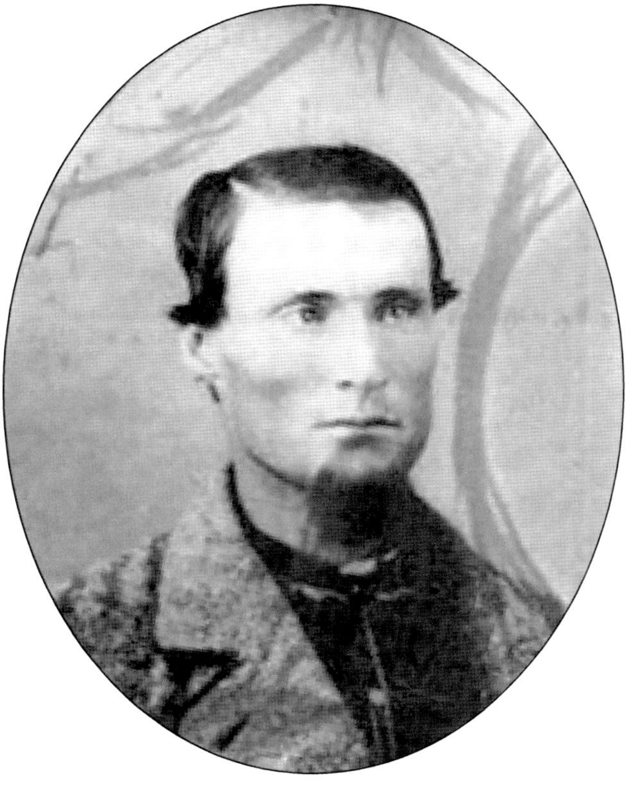

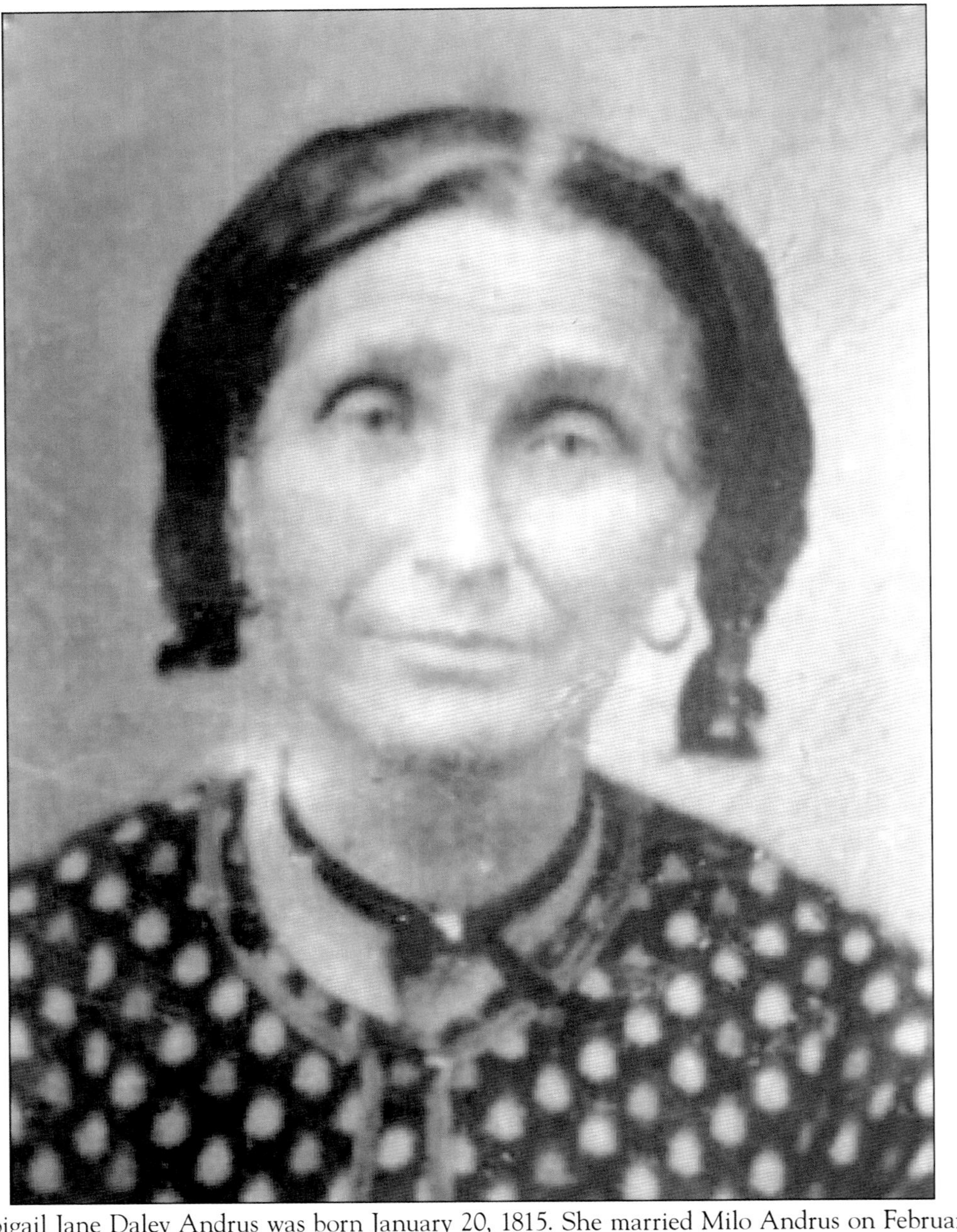

Abigail Jane Daley Andrus was born January 20, 1815. She married Milo Andrus on February 14, 1833. When her husband left with a younger wife to serve a mission abroad, Abigail brought her five children, Mary Jane, Amanda, John, James, and Millenium, across the plains by herself in the Heber C. Kimball Wagon Train Company. Abigail was ill for most of the journey, yet she walked every step, stopping to pick burrs out of her bloody feet. They reached the Salt Lake Valley in the fall of 1848. Abigail and Mary Jane earned money by taking in washing. Her favorite hymn was "Hard Times Come Again No More," the chorus of which is as follows: "'Tis the song, the sigh of the weary, hard times, hard times, come again no more. Many days you have lingered around our cabin door, oh, hard times come again no more." Abigail died in 1894. She is buried in Richmond Cemetery.

Henry Standage was born February 26, 1818, in England. He married Henrietta Rogers on September 19, 1861, and joined the Mormon Battalion, leaving behind his mother and wife. Henry was dedicated to the Lord and was obedient in enduring his many trials and hardships while with the battalion. He served his one-year commitment and then left with many other men to find their families in northern Utah.

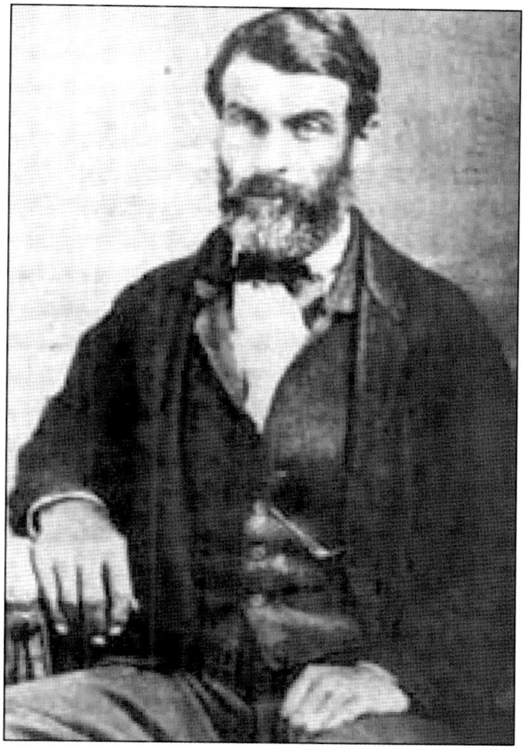

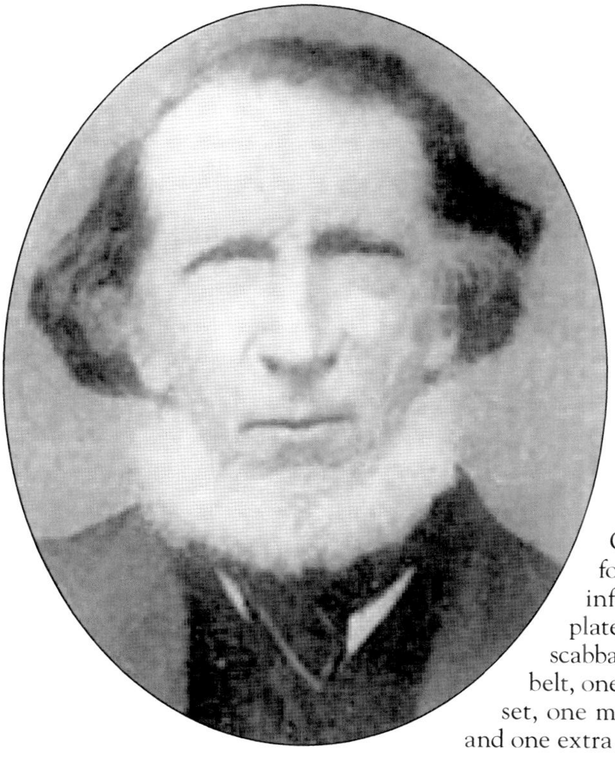

Joseph Dobson was a private of Company A of the Mormon Battalion and later a Richmond resident. He joined on July 16, 1847, in Los Angeles, California. Each soldier was issued the following: one Harpers Ferry musket, one infantry cartridge box, one cartridge box plate, one cartridge box belt, one bayonet scabbard, one bayonet scabbard belt, one waist belt, one musket gun sling, one brush and pike set, one musket screwdriver, one musket wiper, and one extra flint cap.

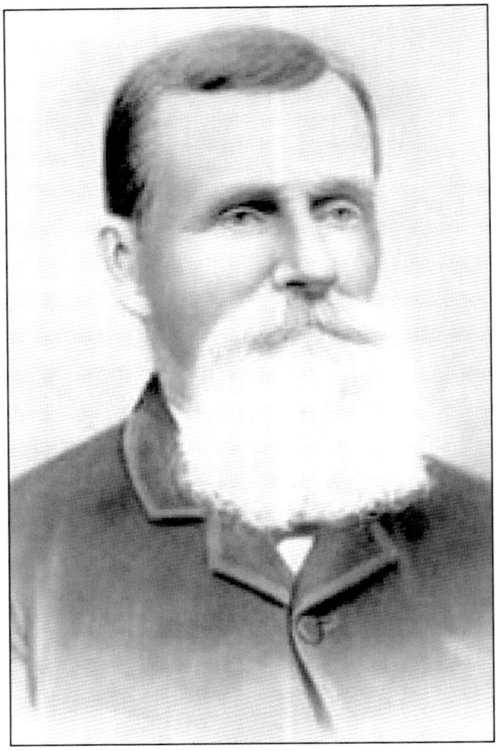

David Pinkney Rainey was born in 1815 in Tennessee. In 1856, he arrived in Utah with Company B of the Mormon Battalion, in which he held the rank of first corporal. He married Dorthea Jane Dennis a year later. They settled in Richmond in 1860, where David was one of the first school teachers. Along with Henry Standage, he taught in a small log building that was located about where the fire station stands on East Main Street today.

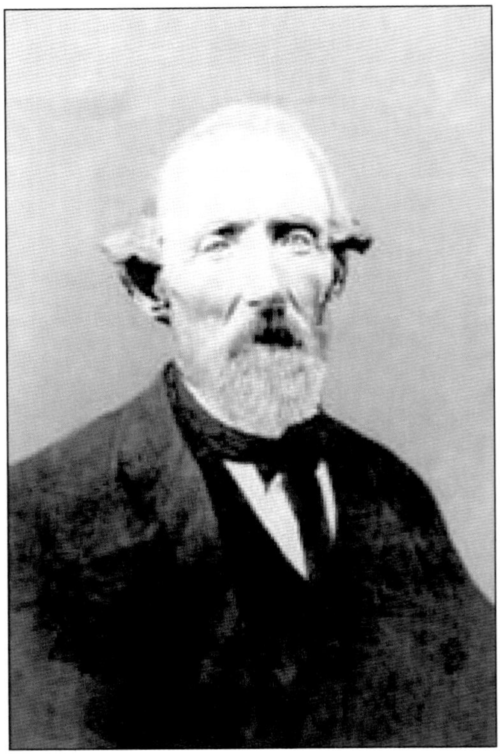

Thomas Richardson was a private in Company E of the Mormon Battalion, serving under Daniel Davis. He served from November 10, 1846, to July 16, 1847. Thomas was one of the 500 Mormons who volunteered to help in the Mexican War effort. Upon the expiration of their term of service, they would be allowed to retain the guns and accoutrements that had been furnished by the government. He later came to Richmond.

William Dorris Hendricks was born in Simpson, Kentucky. At the age of 16, he joined the Mormon Battalion as one of its youngest members. He served in Company D. Hendricks arrived in Utah in 1847, and in 1860, he settled in Richmond, where he was elected as the town's first mayor. He eventually married five women and had 42 children. He died in Richmond in 1909 and is buried there.

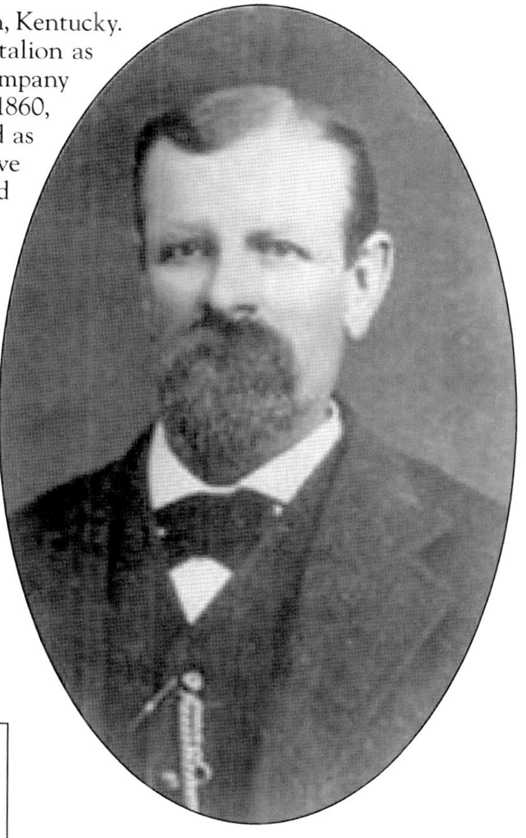

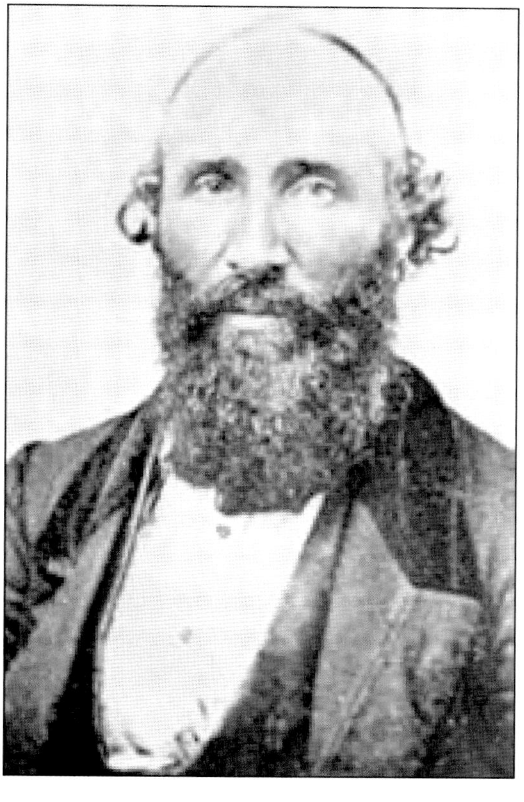

Maj. Howard Egan was born in Ireland on June 15, 1815. At a young age, he followed the life of a sailor. He then settled in Salem, Massachusetts, and worked at rope making. In 1838, he married Tamson Parshley and in 1842, converted to Mormonism. In 1846, he came west, where he joined the Mormon Battalion to participate in the war with Mexico, which had started that same year. Egan eventually ended up in Richmond.

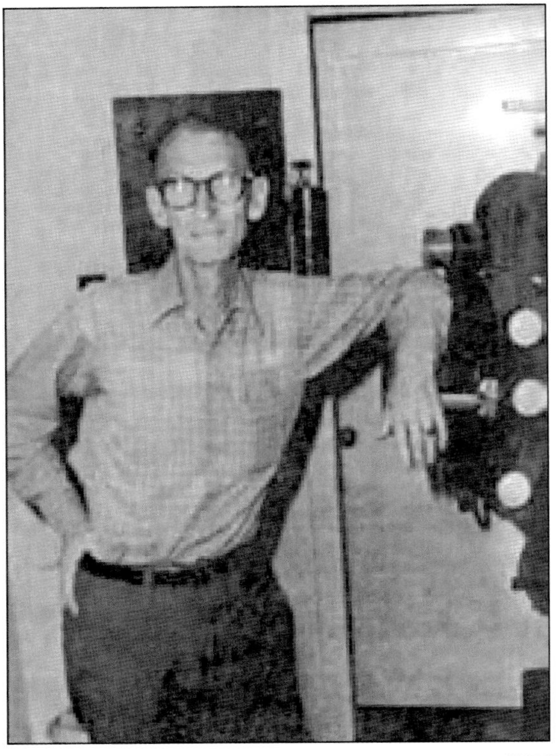

When the theater opened in Richmond on October 6, 1937, Harold "Holly" Albiston was there. He continued to be there every movie night for 46 years. Holly worked as the town projectionist under eight different mayors. Over that time, very little about the machines changed; however, the quality of the film became better. He oversaw the change from lamp houses and low-intensity arcs to high-intensity arcs on the projection machines. This facilitated the showing of modern movies. It was a sad day when the decision was made to close the theater in Richmond. It now sits empty in the city office complex, a remnant of days gone by. Some say they can still see Holly up in the projection room if the lighting is right.

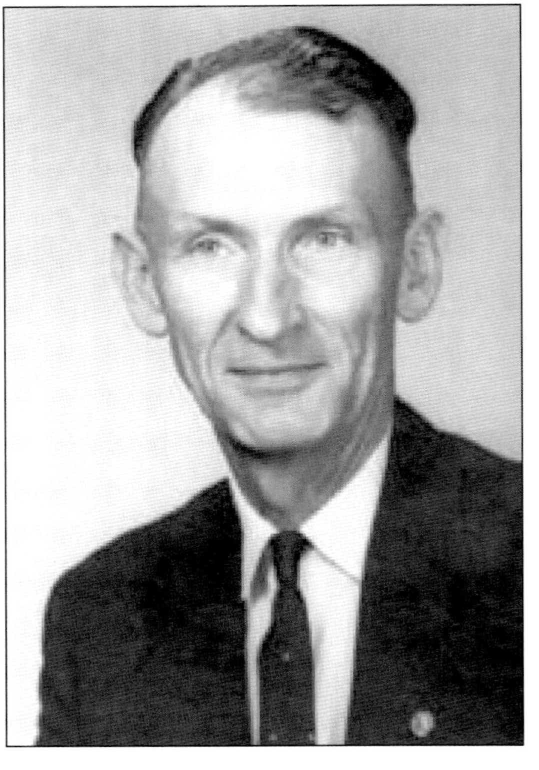

Pictured are Alta Eliza Webb, born June 21, 1899, and Samuel Milton Webb, born November 1, 1902. They were the children of Joseph and Cora Jane Hendricks Webb. Both born and raised in Richmond, Milton later became the Richmond postmaster. Alta died on May 15, 2002, one month short of her 103rd birthday, having lived through the entire 20th century. (Courtesy of Doyle Webb.)

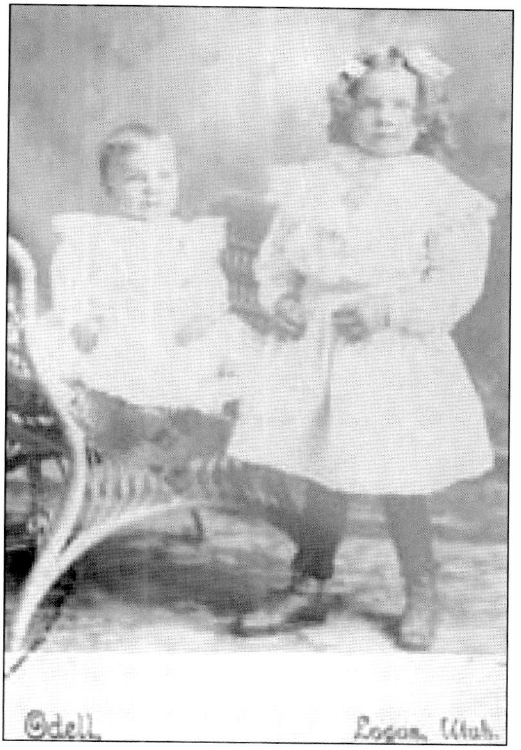

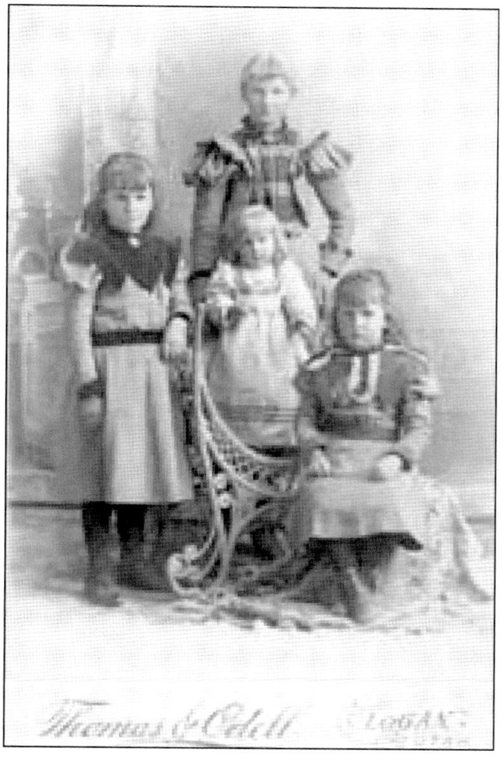

Pictured around 1899 are, from left to right, Flossie Mildred Webb, Elizabeth Elena Webb, Florence Viola Webb, and Lucy Irene Webb, who were the daughters of Eli and Helena Ashment Webb. All were born and raised in Richmond; however, Lucy did not survive to adulthood.

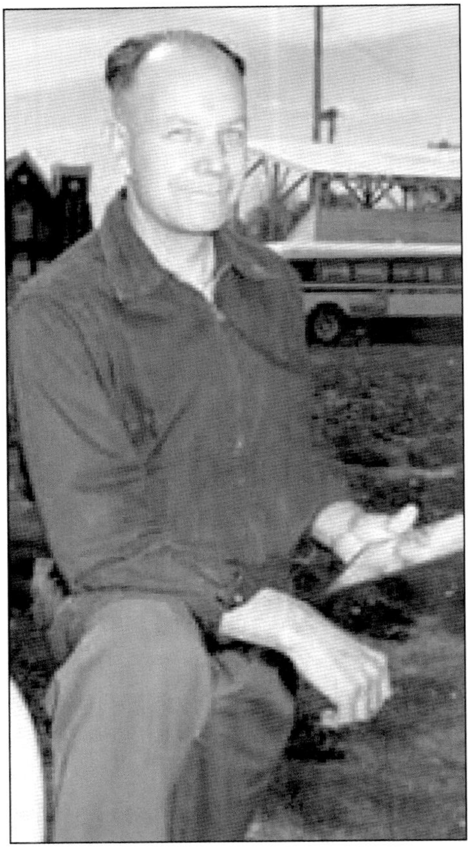

Pictured is Samuel "Milton" Webb, born in Richmond to Joseph and Cora Jane Hendricks Webb on November 1, 1902. Milt served as the Richmond postmaster for many years. He is fondly remembered by the children in town for always having candy in his pockets and for reminding the bishop to end sacrament meeting on time each week by announcing loudly, "Can they see the clock from there?" (Courtesy of Doyle Webb.)

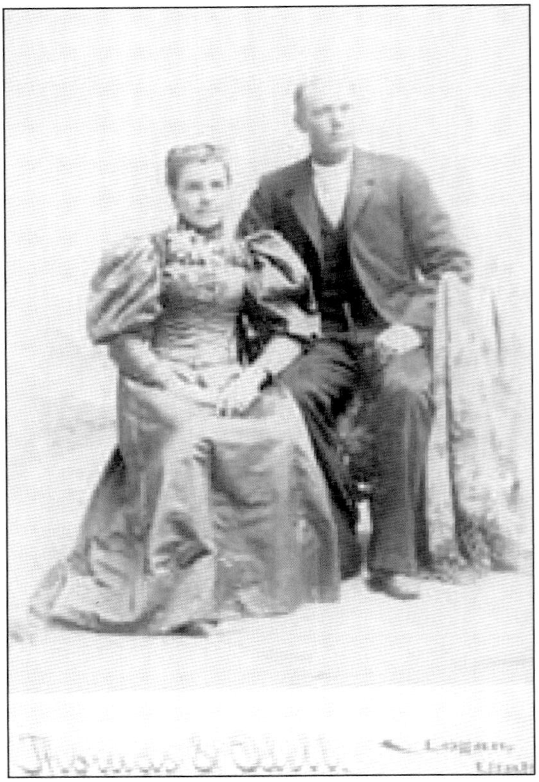

Joseph and Cora Jane Hendricks Webb are pictured here shortly after their wedding in the Logan Temple in 1895. Both were born and raised in Richmond, where they remained the rest of their lives. They were the parents of five children, and many of their descendants still live in town.

Emma Irene Merrill, daughter of Church of Jesus Christ of Latter-day Saints apostle Marriner Wood Merrill and his third wife, Almira Jane Bainbridge, was born in Richmond on July 31, 1880. She had 42 brothers and sisters from her father's eight wives. She married in 1899 and died just five years later at the age of 24.

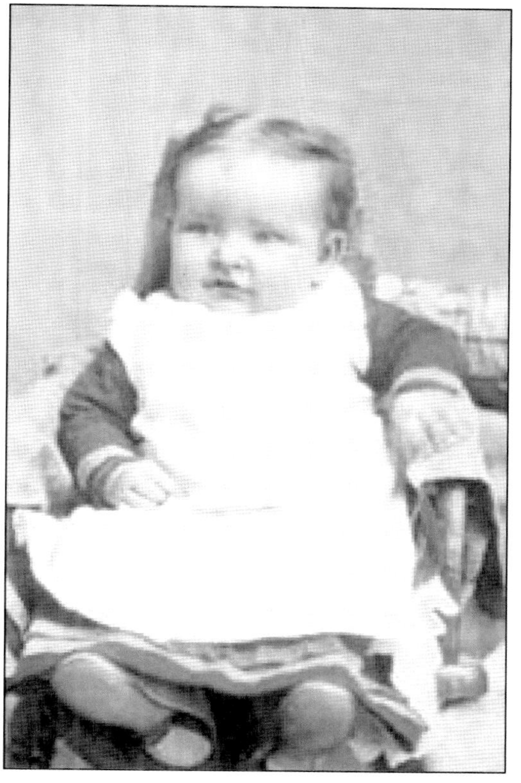

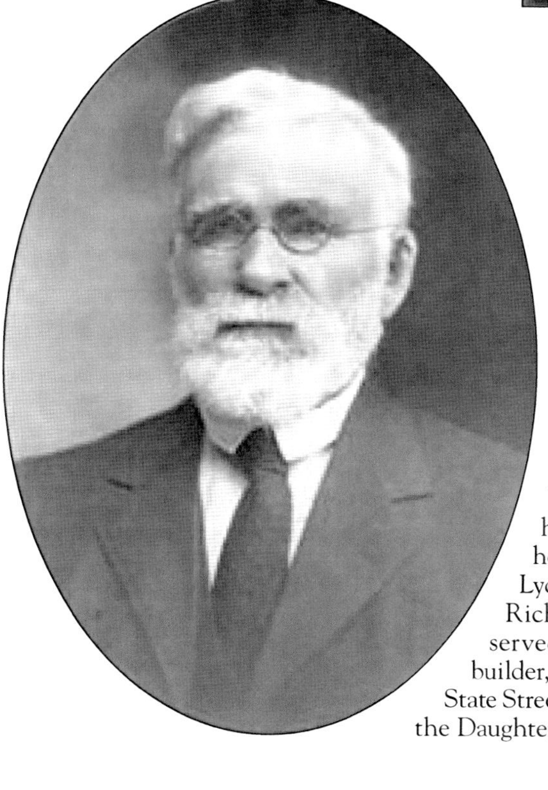

Wallace Kendall Burnham was an early Richmond settler. He arrived in 1860 with his first wife, Philinda Standley, with whom he had five children. He later married her sister Lydia with whom he had 12 children. He was Richmond's first justice of the peace and also served two years as mayor. He was a respected builder, constructing the Tithing House at 25 South State Street. The structure still stands, currently housing the Daughters of Utah Pioneers Museum.

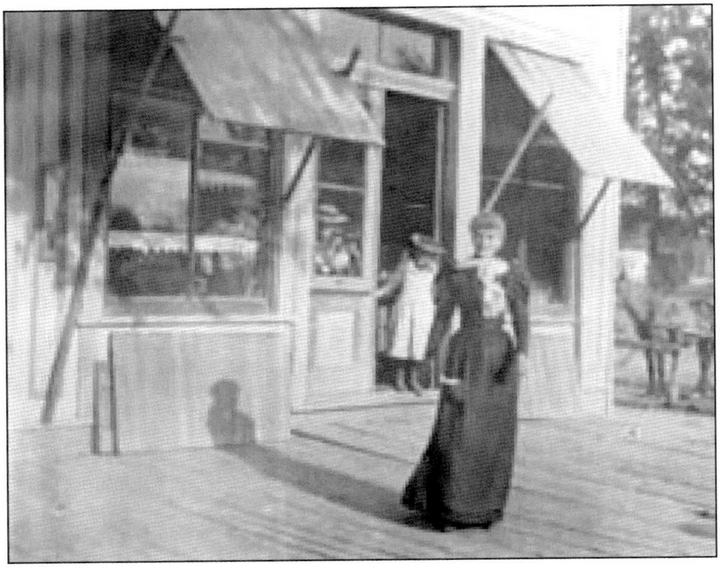

Mary Hendricks Bullen was born in Richmond in 1875 to William Dorris and Alvira Lavon Smith Hendricks. She married Herschel Bullen, with whom she had five children. Mary was prominent in musical and social circles. During Herschel's 26 month mission to Great Britain, Mary worked at the Richmond General Store (pictured) to support him and their family. They moved to Logan in 1897, where she died in 1950.

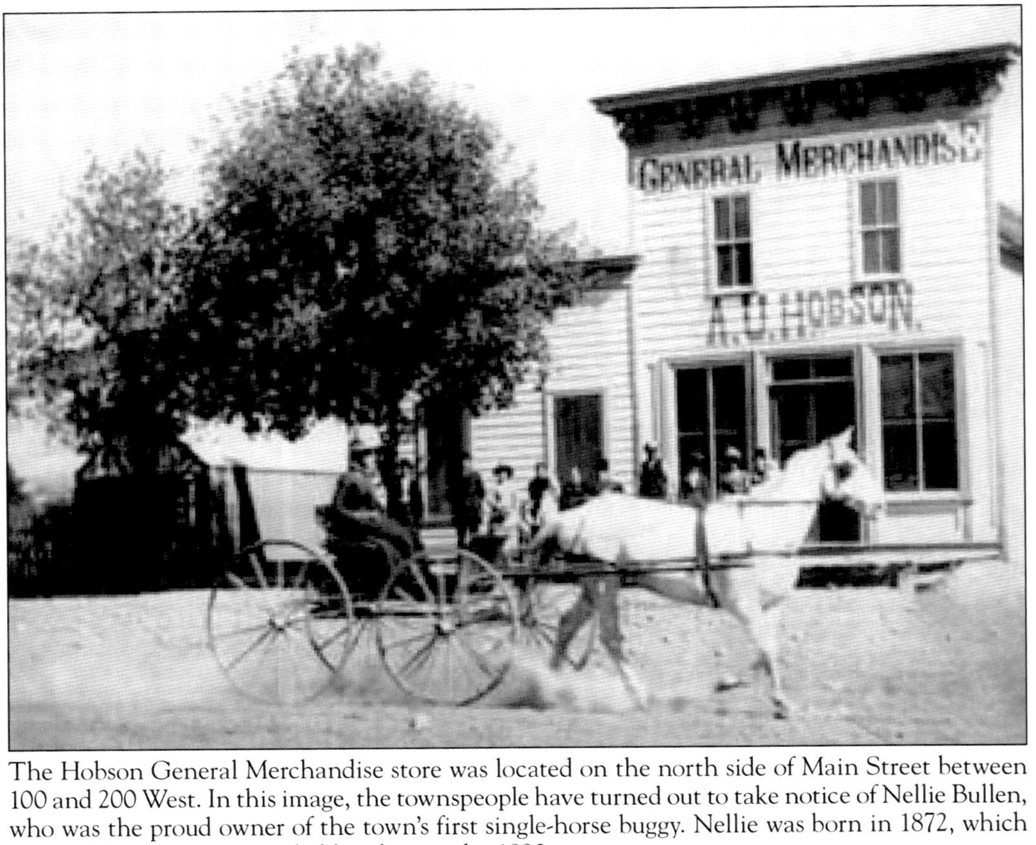

The Hobson General Merchandise store was located on the north side of Main Street between 100 and 200 West. In this image, the townspeople have turned out to take notice of Nellie Bullen, who was the proud owner of the town's first single-horse buggy. Nellie was born in 1872, which means this picture was probably taken in the 1890s.

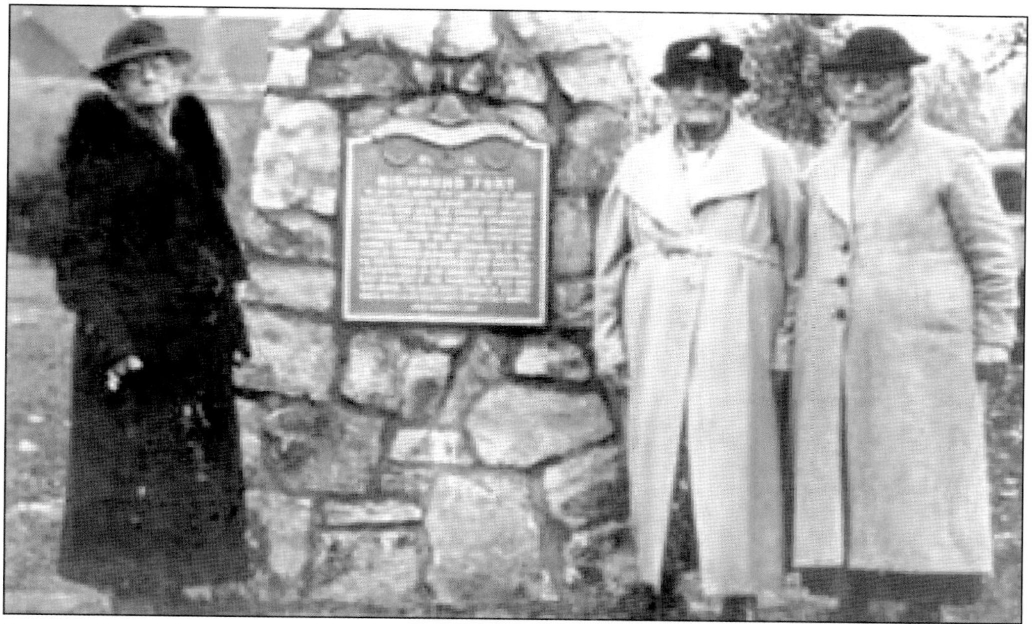

Pictured from left to right are Martha Kingsbury Lewis, Maggie T. Merrill, and Mrs. H.B. Webb at the dedication of the Daughters of Utah Pioneers Monument in the Richmond Park on October 30, 1936. The rocks in the monument were some that had been used in the construction of the old rock school in the 1870s and later in the foundation of the red brick school. They were originally hauled down from nearby canyons. George Anderson was the mason who built the monument.

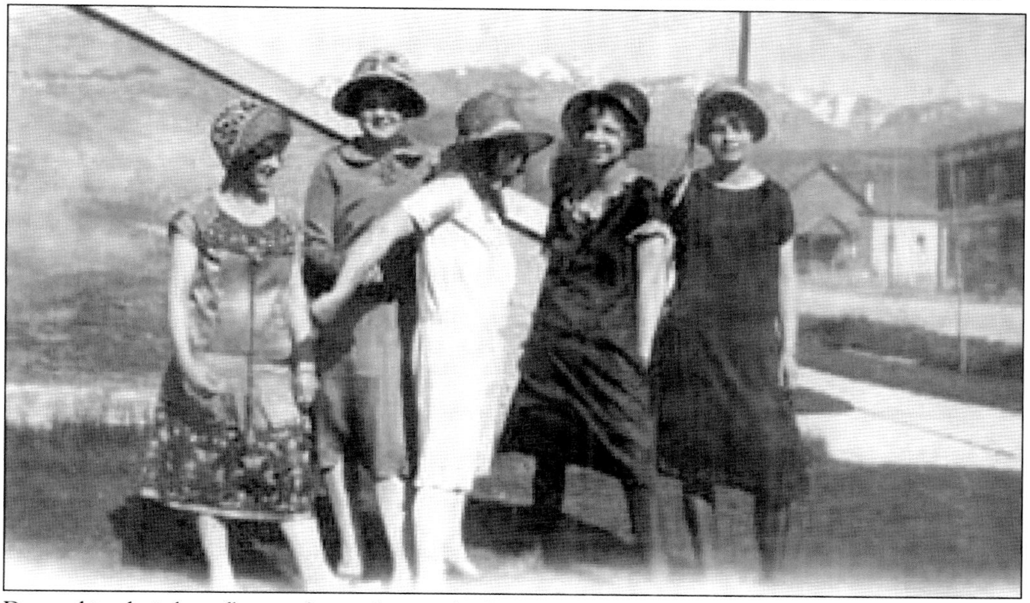

Dressed in their best flapper finery during the Roaring Twenties, this group of teenaged girls poses by the steps of Richmond's Carnegie Library. The fourth girl from the left is Sybil Nelson, and to her right is Fontella Thompson Cartwright, known as "Flonnie." The others are unidentified. In the background is the entrance to the Opera House and the old Richmond Mercantile building. (Courtesy of Richard Bagley.)

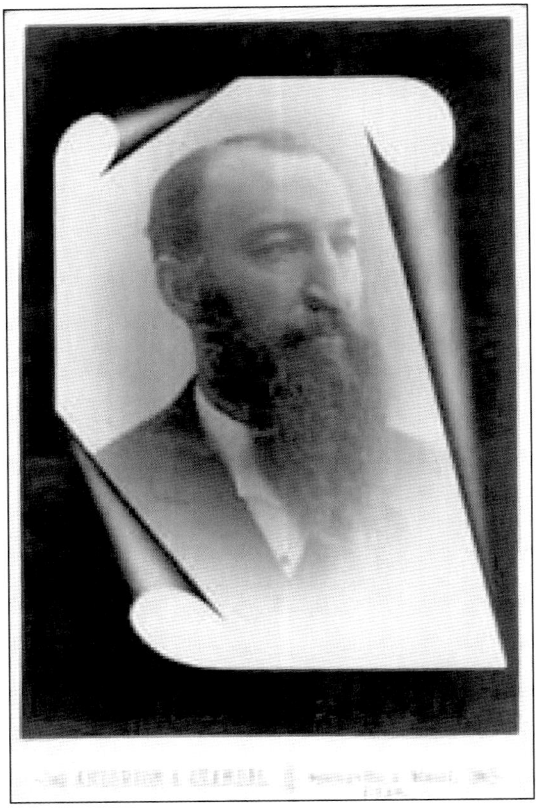

William Herbert Olsten was born in 1848. He was the first certified doctor to practice medicine in Richmond. When Utah gained statehood in 1896, every doctor was required to pass a proficiency test. Dr. Olsten received the highest score in the state. He was married to Lodicy Griffin of Richmond. He died in 1915 and is buried in the Richmond cemetery.

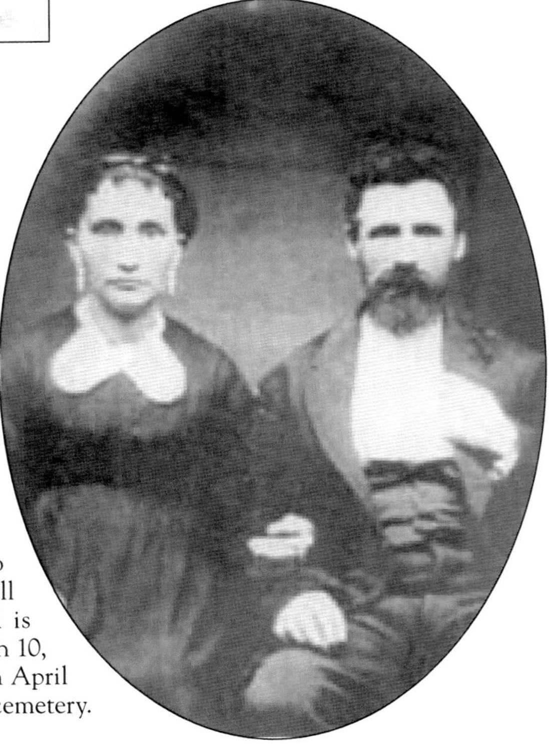

Lola Ann Tylor and John Richardson married on November 23, 1859. In 1863 they moved to Richmond. He owned and operated a sawmill north of town, near Cove. This sawmill is currently under renovation. John died March 10, 1906, and Lola followed a few years later on April 29, 1910. Both are buried in the Richmond cemetery. (Courtesy of Julie Smith Kelly.)

Ann Gregson was born in Bury, England, in 1829. She married John Robinson. In the early 1860s, they moved to Richmond, where they established a home and raised their family. Ann and John were the parents of nine children. Ann died in 1892 in Richmond and is buried in the cemetery there.

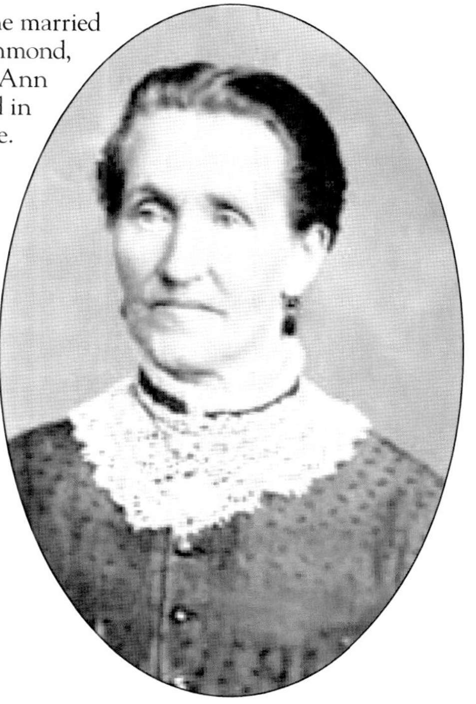

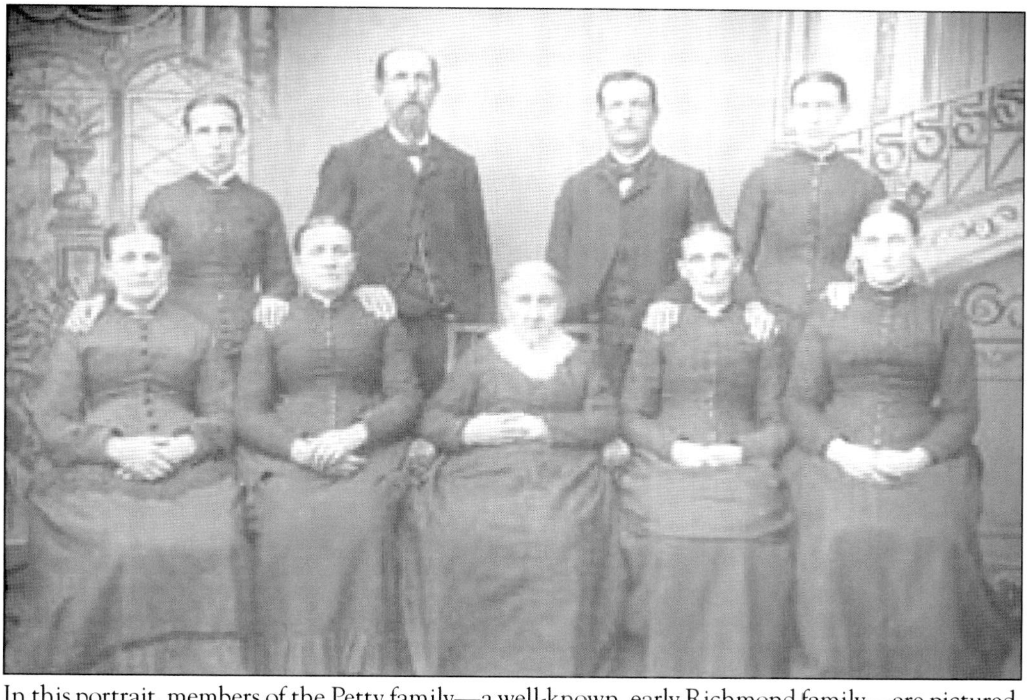

In this portrait, members of the Petty family—a well-known, early Richmond family—are pictured, from left to right, (first row) Mrs. Homer, Mrs. Beckstead, Grandma Petty, Mary Priannah Hillman, and Matlie Lewis; (second row) Maggie Davenport, Lew Petty, Tom Petty, and Louise Egbert. The Petty family was loved and admired by all.

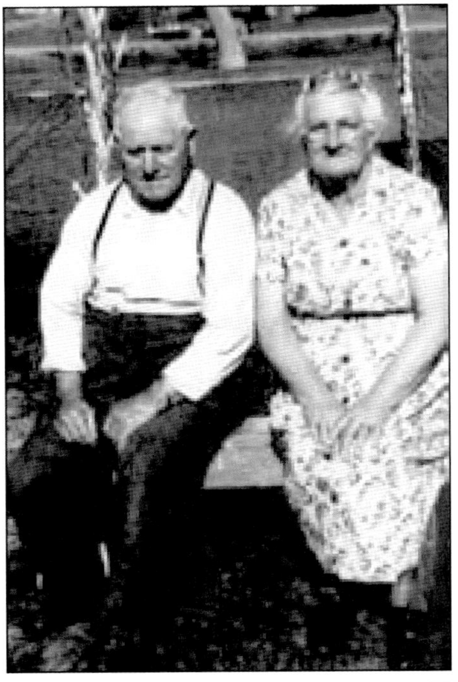

Pictured are James Littlewood Murray and Emeline Thorpe Murray, who came to Richmond around 1910. They first moved into a home about a mile south of town on the highway. Later, they moved to a large home on the corner of State Street and 100 South, where they continued to raise their family of 11 children. Many descendants still reside in Richmond. (Courtesy of Dean Murray.)

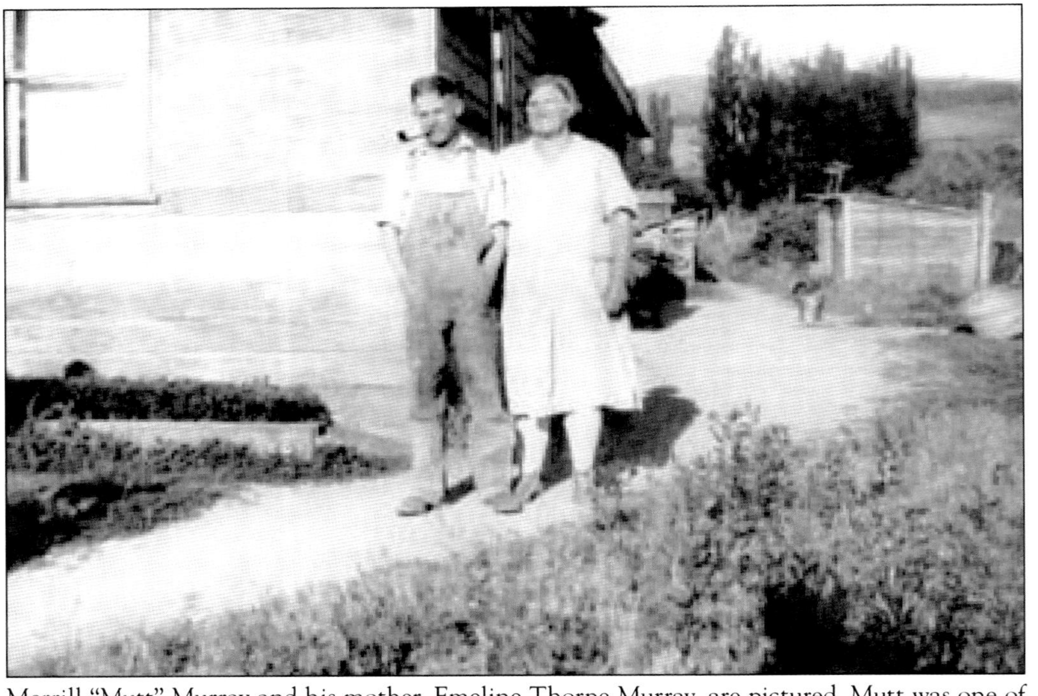

Merrill "Mutt" Murray and his mother, Emeline Thorpe Murray, are pictured. Mutt was one of eight brothers. He may have been short in stature, but he was a giant of a man. He was one of the town's longest-lived and most colorful characters, and he was loved by all who had the pleasure of knowing him. His death left a hole in the town that can never be filled, but the fond memories of him are treasured. (Courtesy of Dean Murray.)

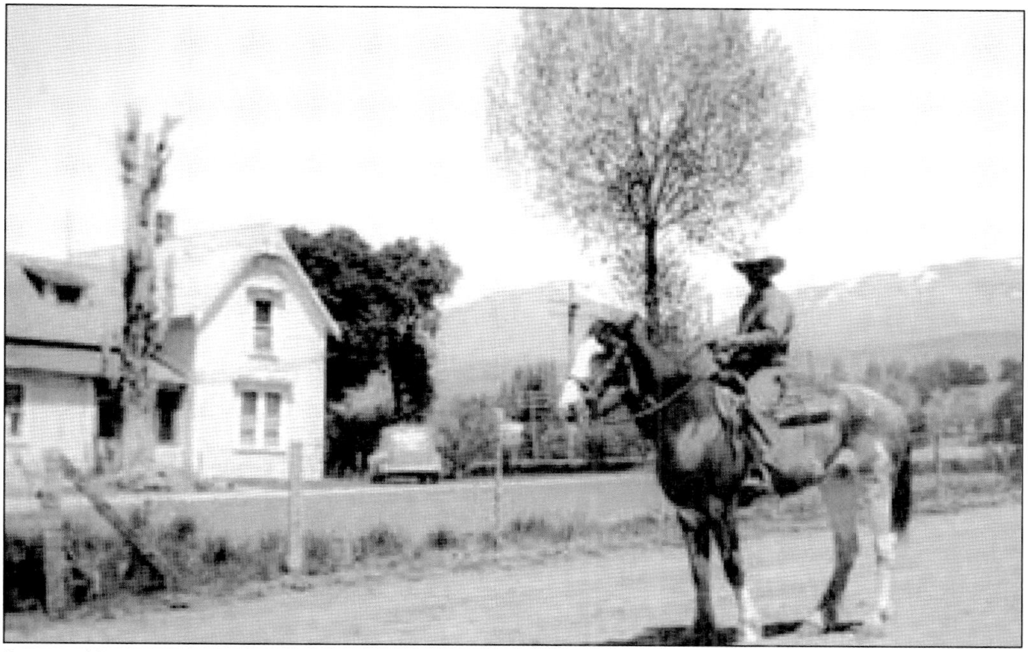

Pictured here is LeRoy "Roy" Murray on his horse in front of the old Carson home, located on the west side of Highway 91, about a mile south of Richmond. Roy was the marshal of Richmond for many years. At one time, Richmond had its own jail, a freestanding metal cage located behind the current Relic Hall. (Courtesy of Dean Murray.)

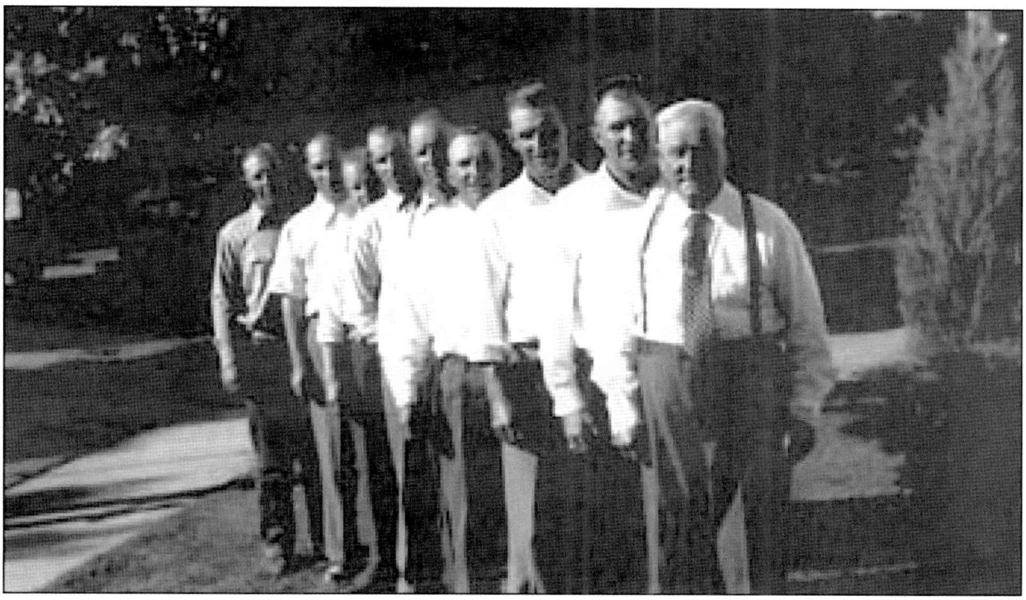

In this image are James Littlewood Murray and his eight sons. They are, from left to right, Leon, Reese, Merrill ("Mutt"), Carl, Lorenzo ("Ren"), James ("Jim"), LeRoy ("Roy"), Even, and James Littlewood Murray (father). The family first lived in the old Carson home on Highway 91 and later moved to town. They took up residence on the corner of State Street and 100 South, where the home still stands. (Courtesy of Dean Murray.)

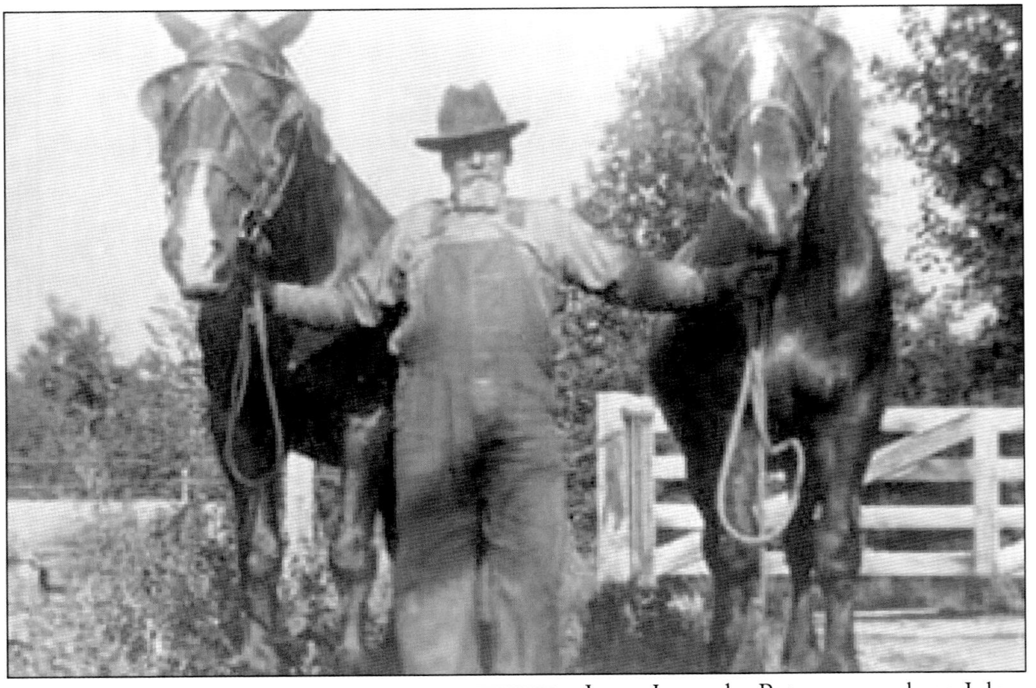

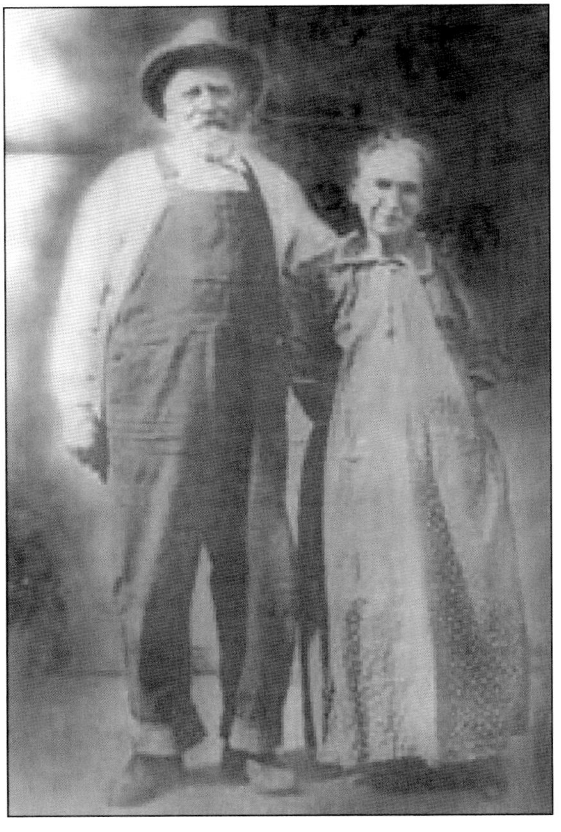

James Lavender Bateman was born July 6, 1855, in Cedar City, Utah. He left his family as a young man to become a freighter, driving a team of eight horses from Corinne, Utah, to Butte, Montana, every six weeks. As far as it is known, he never returned to see his family in Cedar City. He married Susan Violate Richardson on December 31, 1877. She was 13 years old at the time. A severe illness took her hearing soon after, and she was deaf for the rest of her life. They were the parents of nine children, only three of whom lived to adulthood—Leo, Lillian, and Alfred. James was known as a lover of horses and took pride in having the biggest and best teams in the area. Each horse weighed in the neighborhood of one ton. The image at the left shows the couple in their later years. (Both courtesy of Valerie Hatch.)

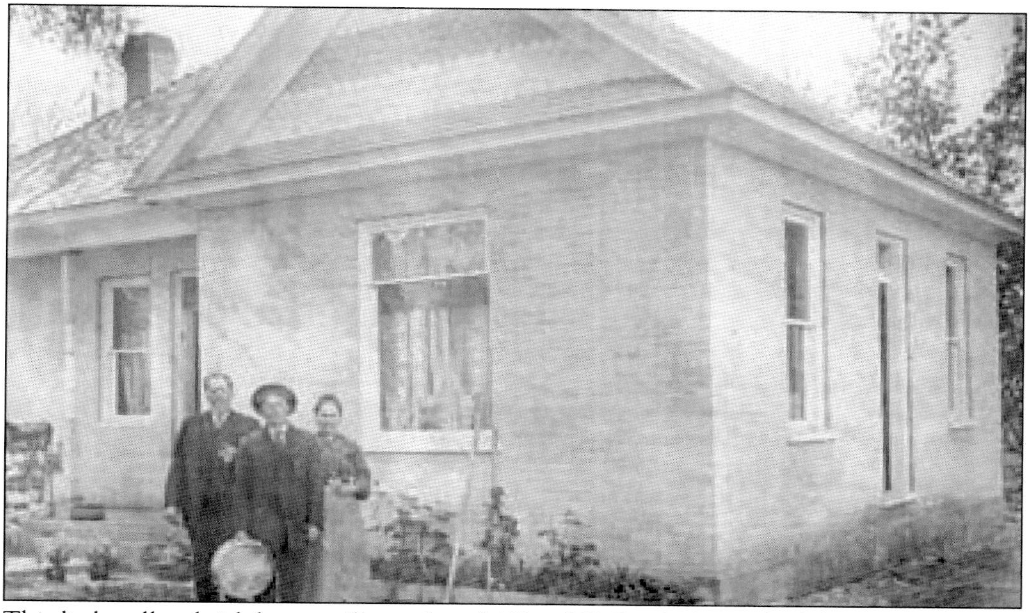

This little yellow brick house still stands at 94 East 300 South. It was built by James Lavender Bateman, pictured here with his wife, Susan Violet Richardson Bateman, and their son Leo Bateman. The house has seen very little change on the outside, except for the addition of a lovely rock wall around the yard. The Batemans' granddaughter Zelda Stoddard resides in the home today. (Courtesy of Zelda Stoddard.)

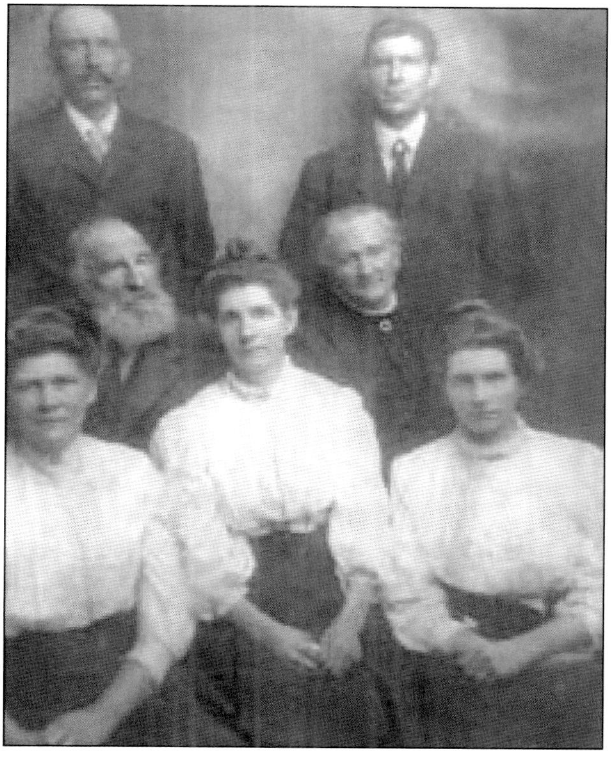

Included in this image of the William Frain Dobson family are, from left to right, (first row) Anna, Elizabeth, and Mary; (second row) William Frain and Ann Hill Dobson; (third row) William Orson and John Moroni. William F. was born in England in 1839. The family immigrated to the United States in 1840 or 1841. William's mother died in Nauvoo, after which William was passed from family to family. He met Ann Hill while crossing the plains to Utah in 1868. They settled in Richmond, where they raised seven children. (Courtesy of L.D. Bowcutt.)

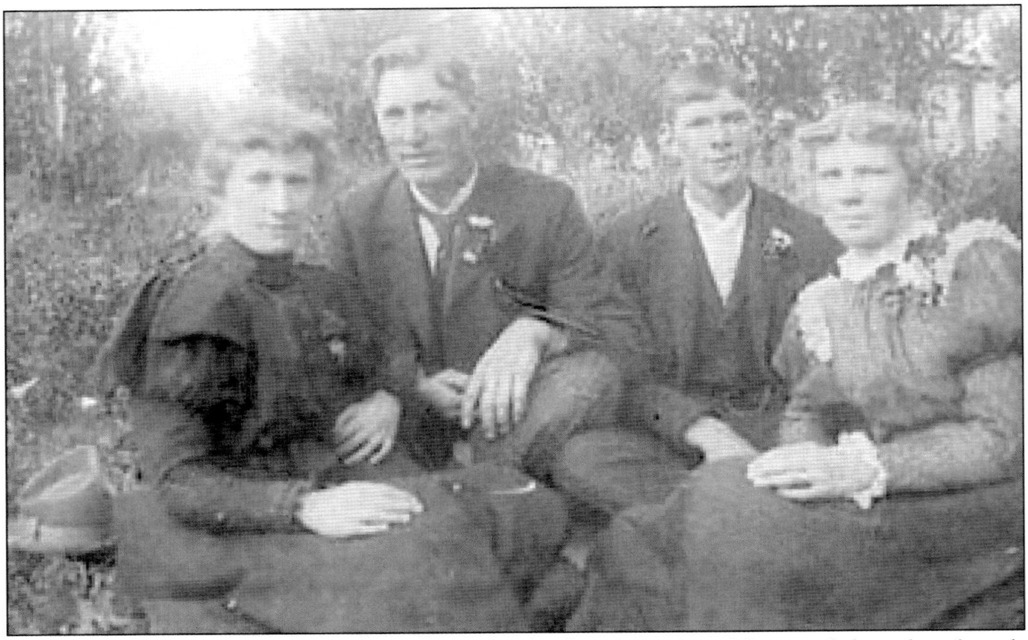

Pictured are, from left to right, Ermma Hyer, her husband, Brigham Hyer, and their dear friends John Moroni Dobson and his wife, Rhoda Christa Peart Dobson. It is believed that this image was taken on the Dobsons' wedding day in the late 1890s. Rhoda died in 1915 at the age of 35, leaving John with several small children. (Courtesy of L.D. Bowcutt.)

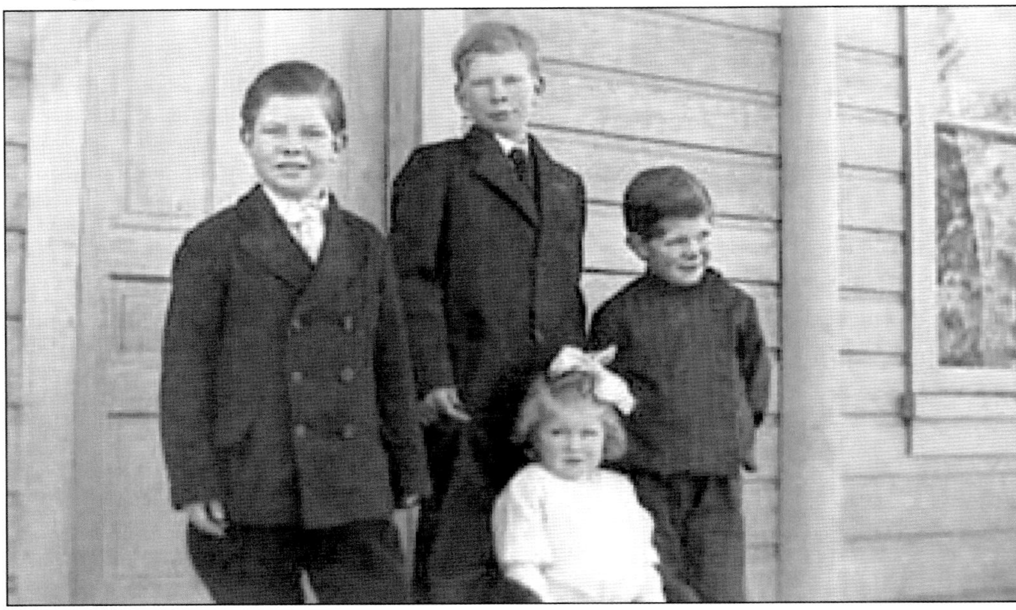

Pictured are, from left to right, Willas "Adrian" Dobson, Milton Dobson, Carmen Dobson, and Orval Dobson, children of John Moroni and Rhoda Peart Dobson. The photograph was taken around 1910 on a Sunday morning before church. Rhoda died about five years later, at which time the children were "farmed out" to be raised by other families. Years later, Adrian would die by his own hand, hanging himself in a barn. (Courtesy of L.D. Bowcutt.)

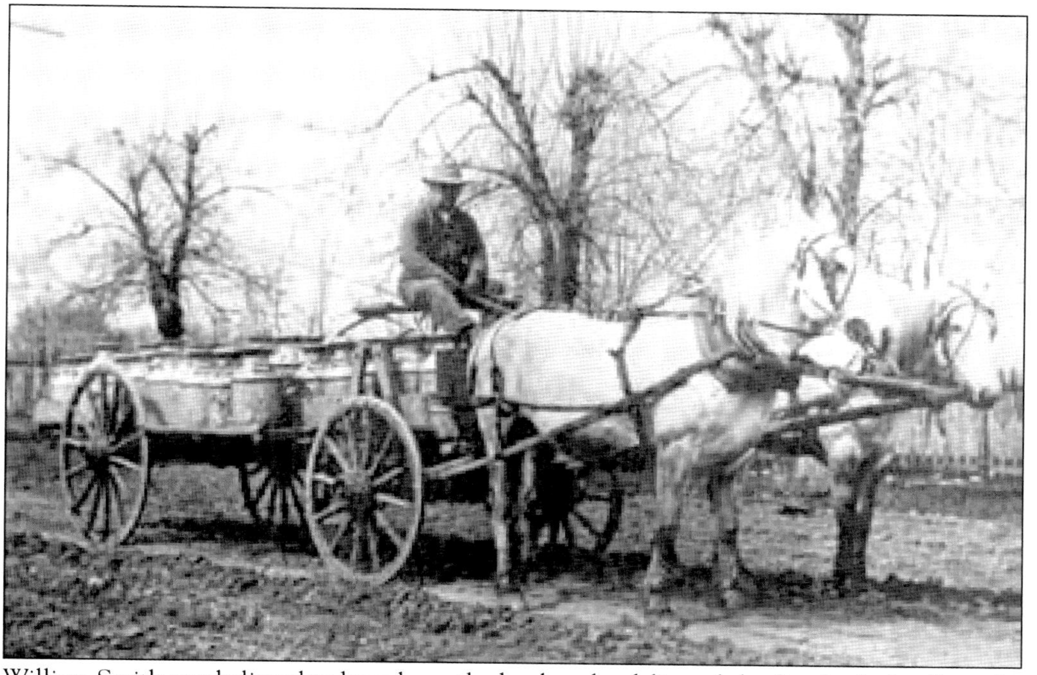

William Smith was believed to have been the hauler who delivered the first load of milk to the new Sego Milk Products plant in Richmond on March 14, 1904. William was the first of three generations of milk haulers to come from the same family. This image and the next two images show the progression from horse and wooden-wheeled wagons to rubber-tired wagons and finally, to the modern truck. (Courtesy of Roger Smith.)

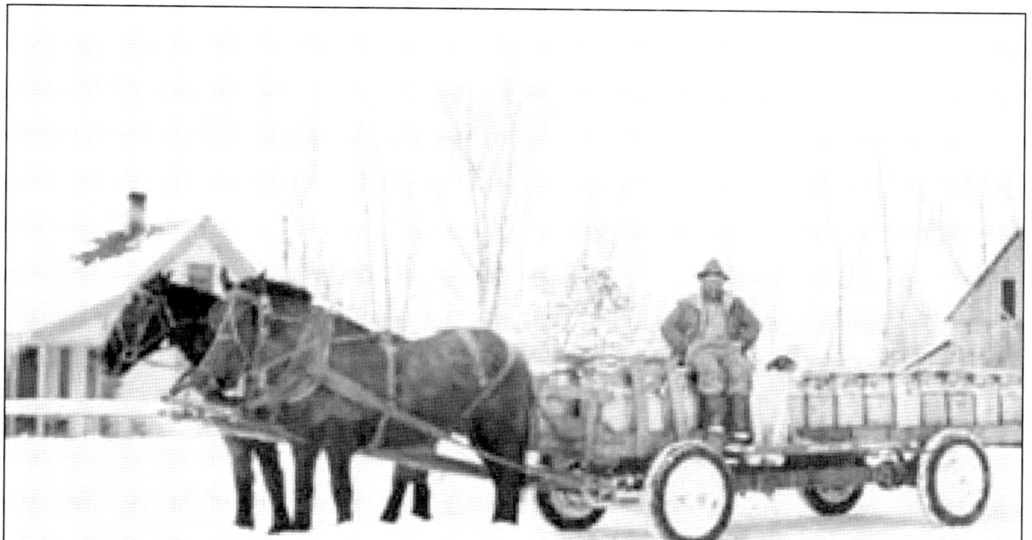

Pictured with his team is Edwin Smith, the son of William and the father of Dean. He hauled milk for the Sego Milk Company and also produced a fair amount of milk on his own farm. Edwin was the second of the three generations of Smith milk haulers for the Richmond Sego milk plant. (Courtesy of Roger Smith.)

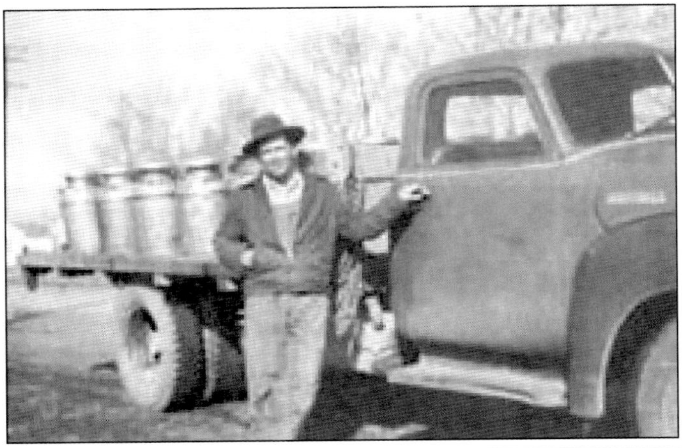

Pictured is Dean Smith, the third generation of milk haulers to haul milk to the Richmond Sego Milk Products plant and the first to use a truck. Milk haulers would drive from farm to farm, picking up the milk each day. Then, after delivering it to the plant, they would reverse their route and drop off the empty milk cans to be refilled and picked up again the next day. (Courtesy of Roger Smith.)

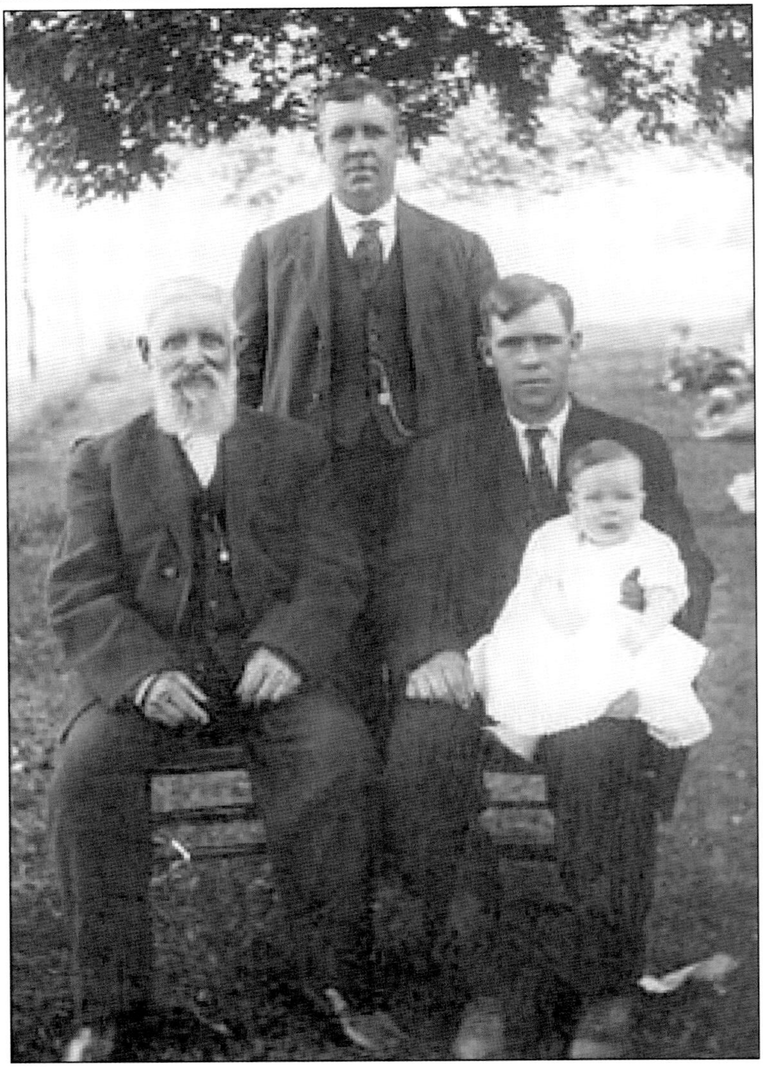

Shown here are four generations of the Smith family. They are, from left to right, Elijah Frederick Smith, William Frederick Smith, Edwin Elijah Smith, and baby Dean Smith. At the time this photograph was taken, it was unusual to have four generations from one family all pictured together, due to the shorter average life spans of the day. (Courtesy Roger and Kathy Smith.)

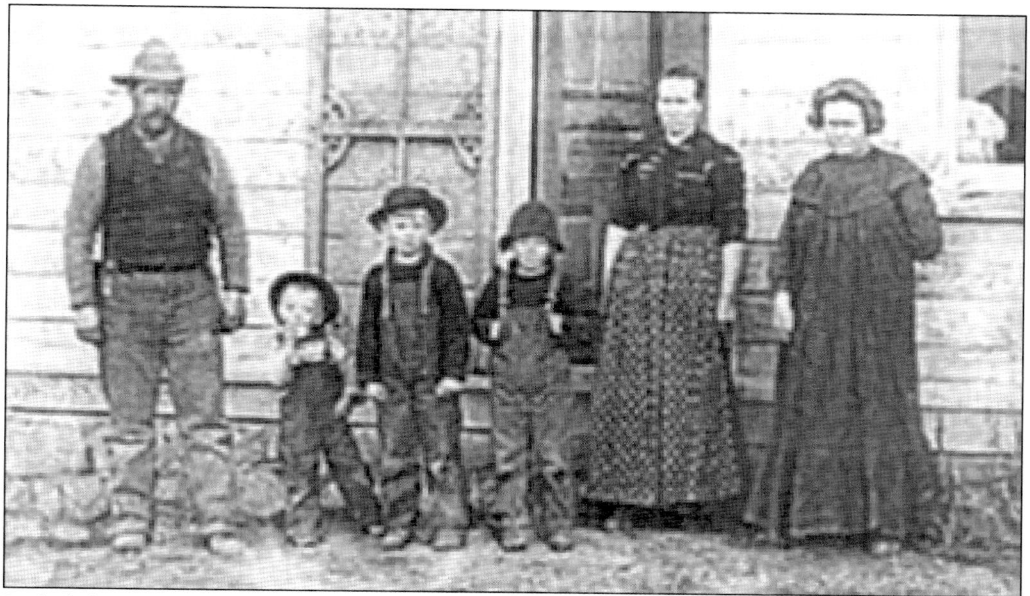

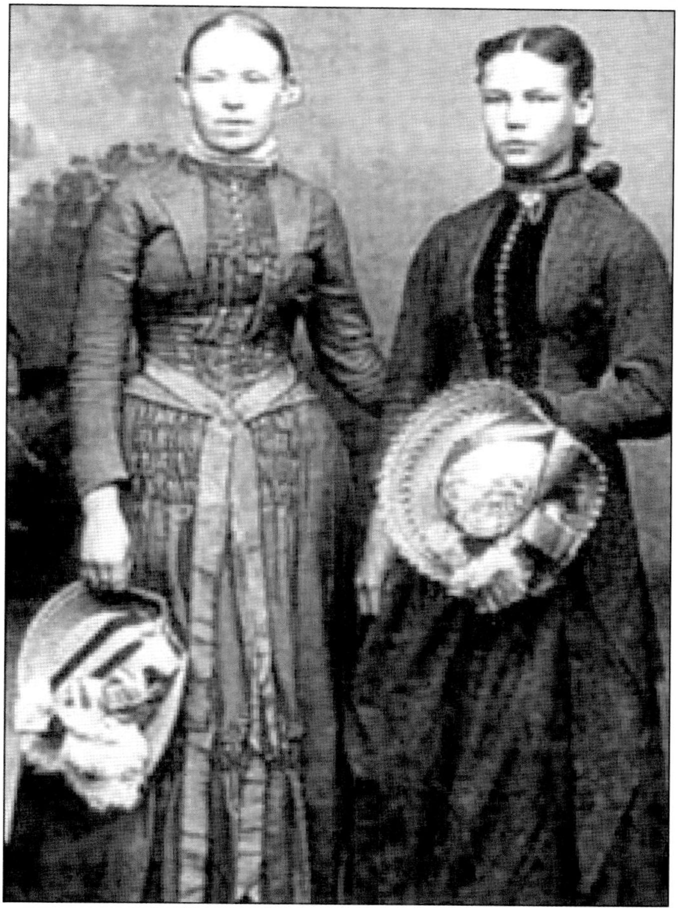

Included in this image are, from left to right, William Frederick Smith (father), Fred Smith, George Smith, Leroy Smith, Sarah Jane Spackman Smith (mother), and Frances Spackman. Sarah Jane and Frances Spackman were sisters. William Frederick and Sarah Jane were married and had a family of three boys, George, Leroy, and Fred. Frances lived with them and was considered part of the family. The rock foundation of the house is visible in the photograph above, as is the clapboard siding. The attire the family is wearing was the usual dress for the time period. Bib overalls were popular for young boys, and hats were also usually worn. Women's everyday wear almost always included an apron or pinafore worn over the dress. The other photograph shows Sarah Jane and Frances in their younger years, dressed in their Sunday best. (Both courtesy of Roger and Kathy Smith.)

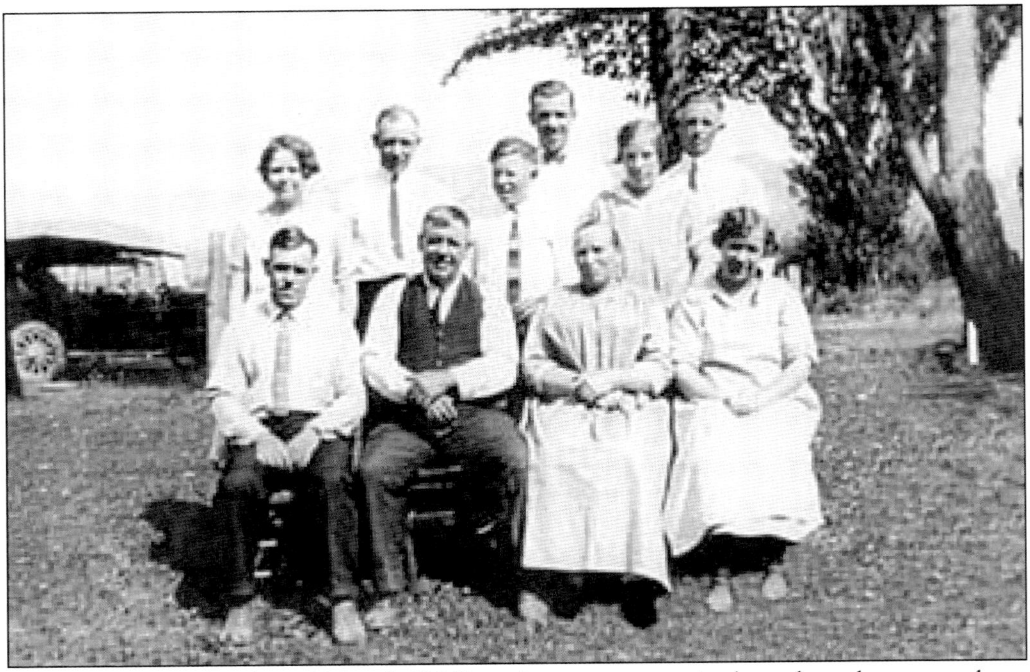

The Smith family lived at 666 South 100 East. As was common in those days, they were a large family living in a small house. Pictured above are, from left to right (first row) Edwin, William F. (father), Sarah Jane (mother), and Mary; (second row) Mildred, Fred, Merlin, George, Amy, and LeRoy. Two cousins, Sarah Jane and Frances Spackman, also lived with the family. The cousins were housed in a small outbuilding called a summer kitchen. The family referred to it as "the shanty." It was just yards away from the house. The house still stands, and was occupied by Mildred Means for many years. It has recently undergone extensive remodeling. (Both courtesy of Roger and Kathy Smith.)

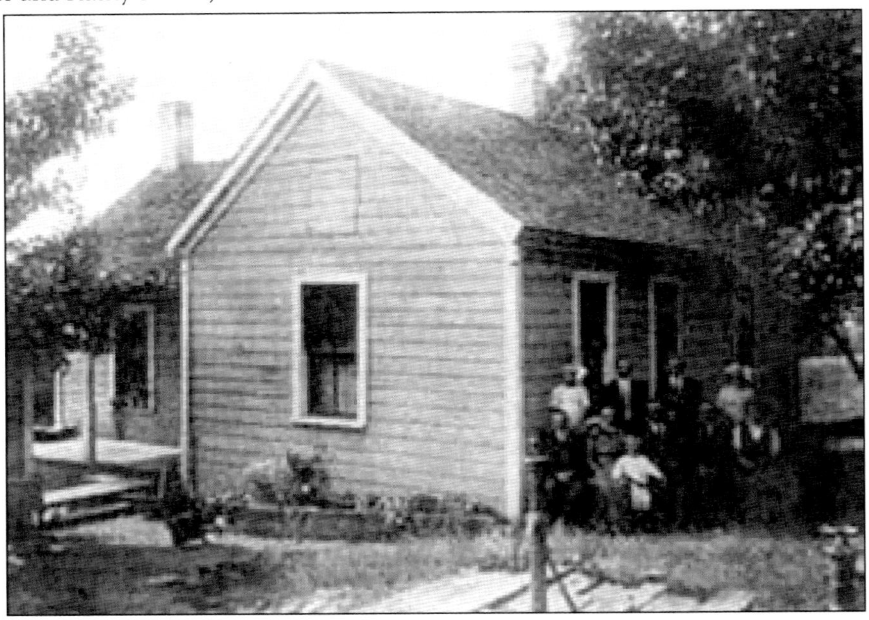

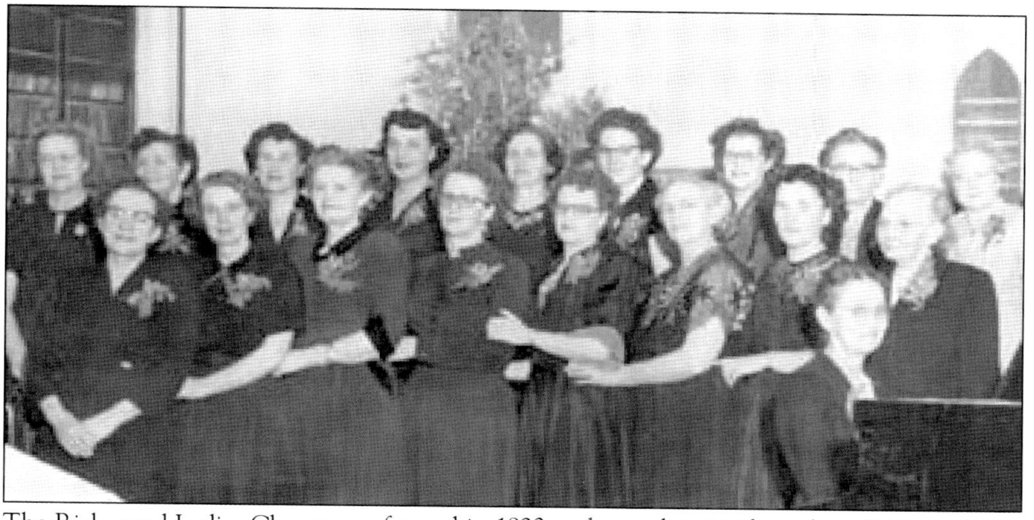

The Richmond Ladies Chorus was formed in 1923 and stayed active for at least 50 years. They are pictured here in 1952. Included in the image are, from left to right (first row) Maud Merrill, Florence Lewis, Edna Lewis, Leona Bullen, Juness Christensen, Ellen Pack, Leora Smith, Anna Johnson, and Emma Hicken; (second row) Alba Webb, Aldean Smith, Emma Bell, Connie Bullen, Lona Smith, Louise McCarrey, Lucille Lewis, Bertha Hendricks, and Lavine Galbraeth. Not pictured are Adonia Dennis, Laura Tanner, and Alda Brown.

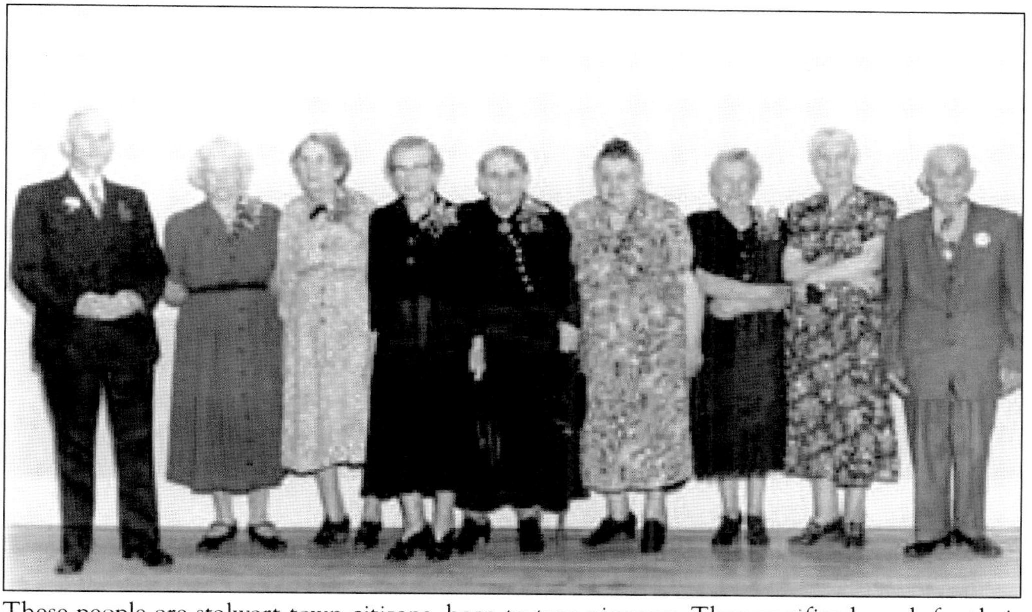

These people are stalwart town citizens, born to true pioneers. They sacrificed much for their families, faith, and community. They are, from left to right, William H. Lewis, Mrs. Carlson, Martha Aylsworth, Susie Stoddard, Mrs. Farnes, Lucinda Bair, Lottie Sullivan, Mary Bell, and Frank H. Traveller.

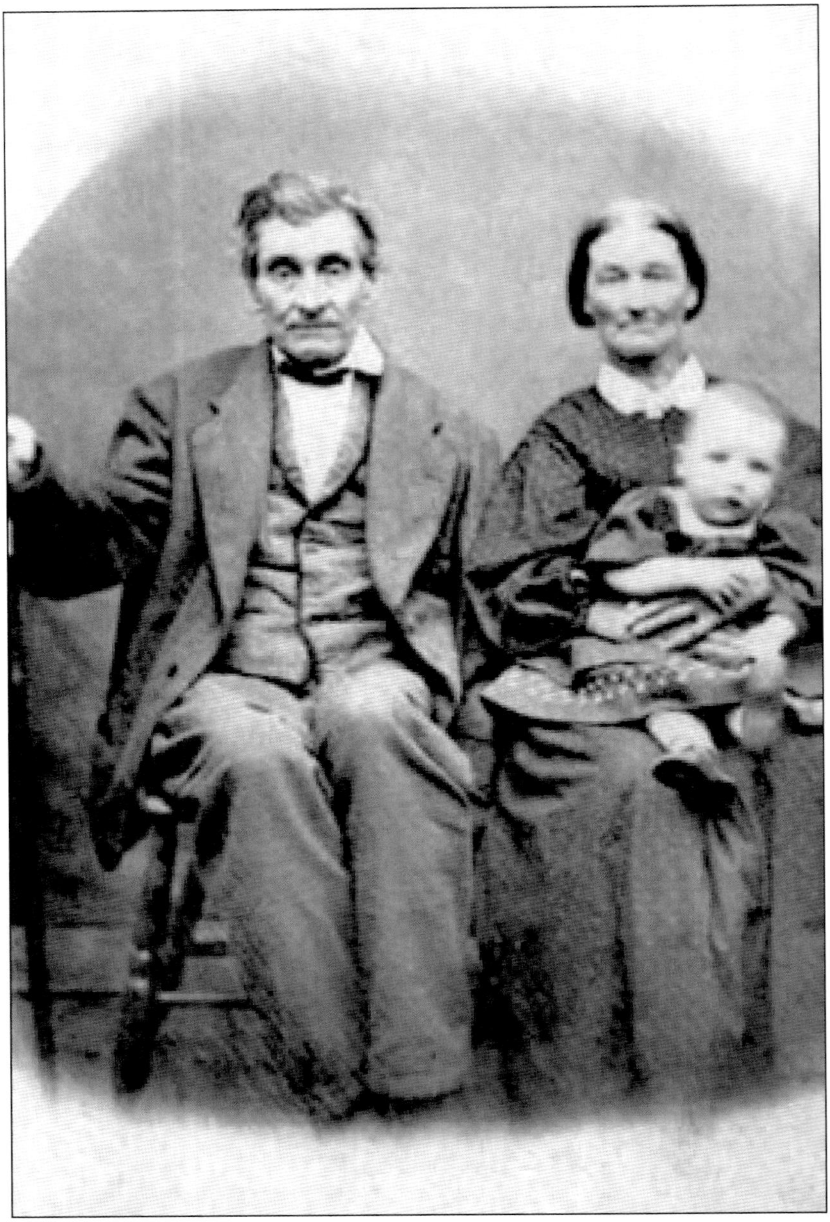

James and Drusilla Hendricks are pictured with baby Elizabeth Harriet Hendricks. James was shot in the neck at the battle of Crooked River and was never able to work again. Thus, the burden of earning a living and most other responsibilities fell on Drusilla. There were five children in the family, and each child had assigned duties to carry out. William, the oldest son, was 12 years old when he was put to work hauling rock for the Nauvoo Temple. His work paid for the family's tithing. Drusilla also let William sign on with the Mormon Battalion at the age of 16, one of the youngest to enlist. Drusilla was a very strong woman, enduring much in life. She was stalwart in her faith and believed that God would see her through. Drusilla died on May 20, 1881, and was laid to rest in the Richmond cemetery. The local camp of the Daughters of Utah Pioneers bears their name today, the James and Drusilla Hendricks Camp.

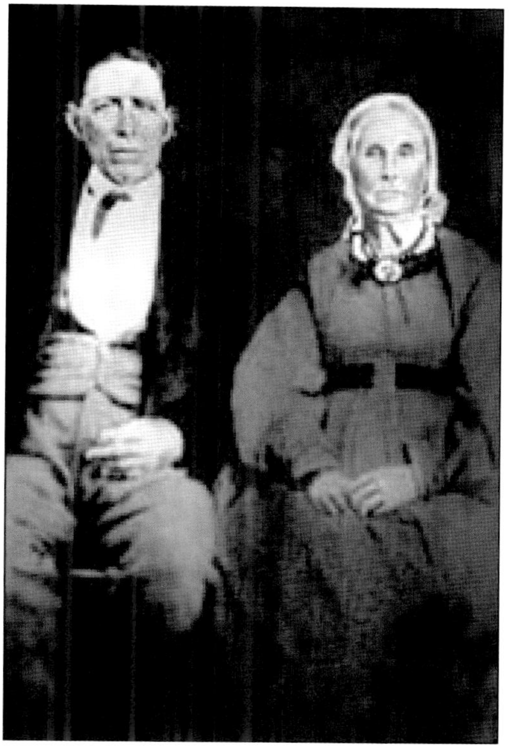

James and Almira Phelps Davenport settled in Richmond in the fall of 1861. They were the parents of 11 children. They were both endowed in the Nauvoo Temple on December 31, 1845. They were later sealed in Brigham Young's office on February 3, 1846, four days before the Nauvoo Temple was closed. The temple was later destroyed by a mob. (Courtesy of Karen Rawlings.)

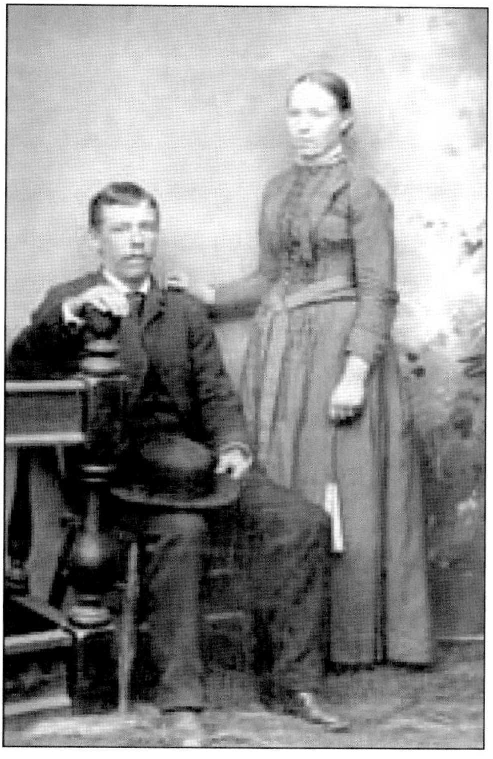

Pictured here are Andrew Feltman and his wife, Mary Alice Bell Feltman. They resided on a farm located in southeast Richmond. Andrew was born in Switzerland on November 15, 1843. Mary Alice was born in Grantsville, Utah, on April 26, 1859, to Mathew T. and Jane Metcalf Bell. Andrew and Mary Alice are both buried in the Richmond cemetery. (Courtesy of Judy Tripp.)

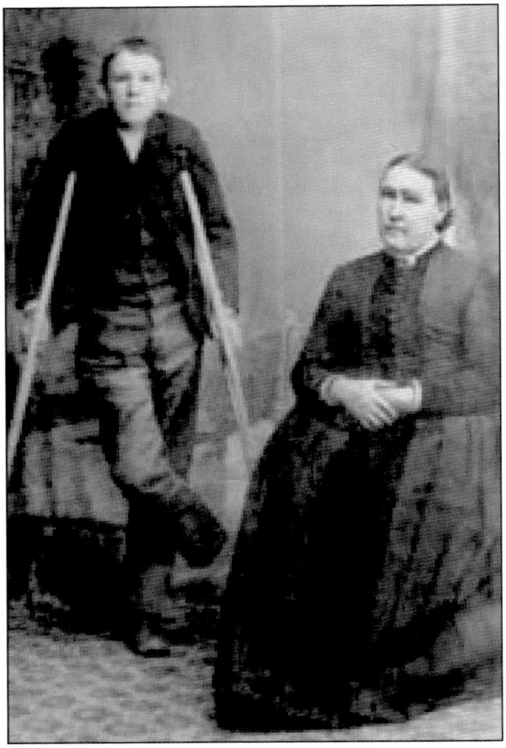

Mary Ellen Wood Allsop is pictured here with her son Reuben Allsop. In her history it states, "Her son, Reuben, suffered from an injury that made it necessary to have his right foot removed. This was done in the home, with Mary Ellen being the nurse." She and her husband, John Allsop, had 11 children. (Courtesy of Karen Rawlings.)

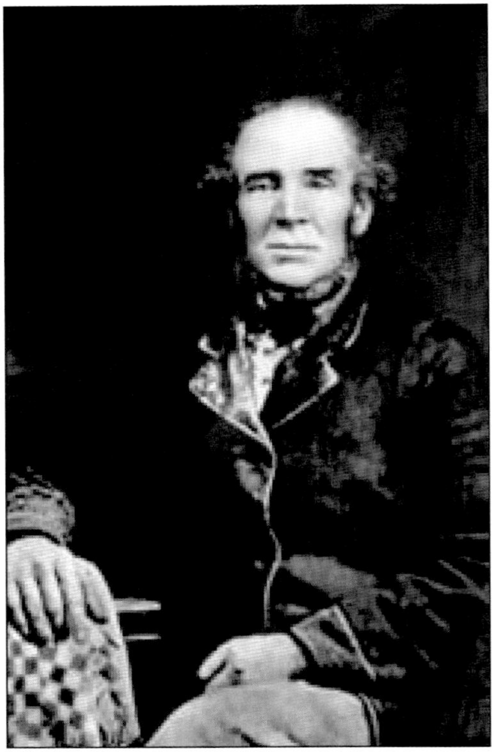

John Allsop was born in Nottingham, England, on September 20, 1923. He immigrated to Utah in 1854 and moved to Richmond with his wife, Mary Ellen Wood Allsop, in the spring of 1860. He was a carpenter and furniture maker. He died on October 25, 1876, and is buried in the Richmond cemetery. (Courtesy of Karen Rawlings.)

In this image are Enoch Bartlett Tripp and his wife, Julia Ann Bowman Tripp. Enoch came to Richmond at the same time as his brother William Robert Tripp. They were both farmers and had large families. They also traveled back and forth to the East Coast to tend to other business ventures. (Courtesy of Judy Tripp.)

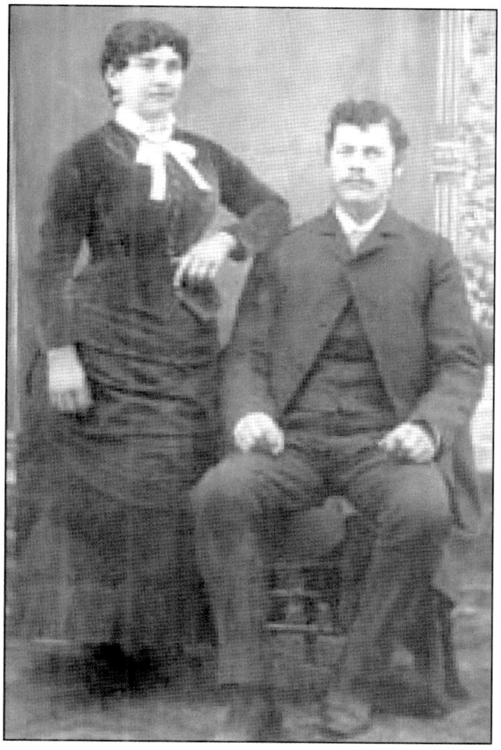

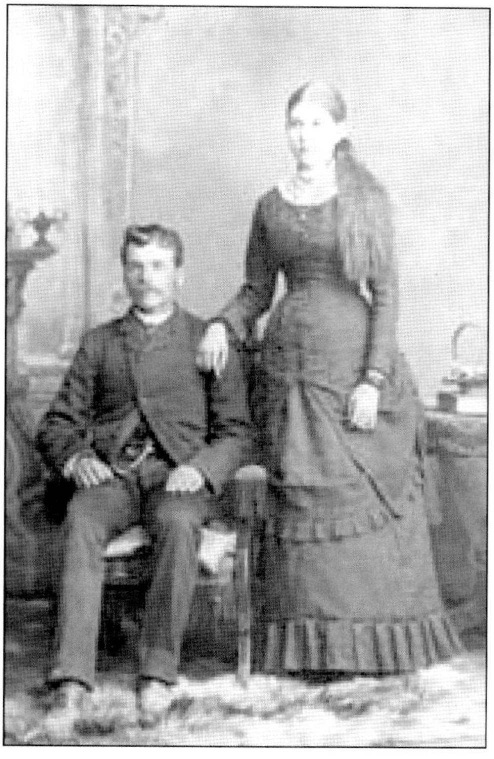

Pictured are William Robert Tripp and his second wife, Martha Ann Cotterell Tripp. Martha was the daughter of Joseph and Sarah Ann Bowman Cotterell. This image is special, as it is very unusual to see a woman photographed with her hair down during this period. (Courtesy of Judy Tripp.)

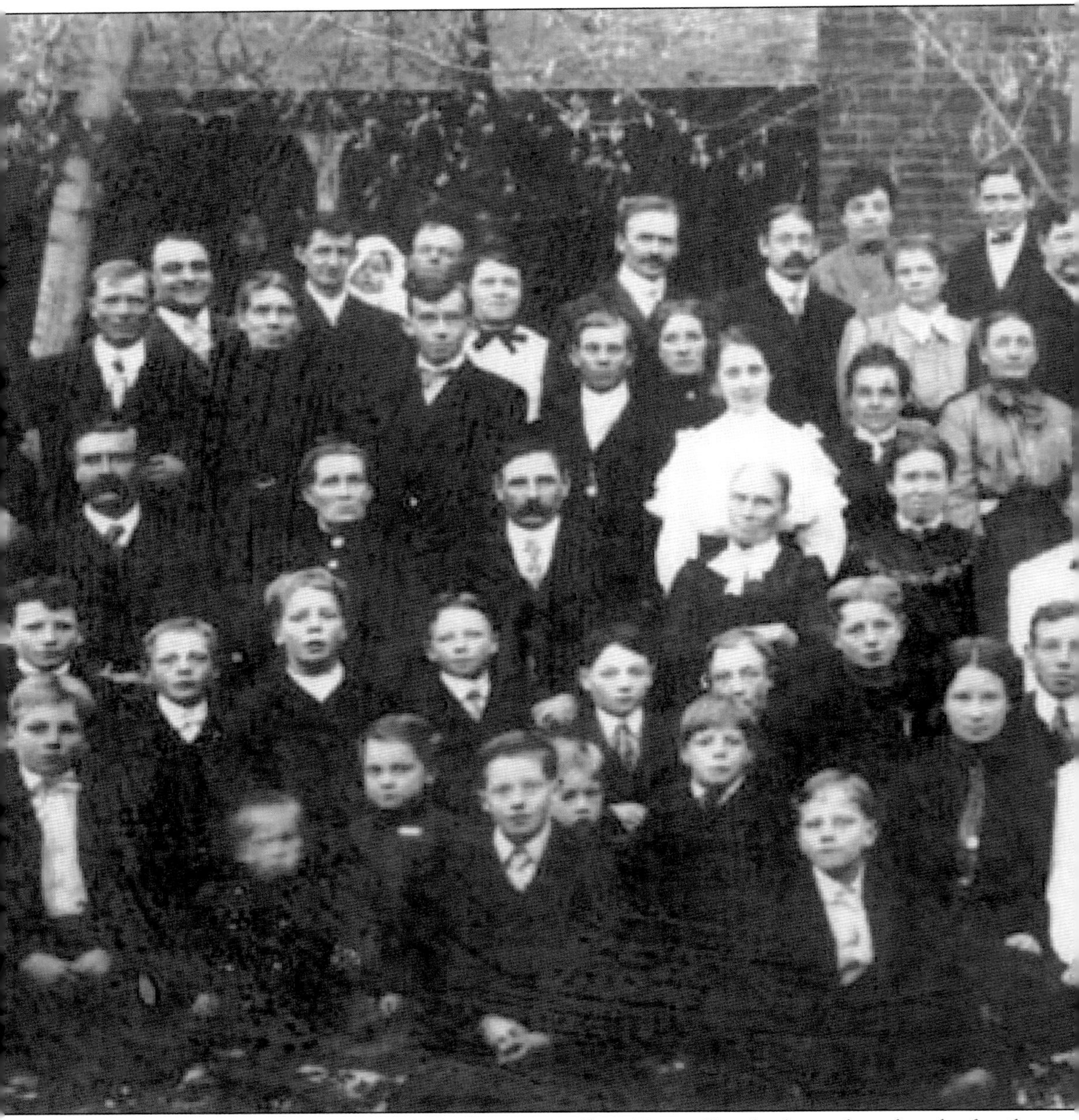

In 1905, the family of Richmond's first mayor, William Dorris Hendricks, gathered at the family home on the corner of Main and State Streets. William, with the white beard, is seated fifth from the right in the first row of adults. On his right are three of his wives, Eleanor Anna Maybin, Almira Davenport, and Alvira Lavona Smith. On his left are wives Mary Jane Andrus (white scarf) and Christine Olsen. The Hendricks family played a prominent role in the settling and development

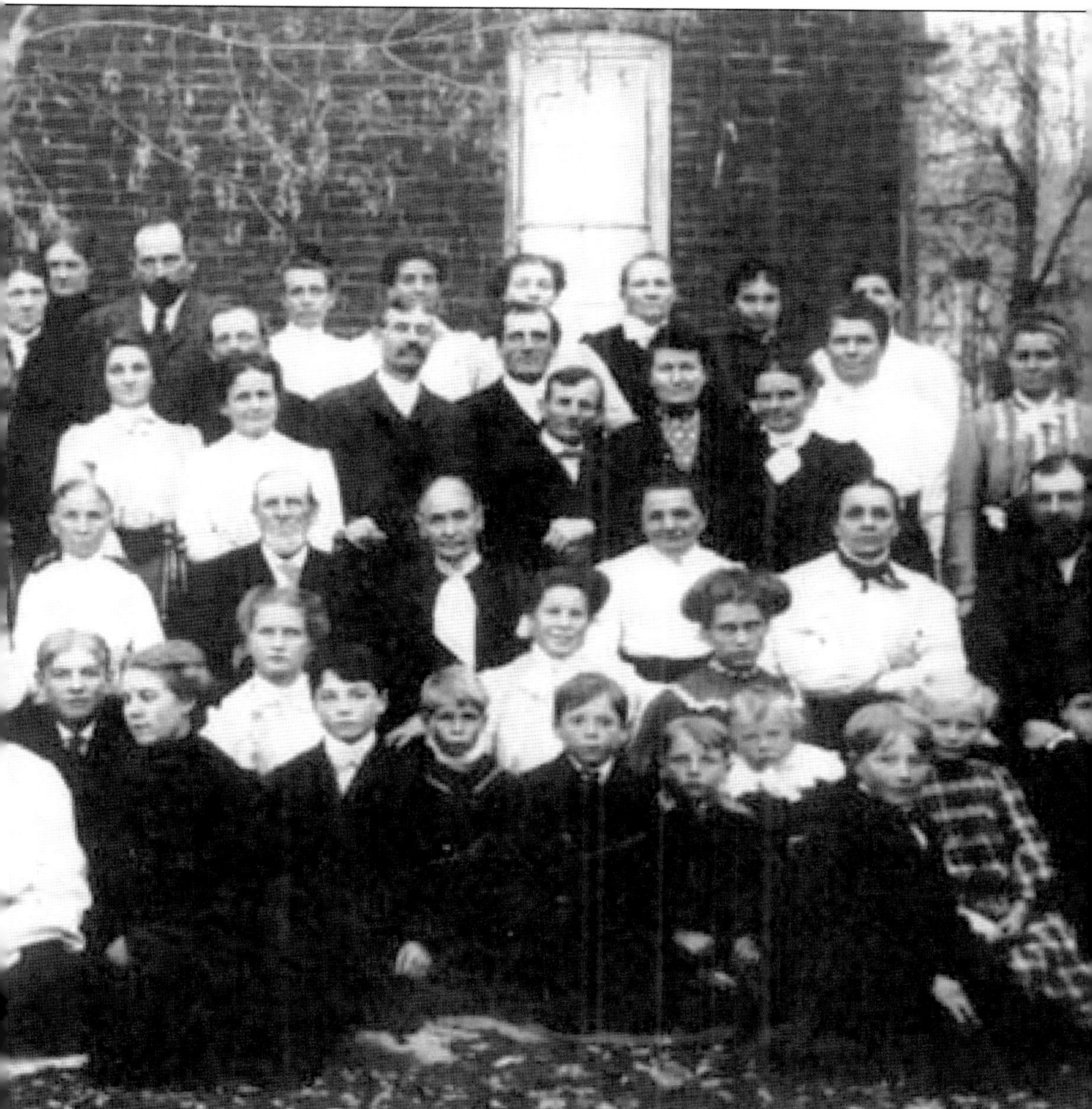

of the town. They owned and operated many businesses, held many public offices, and served in numerous church callings. Mary Jane Andrus Hendricks spearheaded the fundraising for the construction of the Relief Society Building, which still stands today. The Hendricks influence remains strong in Richmond, with many descendants still residing in the area. The family continues to hold a large reunion in town every summer. (Courtesy of Hendricks family.)

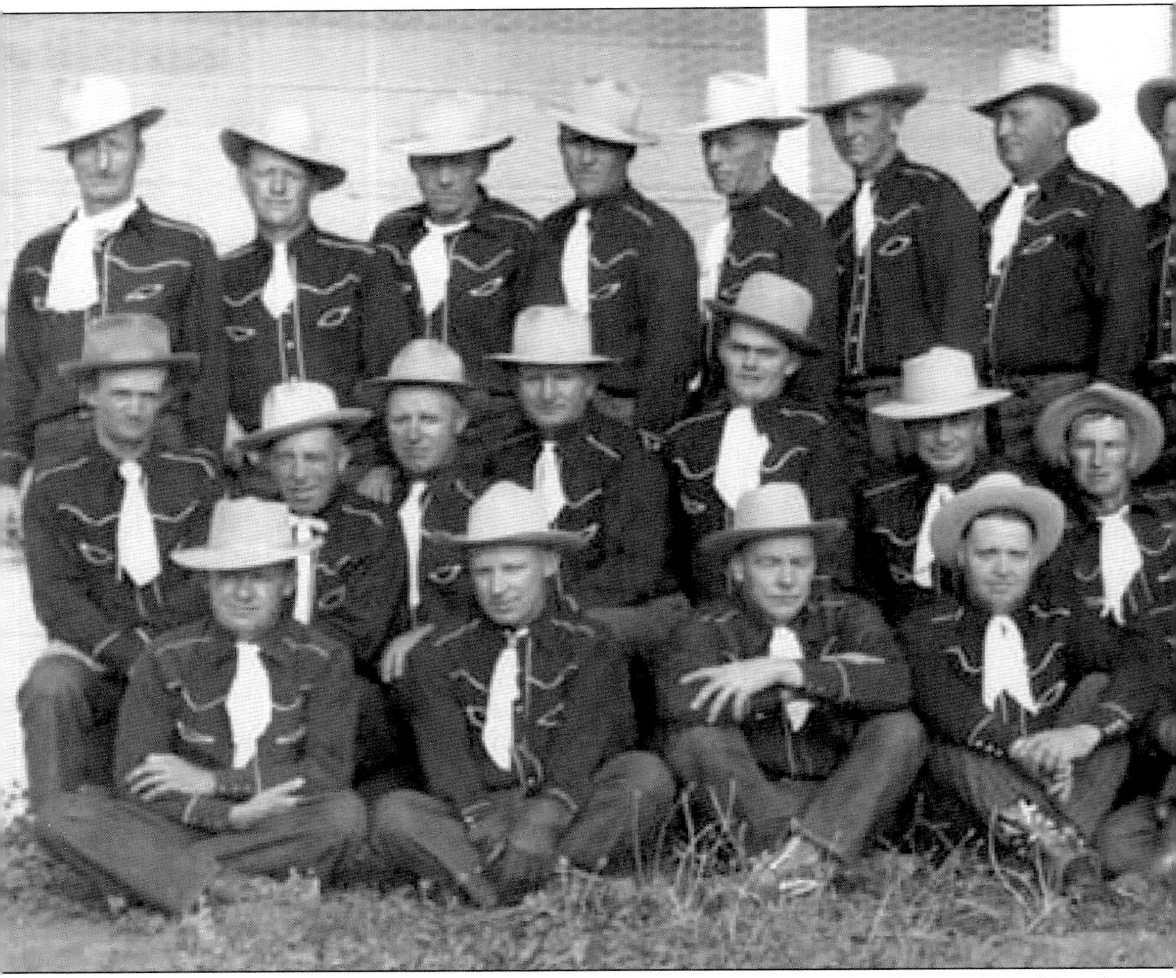

The members of the Richmond Riders Club in 1947 are, from left to right, (first row) Myrl Smith, Merrill Murray, William Nivison, Rulon Thompson, Thomas Whittle, Elmer Skidmore, Ned Spackman, James T. Murray, Cyrus Skidmore, and Amos Bair; (second row) Champ Webb, Farron Spackman, Lorenzo Murray, LaMont Bair, William Harris, Bryan Hendricks, Robert Hoppie,

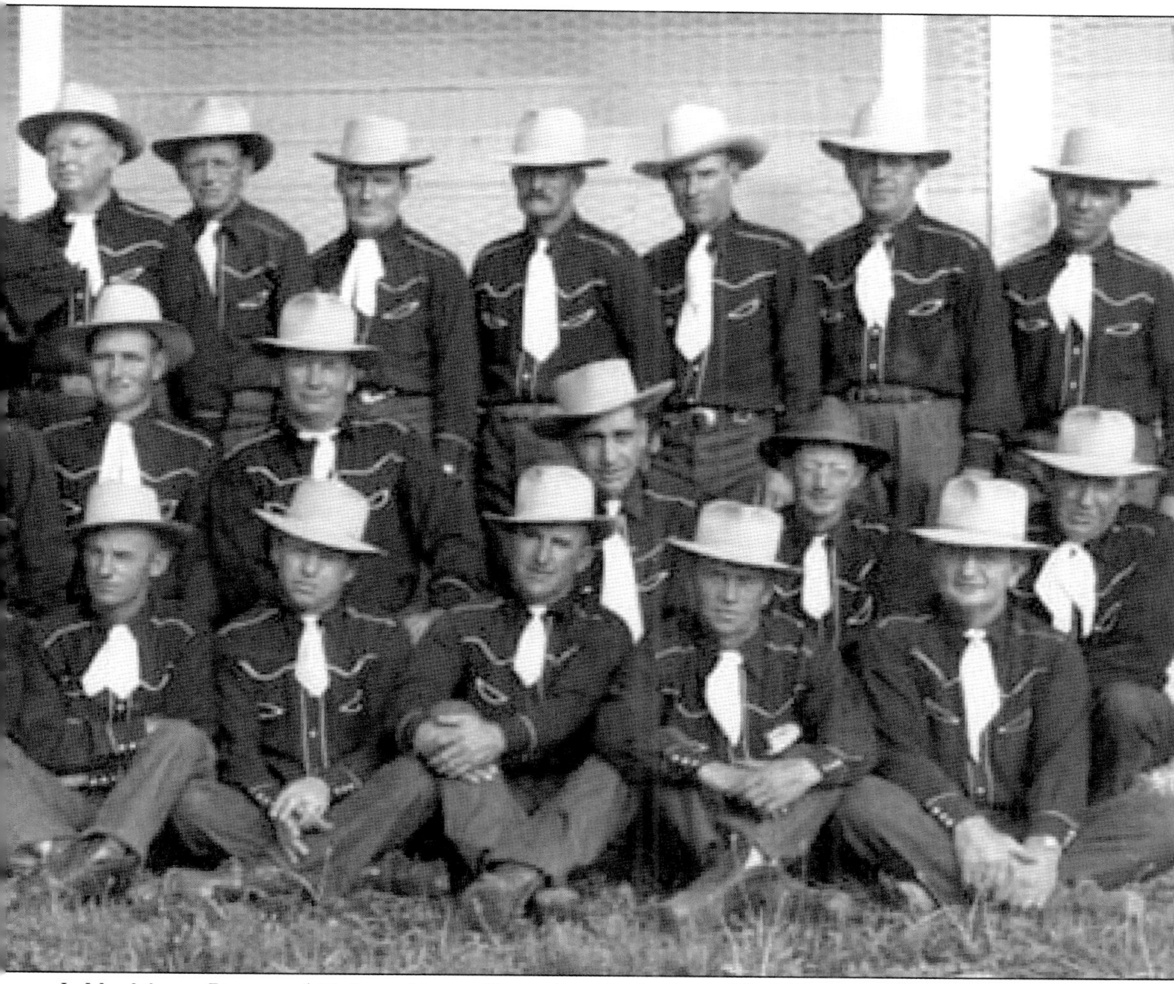

LaVor Moon, Raymond Nelson, Henry Plant, Joseph Andrus, Clark Rigby, and Judd Anderson; (third row) Arnold Egan, Noel Stoddard, Harold Christofferson, Jed Robinson, Ivan Christensen, Albert Hill, Vern Tripp, Reed Harris, Ern Tripp, LaMar Spackman, John Whittle, George Webb, LeRoy Murray, and Owen Nelson.

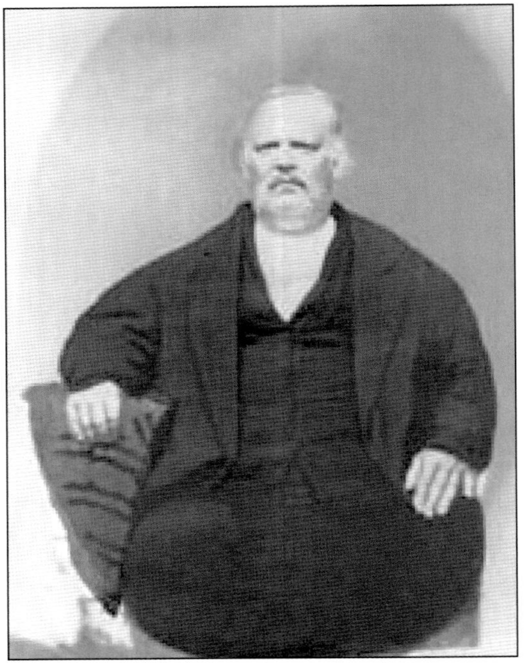

A veteran of the Indian Wars, John Bair helped settle Richmond in 1859 after scouting out the area several years earlier. He developed a good rapport with the local Indians, who called him Chief Bear John. His professions included shoemaker, lawyer, and farmer. He had six wives and at least 32 children.

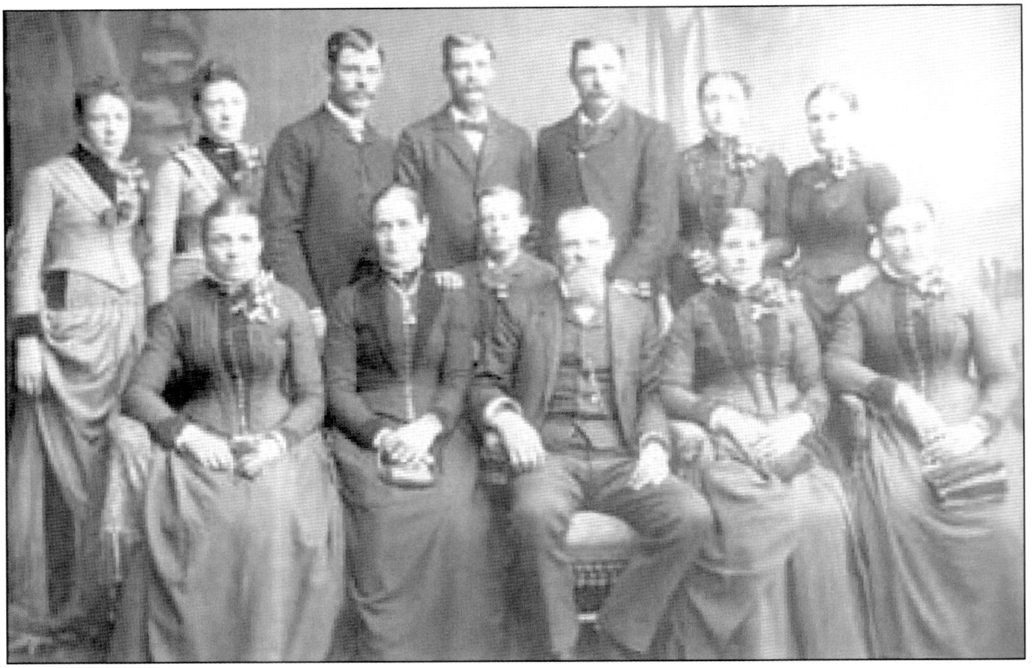

William Dorris Hendricks and first wife Mary Jane Andrus Hendricks were married at the Warm Springs Bathhouse in 1851. They moved to Richmond in 1860, and he was elected as the first mayor in 1864. He had four more wives and played the violin at dances. Pictured is William and Mary Jane's family. From left to right are (first row) Mary Jane, Mary Jane Andrus, George Gideon, William Dorris, Hila Hannah, and Eliza Abigail; (second row) Chloe, Drusilla, William Henry, Milo Andrus, Brigham Andrus, Charlotte, and Elizabeth Mahala.

Two

From Nothing to Something

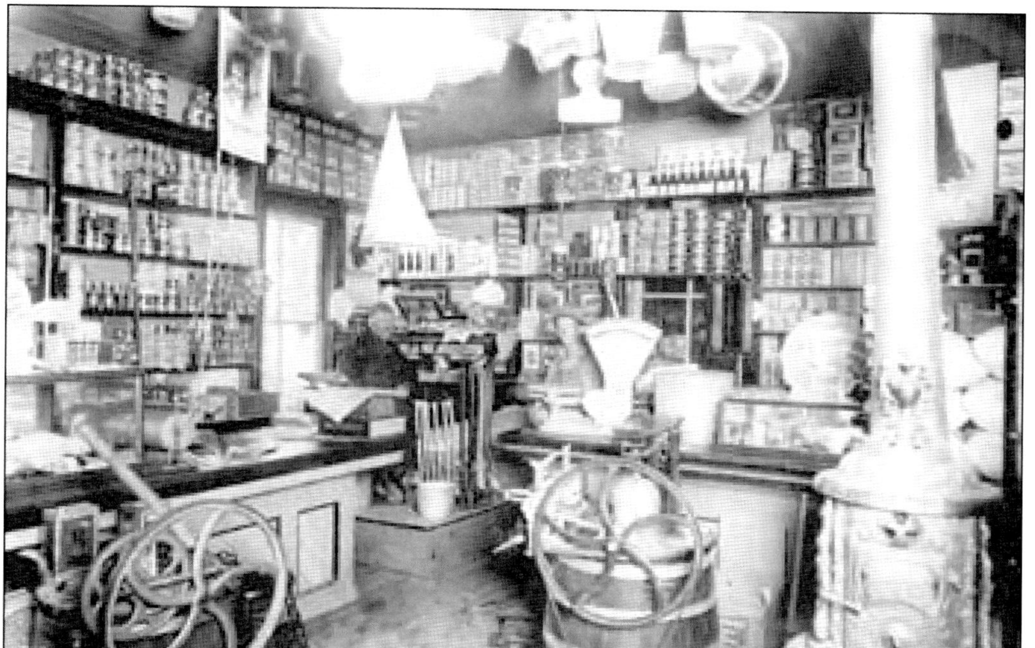

This photograph of the interior of one of the stores in Richmond was taken about 1920. The clerk seated at the desk is Tinker Thompson, and the young boy (possibly a delivery boy) is Merrill "Mutt" Murray. Above the window on the left are boxes of Kellogg's Corn Flakes, and a little to the left are cans of MJB coffee. To the right of the window is a Winchester calendar.

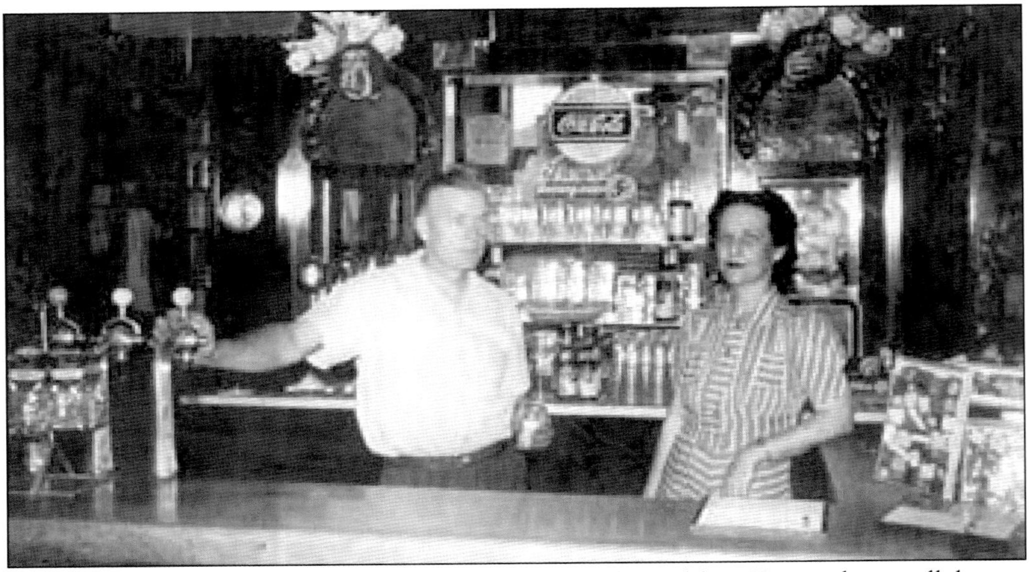

Pictured are William and Marie Nivison. They came to Richmond from Kansas, driving all the way on dirt roads and fording streams when necessary. In 1937, they bought the drugstore and liquor store from the Lundahls. The payment consisted of all the profits from liquor sales, and they kept what they could make from the drugstore and soda fountain. (Courtesy of Howard Nivison.)

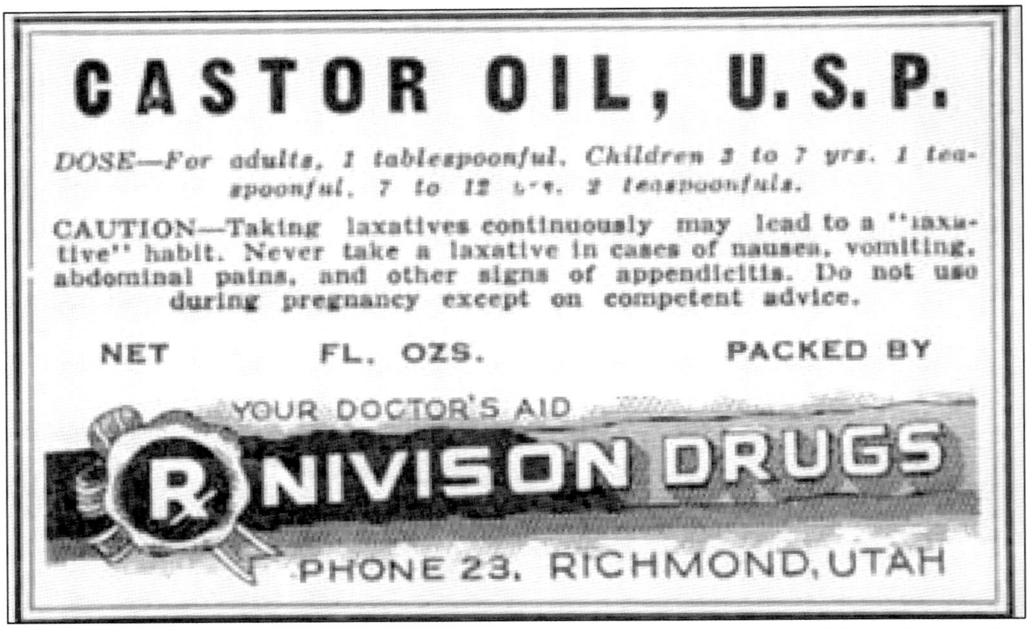

This is a prescription label for castor oil from Nivison Drugs. The label reads as follows: "Dose—For adults, 1 tablespoonful. Children 3 to 7 yrs. 1 teaspoonful. 7 to 12 yrs. 2 teaspoonfuls. Caution—Taking laxatives continuously may lead to a "laxative" habit. Never take a laxative in cases of nausea, vomiting, abdominal pains, and other signs of appendicitis. Do not use during pregnancy except on competent advice."

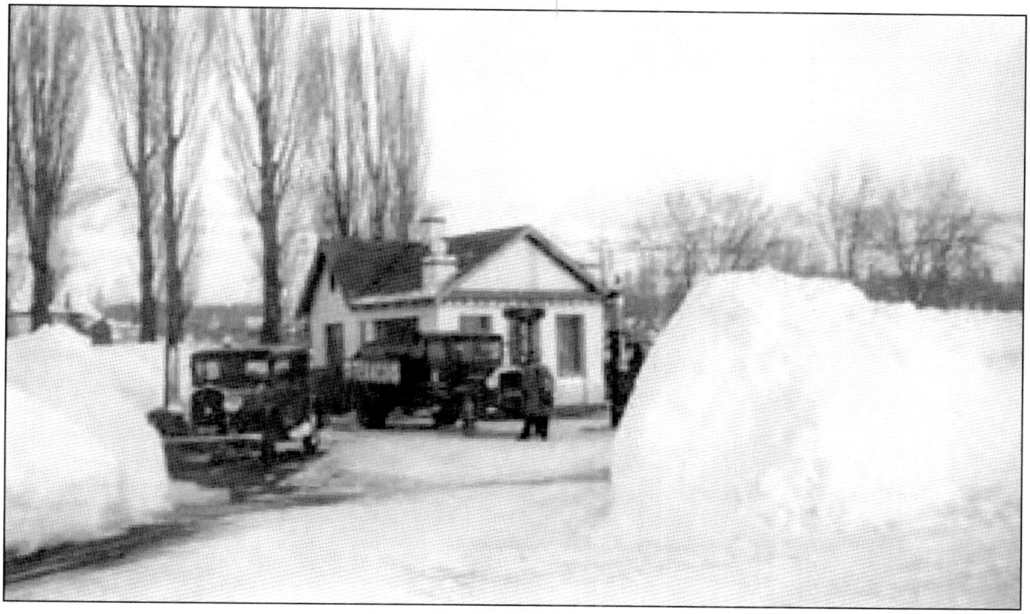

Grant L. Bagley operated one of the earliest service stations and automobile repair garages in Richmond. It was located on the highway at 100 South. Grant rented the building from E.J. Wilson. When Grant started the business in 1929, it consisted of the sale of gasoline and oil. During the 1930s, an addition was built for service and oil changes. In the 1940s, a major renovation was made, and the business became an appliance store and a service and repair facility with a new double bay. Albert Bateman was the full-time mechanic for 10 to 15 years. This station was very loyal to the Texaco brand and remained a Texaco station for its entire existence. (Both courtesy of Richard Bagley.)

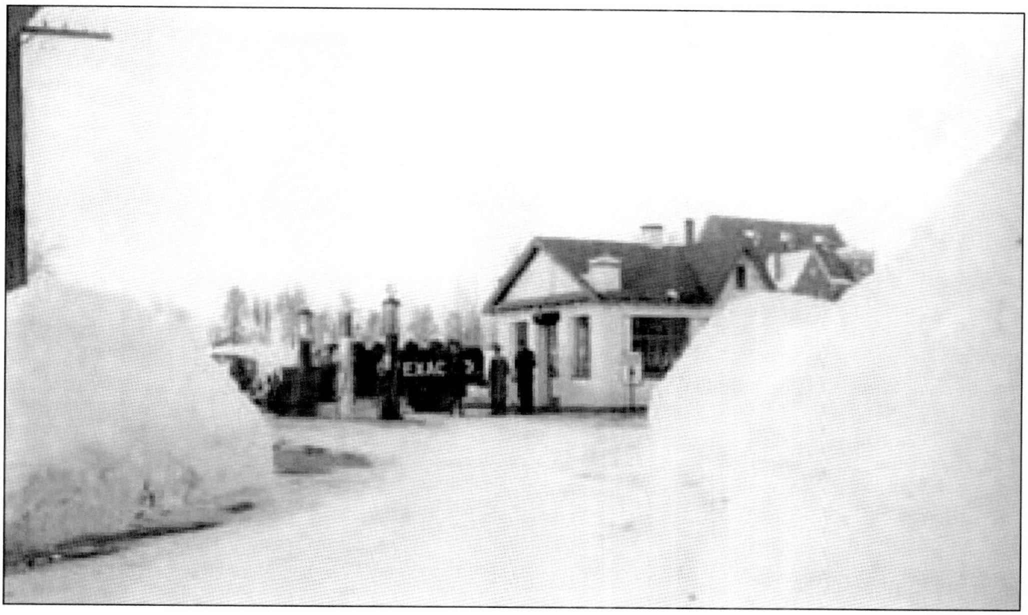

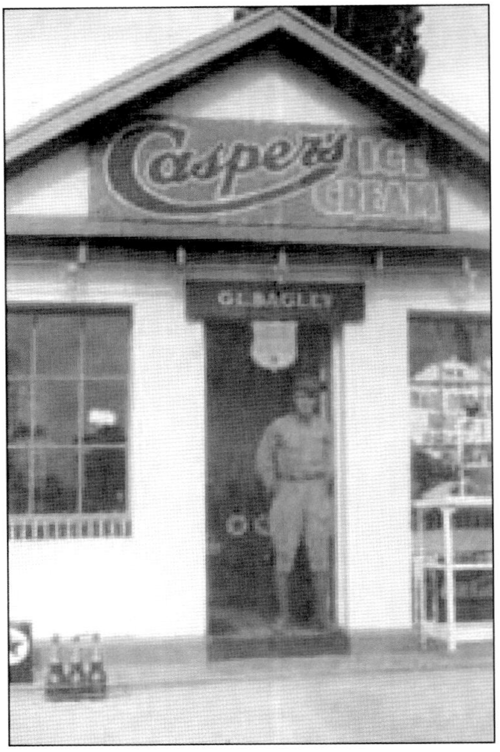

Grant L. Bagley is pictured standing in front of his Texaco station. Grant was proud of his association with Texaco and was always seen in his Texaco shirt. He moved to Richmond in 1928 and entered the business world by opening his service station the next year. After his death in 1949, Evan Spackman, Grant's right-hand man, took over and ran the station at the same location for many years. (Courtesy of Richard Bagley.)

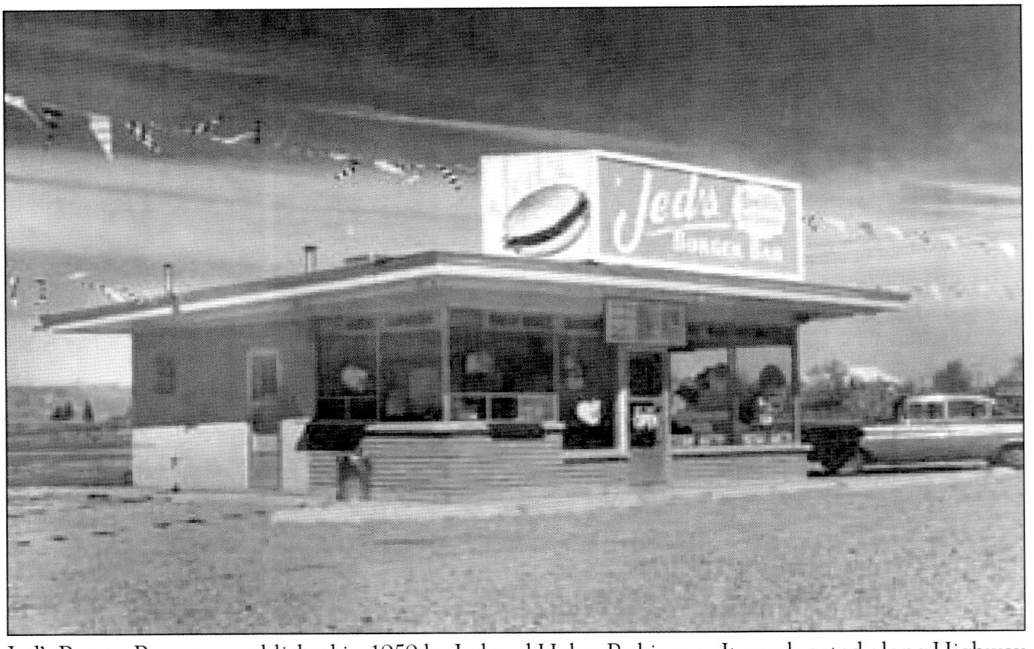

Jed's Burger Bar was established in 1959 by Jed and Helen Robinson. It was located along Highway 91, the perfect spot for a drive-in. Jed's served all ages. It was the perfect teenage hangout, and the older folks enjoyed stopping in for a root beer float. Their hand-cut french fries were legendary. The film *Napoleon Dynamite* featured scenes shot inside. (Courtesy of Richard Bagley.)

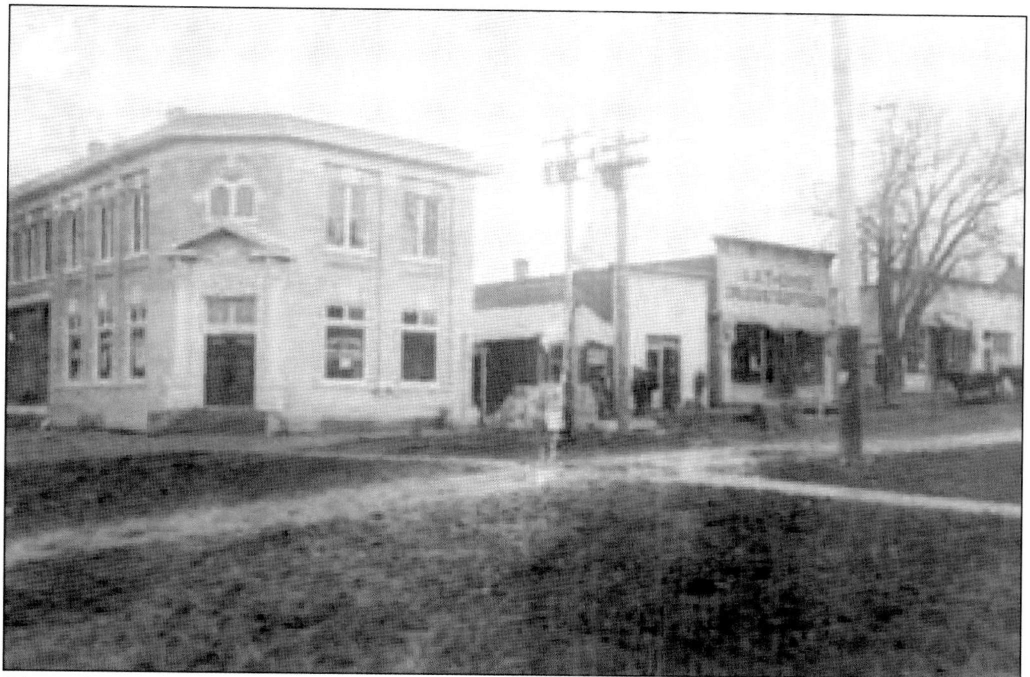

These three photographs are of the north side of Main Street, east of State Street, all taken from about the same vantage point. The two-story bank on the corner was built in 1908, and it is believed the first photograph was taken shortly thereafter. Note the deep mud on the unpaved roads and the horses tied to the hitching post. The second picture was taken some years later, after the roads were paved, although this is not apparent because of the snowy conditions. The third photograph is more current and depicts the same section of the block as it appears today. The second story of the bank was removed in the 1960s. The A.A. Thomas drugstore still stands and is now a private residence. Faded letters on the side can still be read, "Richmond Pharmacy, Sweet's Chocolates, Sold from Alaska to Australia." (Both courtesy of L.D. Bowcutt.)

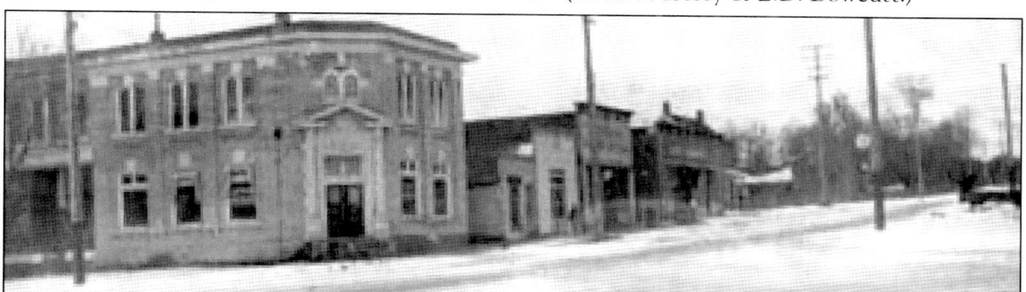

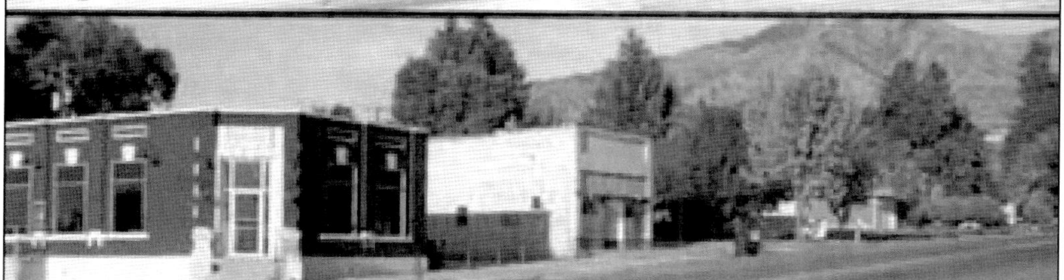

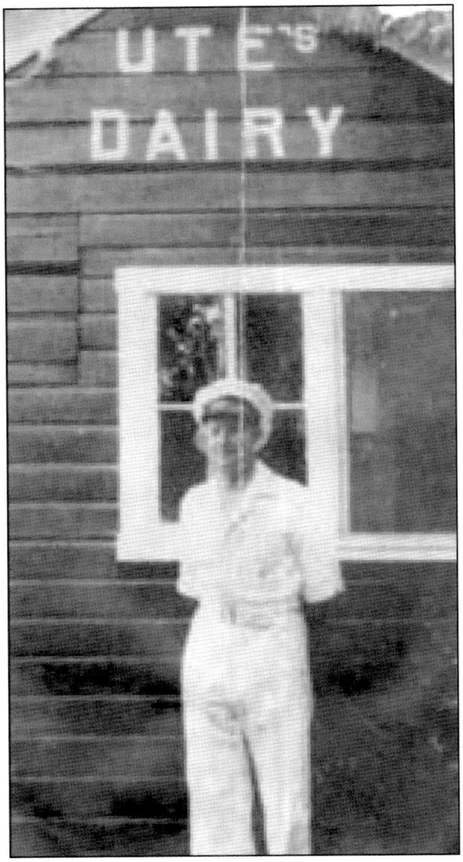

Ulyess "Ute" Lewis founded and operated Ute's Dairy in Richmond for many years. The dairy was located on the corner of 100 West 100 South, across from Park School. Ute's son Lex remembered his dad as a hard worker, a good storyteller, and a bit of a feisty character. (Courtesy of Lex Lewis.)

This delivery truck, used by Ute's Dairy, is parked in front of the Lewis family home, which was located on the northeast corner of 100 West 100 South. Ute's son Lex recalls riding on the running boards as a child and hopping off to put bottles of milk on customers' front porches. (Courtesy of Lex Lewis.)

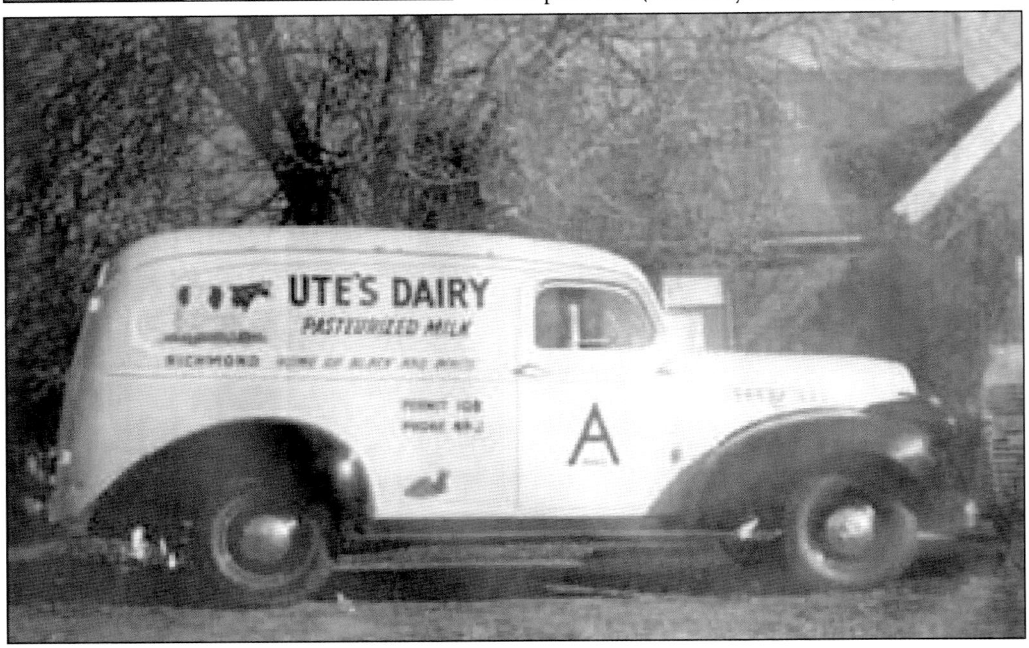

A US post office was established in Richmond on June 15, 1864. A small building was erected on the southwest corner of 100 East and Main Street. Several years later, it was moved to this building, which was located just east of where L.D.'s Café is now, and later, when the post office was moved to a new building, this small building became part of Theurer's Store.

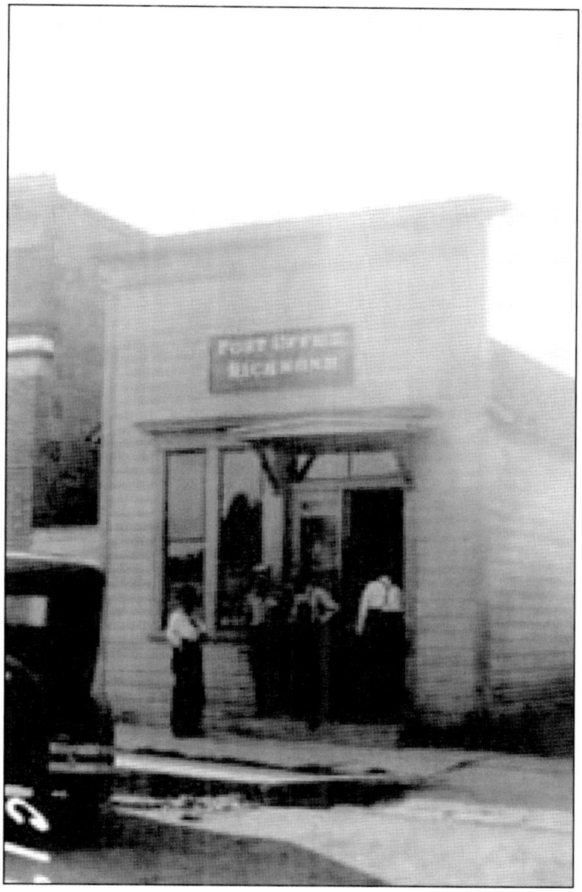

The Richmond State Bank was built on the northeast corner of Main and State Streets in 1908. David Eccles, a resident of Ogden, acted as president, with J.W. Funk as vice president. The cashier was George G. Hendricks. The bank was later acquired by First Security and then by Wells Fargo before it closed in the late 1990s. The bank still stands, although the second story, where the town telephone operator worked, has been removed.

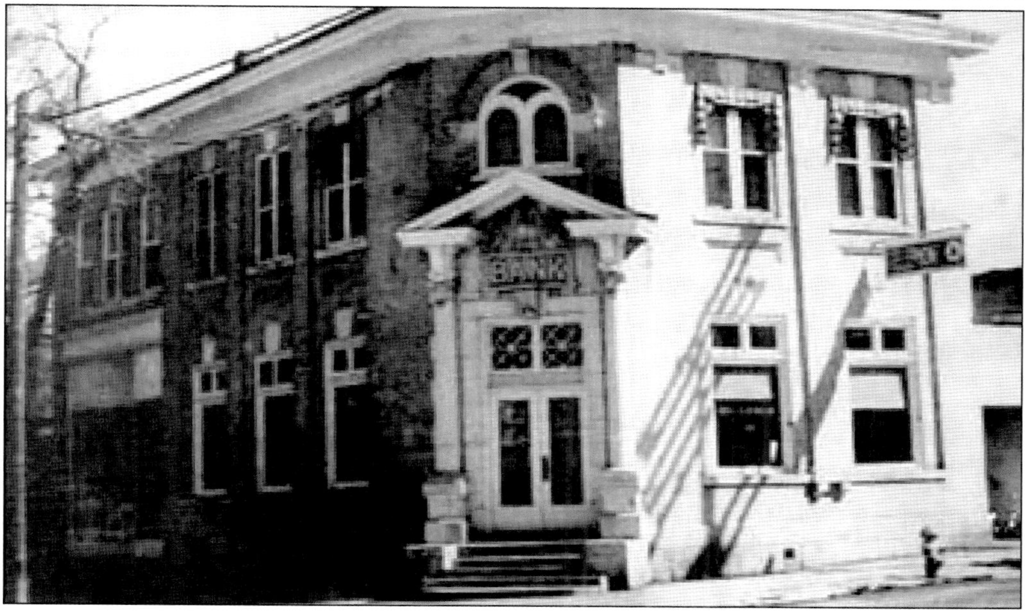

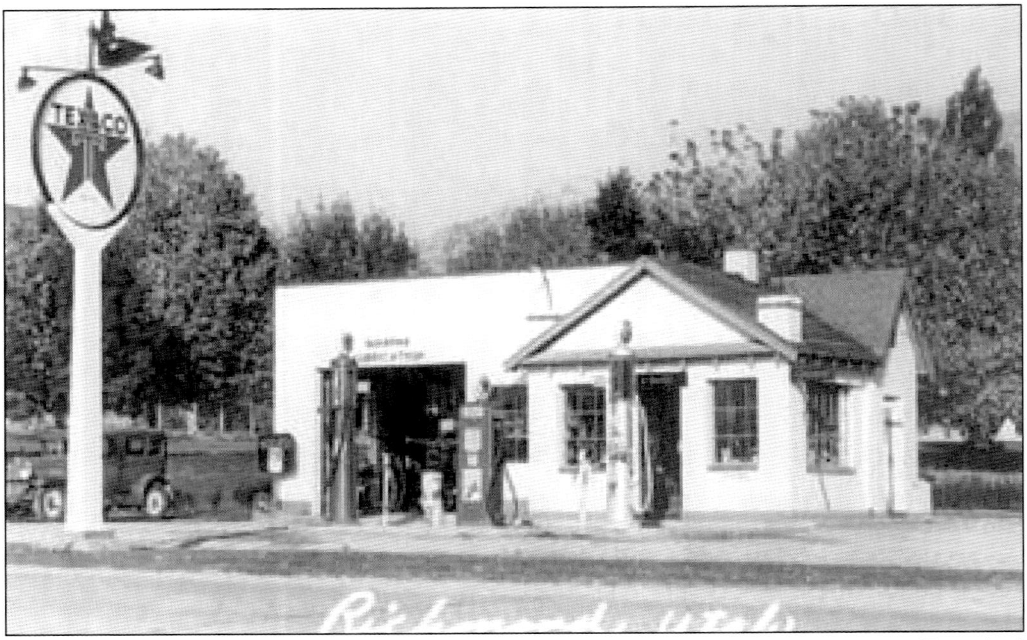

In 1939, Evan Spackman began working for Grant L. Bagley at the Texaco Station. Evan had many good experiences working with Grant and enjoyed being employed there. When Grant passed away in 1949, Evan was able to become the proud owner of the service station. It then was renamed Evan's Texaco. The location of 95 South Highway 91 was a great spot to sell gasoline. Evan was known for taking care of a lot of kids who got flat tires on their bicycles. He would patch their tires and refill them with air at no charge, sending the children on their way. Evan was a very good-hearted man and treated his customers with honesty and respect. The photograph above was taken in 1949 and the photograph below in 1955. (Both courtesy of Marva Dawn Alvey.)

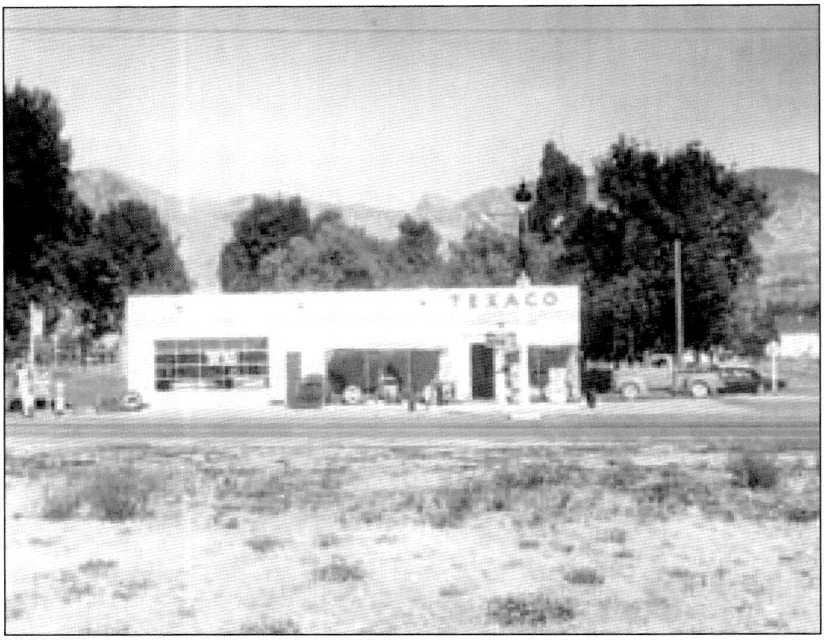

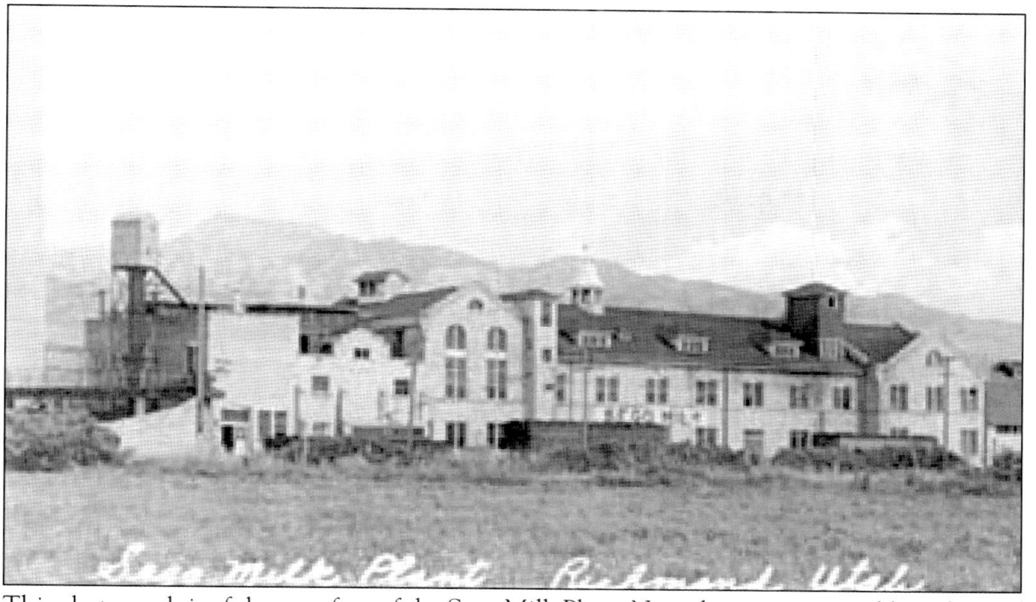

This photograph is of the west face of the Sego Milk Plant. Note the train cars visible in front of the plant. The train stopped there regularly to pick up the processed and canned condensed milk for distribution throughout the western United States. The train also dropped off empty cans and other supplies needed in the condensing process. (Courtesy of Cheri Housley.)

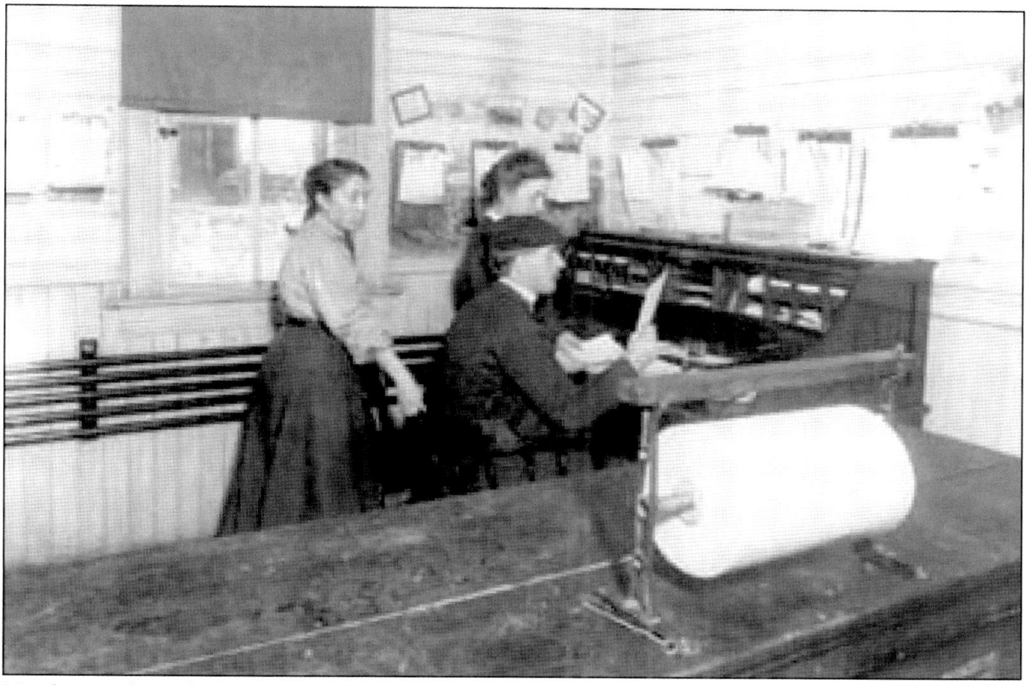

Hard at work in the creamery office of the Utah Condensed Milk Company in 1907 are Robert Ireland (butter and cheese division manager) and office workers Miss Merrill (left, first name unknown) and Lillian Bair. This room served not only as an office but also as a cheese and butter wrapping area during peak production times.

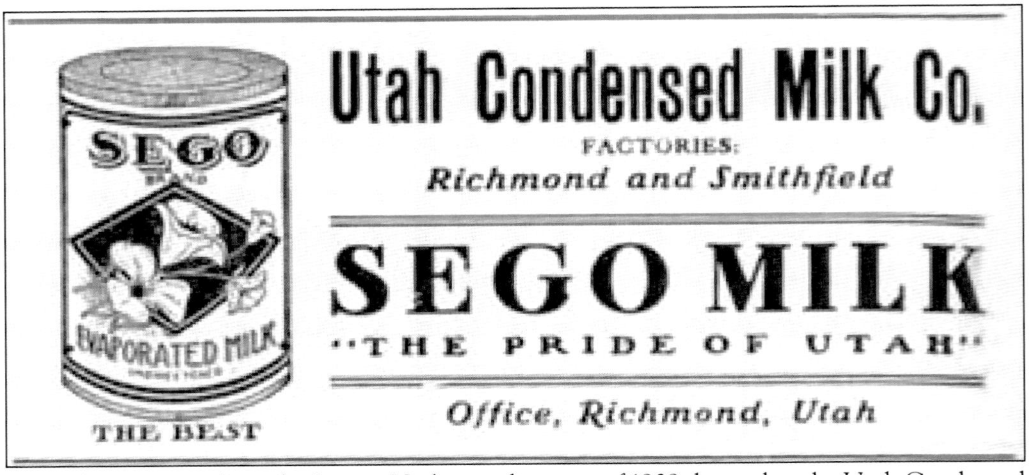

This advertisement from the Logan, Utah, city directory of 1909 shows that the Utah Condensed Milk Company and the Sego Milk Company operated simultaneously out of the Richmond Plant for a time. The plant was the largest in operation west of the Mississippi River for many years. The sego lily is the Utah state flower from which the company derived its name.

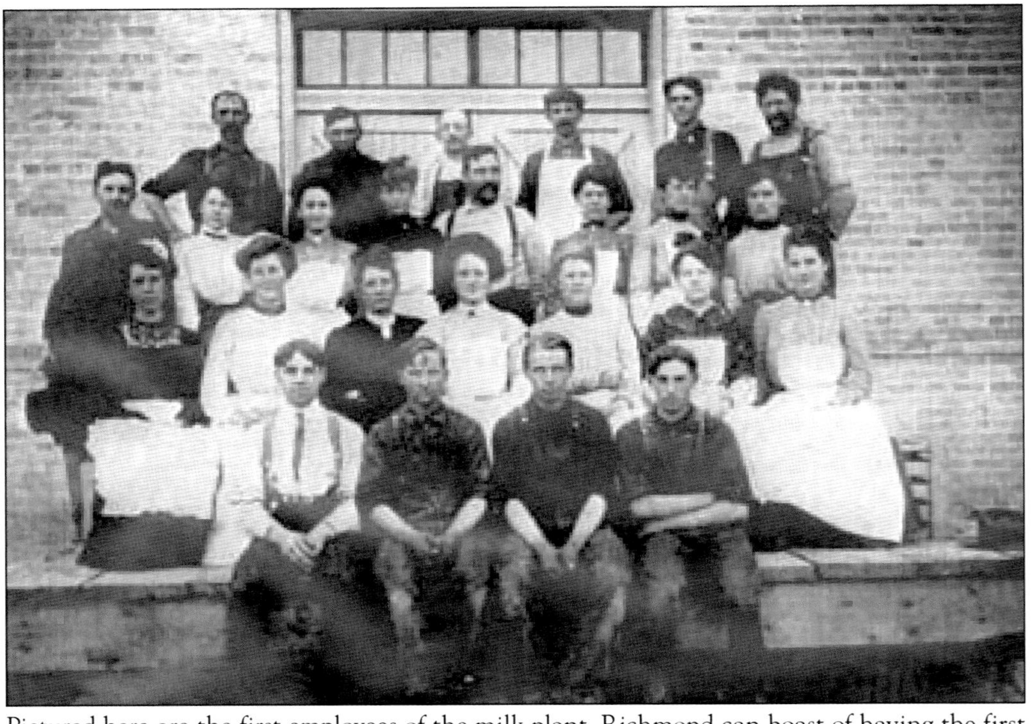

Pictured here are the first employees of the milk plant. Richmond can boast of having the first incorporated dairy company, established in June 1892, in Utah. In fact, there were two. They were known as Cache Valley Dairy Company and the Union Creamery Company. The dairy included the first centrifugal separator and Babcock tester used in Utah. (Courtesy of Zelda Stoddard.)

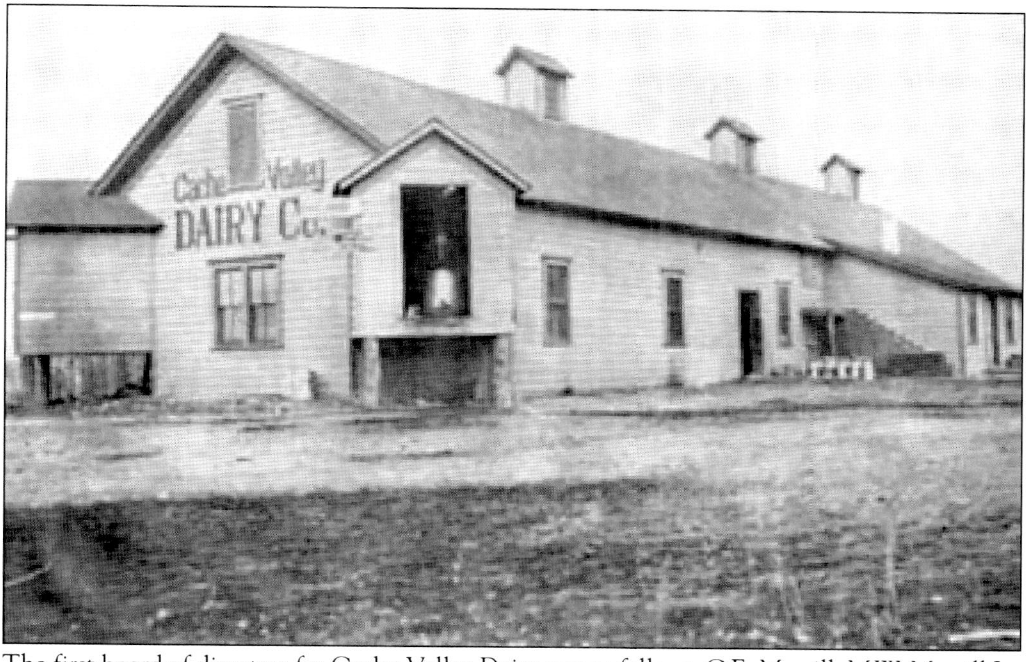

The first board of directors for Cache Valley Dairy was as follows: C.E. Merrill, M.W. Merrill Jr., M.W. Merrill, W.H. Lewis, B.F. Bingham, and Alma Merrill. They ran a state-of-the-art plant and pioneered many processes.

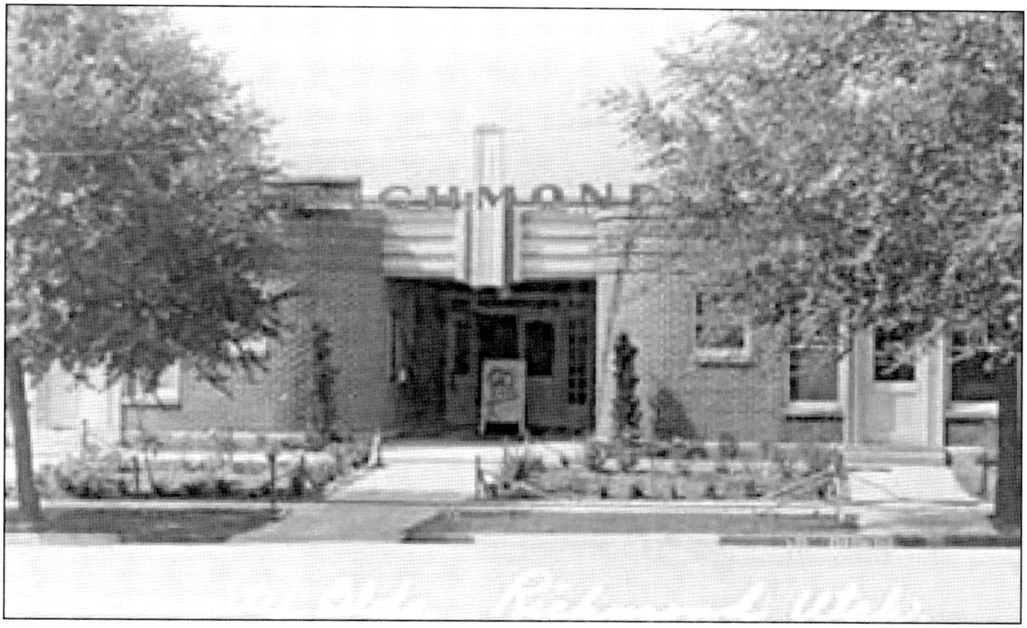

The Richmond Community Building was built in 1936 and 1937 and would serve many different purposes. It had office space, a theater, a large recreation room, and a kitchen. The contract was awarded for a cost of $32,000. This photograph shows that the dentist office on the left was occupied by G.E. Merrill. On the right was the post office. A freestanding marquee advertised the weekly movie.

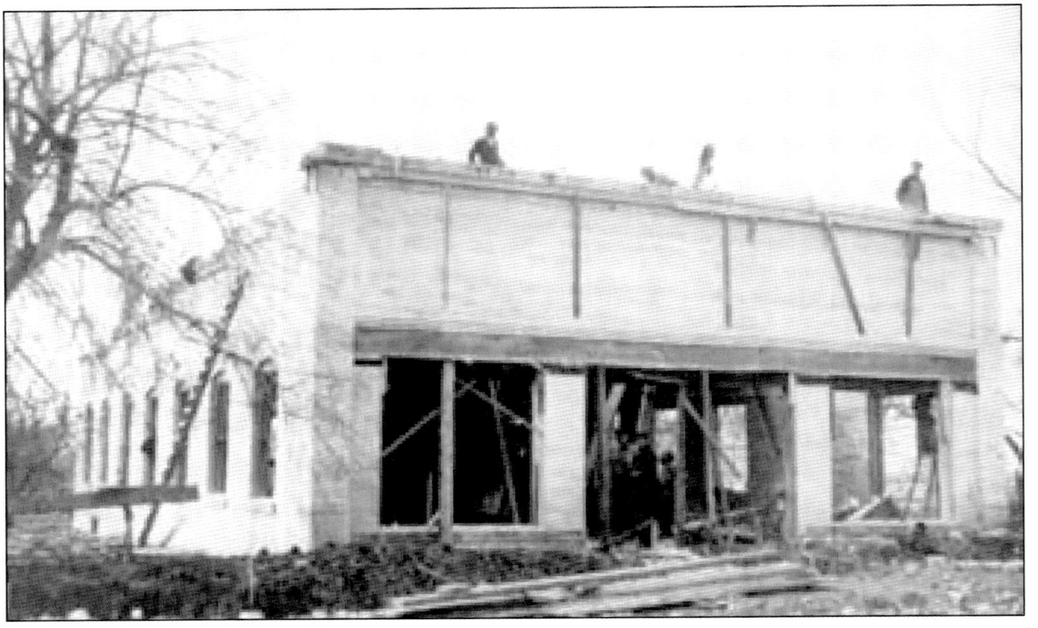

Plant Auto was built around 1915. Owen Henry Thomas Plant Jr. and his crew worked diligently on the construction. Everything was done by hand. There were no cranes or power tools to make the job easier. The completed project was a welcome addition to Richmond. At one time, there were close to 5,000 residents in town, many of them wanting to buy cars. Locals also took advantage of the two drugstores, a millenary shop, Olsen's Meat Market, Monson Lumber, Sweet's Chocolate, a barbershop, several co-ops, and an appliance store that was owned by the Lewis family. Many other stores and businesses catered to the needs of Richmond during its boomtown days. (Both courtesy of Favell Plant.)

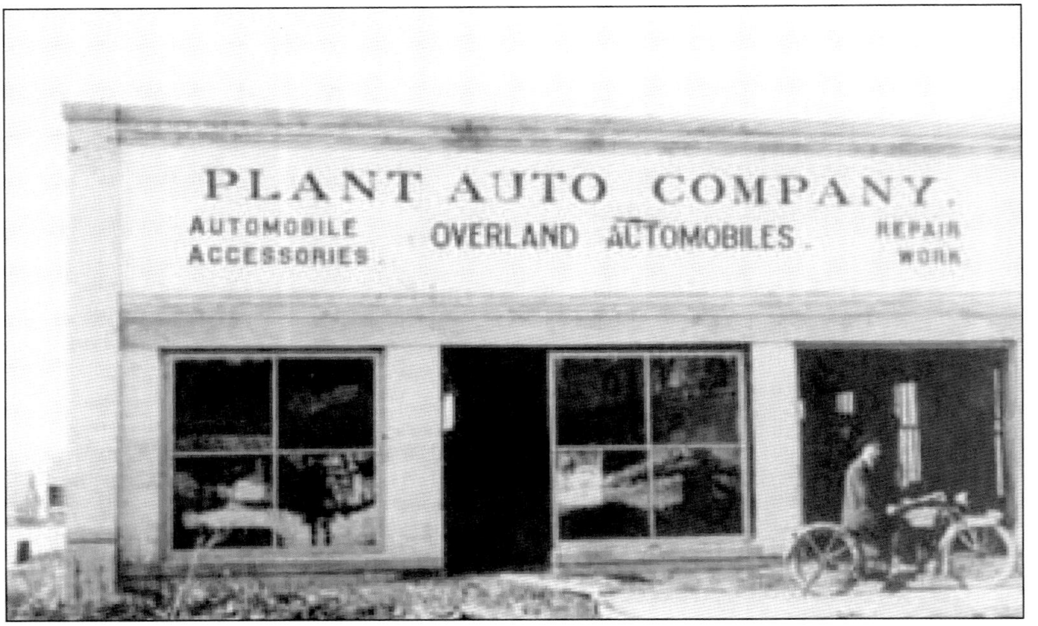

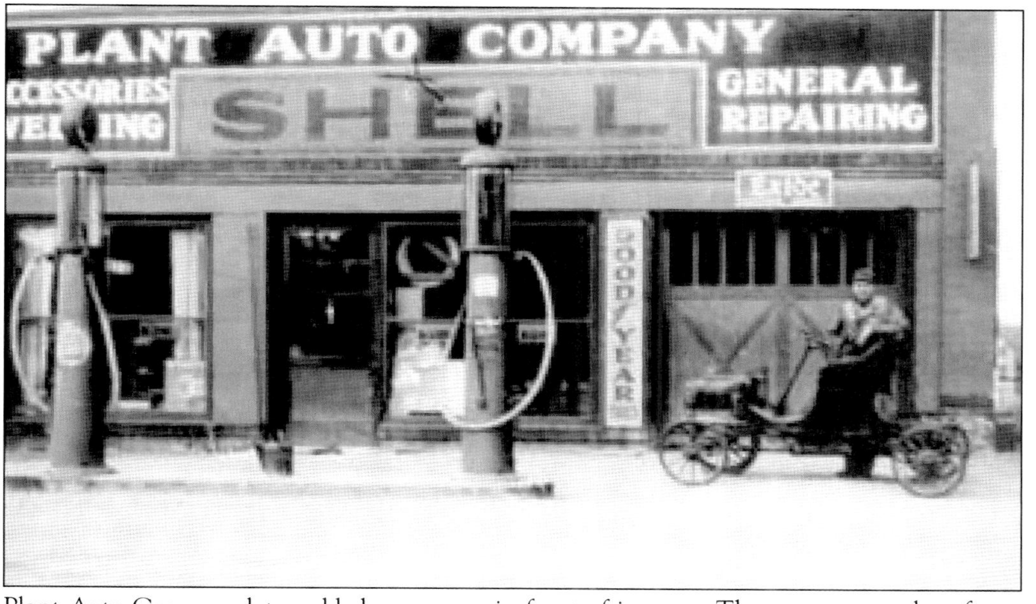

Plant Auto Company later added gas pumps in front of its store. There were not a lot of cars in Richmond at the time, but the convenience of being able to buy gas in town was a welcome addition. Also, being located on Highway 91 made it the perfect spot to attract motorists passing through town. (Courtesy of Favell Plant.)

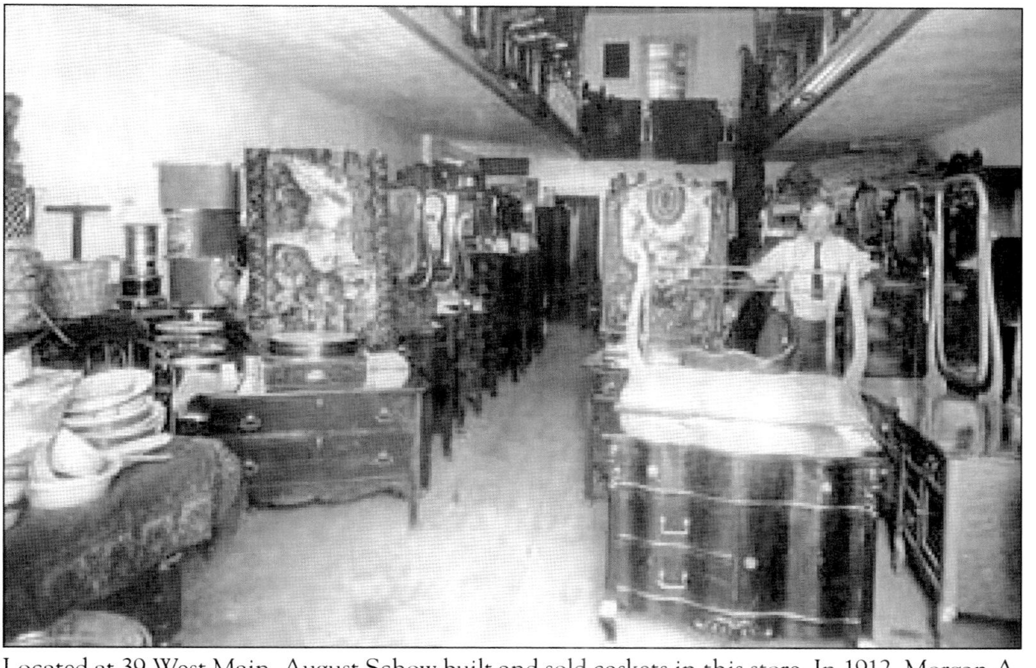

Located at 39 West Main, August Schow built and sold caskets in this store. In 1912, Morgan A. Knapp bought it. In 1919, it was sold to Eli Webb, who sold it to his son Eugene in 1934. In 1945, Bob Hoppie bought it and turned it into a pool hall. In 1955, it was sold to Russell Bowcutt. In 1959, Russell's son L.D. took over. Then, in 1962, L.D. remodeled it and turned it into L.D.'s Café, home of the best food in town to this day. (Courtesy of L.D. and Ann Bowcutt.)

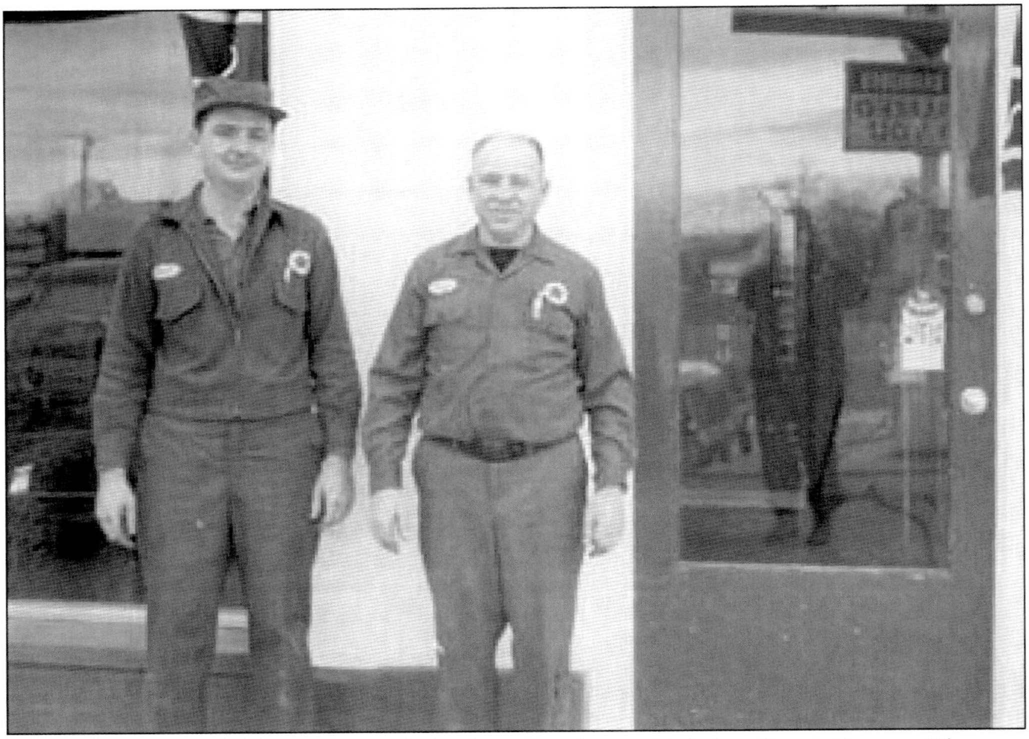

In 1956, Dee Bair (left) went to work for Evan Spackman (right) at Evan's Texaco. They are posed together in this image from 1965. Dee worked under Evan for 20 years. In 1971, the station was moved down the street to where Plant Service Station had been (below). The bigger building allowed them to expand the business. Evan retired on his 65th birthday in 1971 but retained ownership of the station until 1976, when Dee bought it. Dee ran a very courteous operation, and his reputation soon drew loyal customers from all parts of the valley. Dee's son Randy Bair came to work for him in 1977 and worked by his side until August 2000 when Dee retired. Randy then took over the business and ran the Texaco station until July 24, 2005. (Both courtesy of Marva Dawn Alvey.)

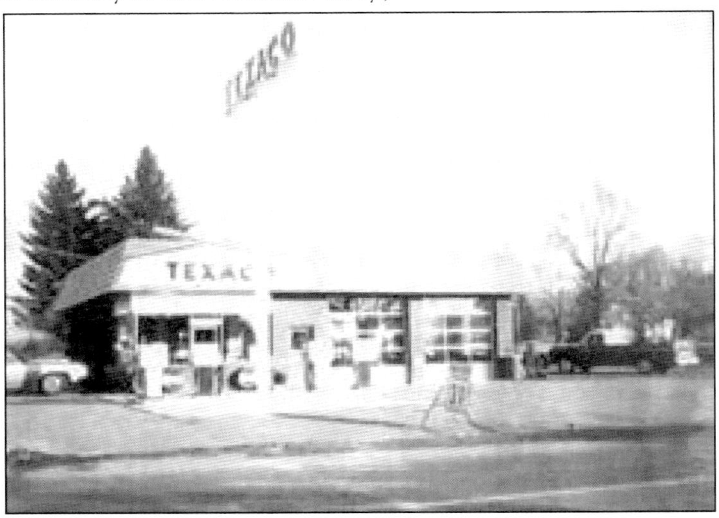

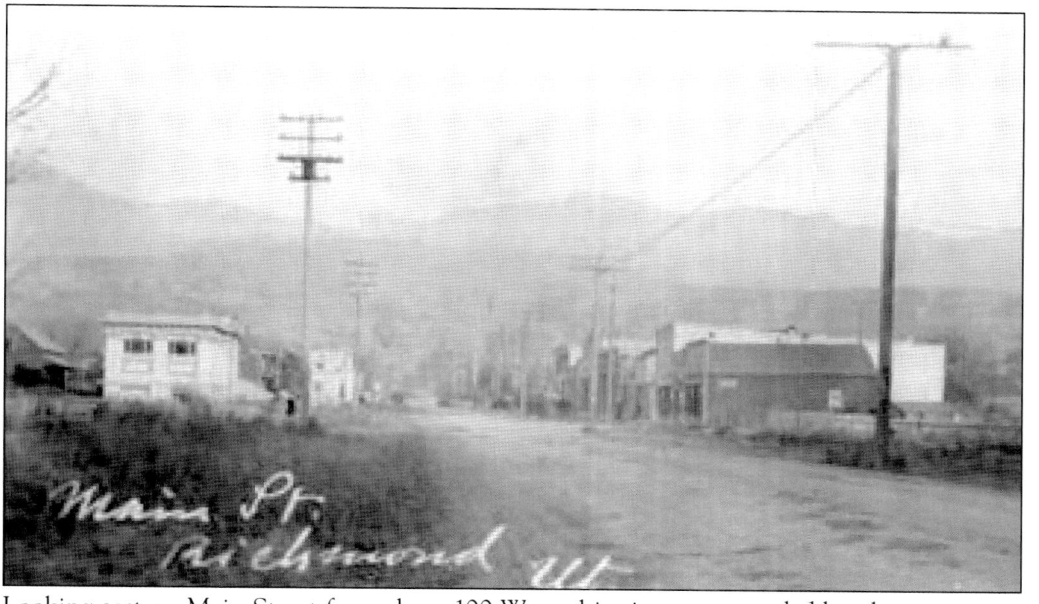

Looking east on Main Street from about 100 West, this picture was probably taken sometime between 1914 and 1920. Where trees had lined the street just a few years before, there are none at this time. The house of William Dorris Hendricks is seen just east of the Carnegie Library. It was torn down in order to make way for the Community Building in 1937.

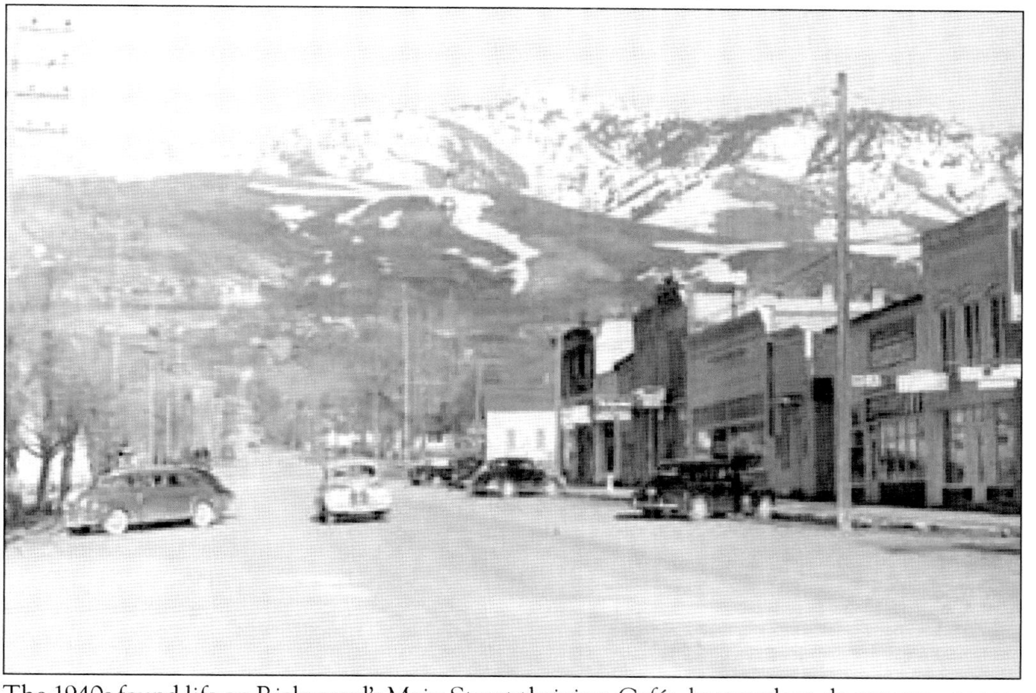

The 1940s found life on Richmond's Main Street thriving. Cafés, beer parlors, drugstores, grocery stores, the old post office, and many other businesses lined the south side of Main Street. Anything needed could be obtained right in town, making trips to the "big city" of Logan only rarely necessary. This photograph was taken in May 1949.

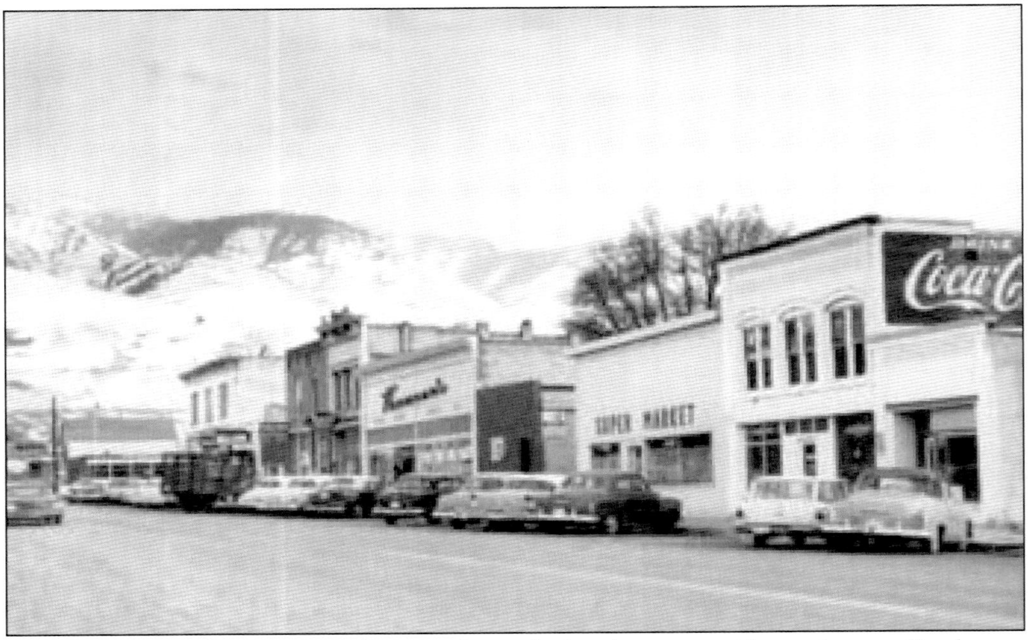

By 1960, Richmond's Main Street business district had undergone significant changes. Roads were paved, a new post office had been constructed, and modern signage was going up on the stores. Note the electric signs for Hotpoint Appliances, Farr Ice Cream, Coca-Cola, and Rexall Drugs, as well as the one on Theurer's Grocery. (Courtesy of Cheri Housley.)

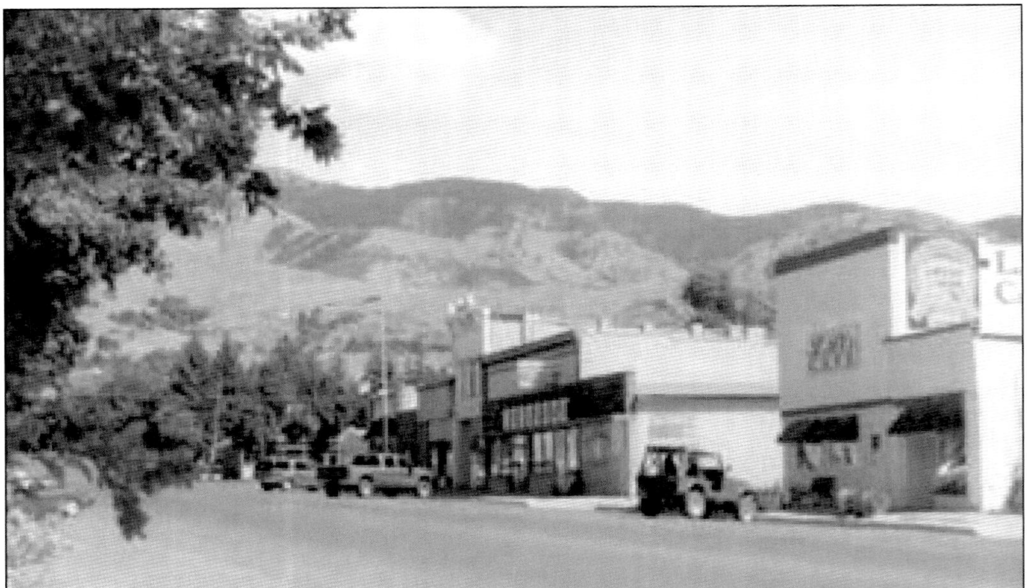

This is the south side of Richmond's Main Street as it appeared in 2010. From the right are L.D.'s Café, the Theurer's Grocery building (which closed in 2007), the Utah State Liquor store, River City Home Brew, and Grandma's Corner Bakery. What was once a thriving business district has dwindled over the years, leaving only these few shops in the heart of town. (Courtesy of Kathy Jones.)

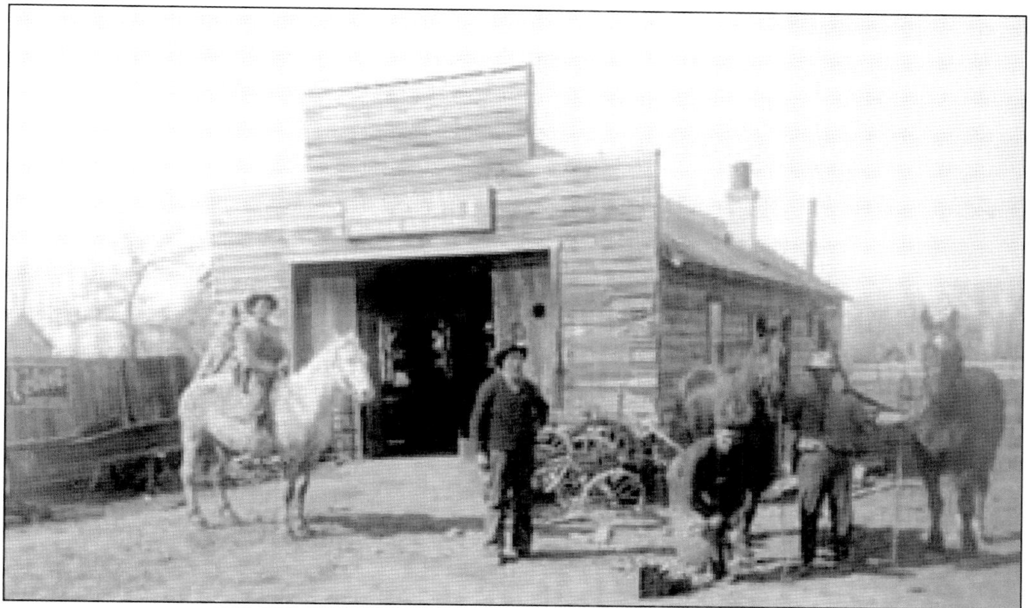

The B.L. Peart General Blacksmith and Horseshoeing Shop was a successful Richmond business for many years. Benjamin Loss Peart arrived in Richmond in 1869, bought a sawmill and a shingle mill, and opened this shop. His son Joseph, pictured shoeing a horse in 1910, ran the blacksmith shop until 1955, although in later years it evolved into a farm machinery repair shop. (Courtesy of J. Willard Marriott Library.)

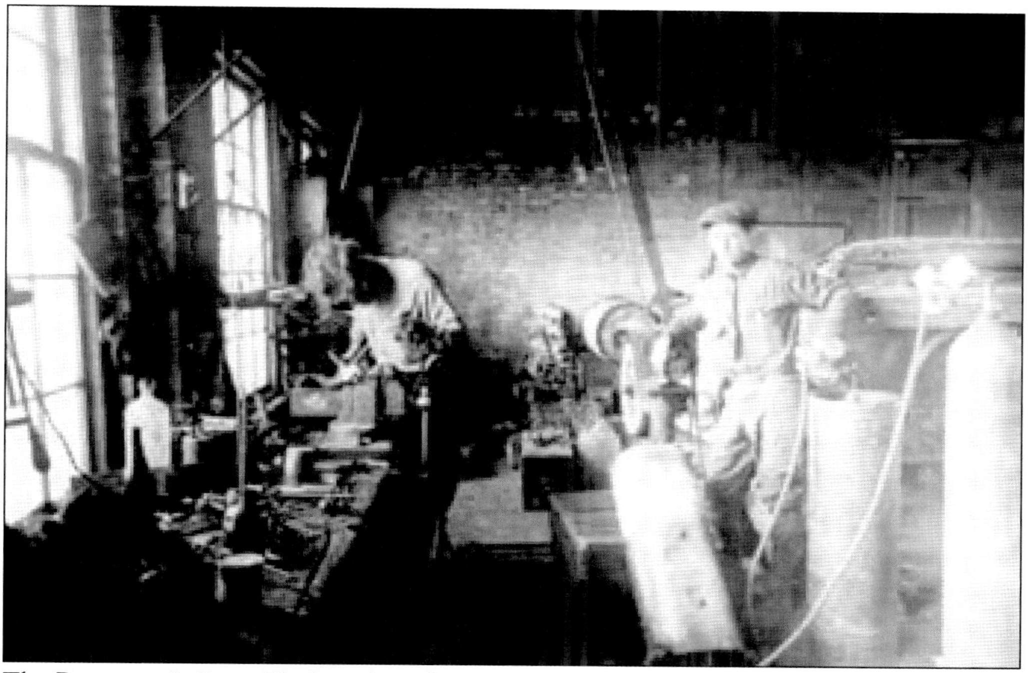

The Benjamin L. Peart Blacksmith and Horseshoeing Shop is pictured about 1910. Benjamin married Elizabeth Christiana Ashment on October 9, 1869, in Salt Lake City. Benjamin also owned a sawmill and shingle mill in High Creek Canyon. Elizabeth cooked for the mill hands.

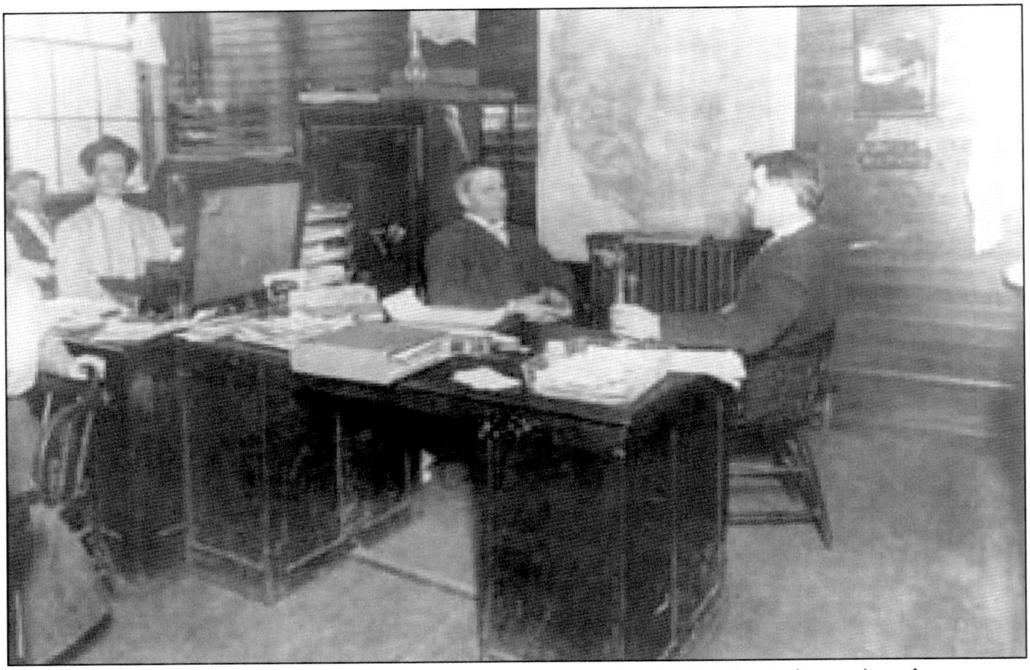

Above, in the office, are Sego Milk Company president Charles Z. Harris (center) with secretary Linnie Telford and manager of the butter and cheese division Robert Ireland. The image below was taken in 1907, during the early days of the company. Some of the company's first employees are included in the photograph. They are, from left to right, (first row) Albert Thompson, Ernest Johnson, unidentified, Victor Johnson, William Barnett, Joseph Albiston, Matthew Feltman, and Frank W. Traveller; (second row) Justin Skidmore, Minnette Andersen, Bertha Shepard, C.E. Merrill, Charles Z. Harris, Robert Ireland, S.W. Hendricks, Frank Stout, Mabel Covey, and Amelia Spence; (third row) Sarah Merrill, Ethel Buxton, Nettie Feltman, Nina Boman, Rozina Woodland, Sarah Johnson, Irene Rainey, unidentified, Chris Knutson, and Mr. Hirst; (fourth row) LePrele Buxton, Clara Bair, Jerusha Bair, Dan Kennedy, Ada Peart, Charles Peterson, Flora Burnham, Maggie Johnson, Inez Egan, Frank Covey, Claus Anderson, Neils Peterson, Edgar Merrill, and John Watson.

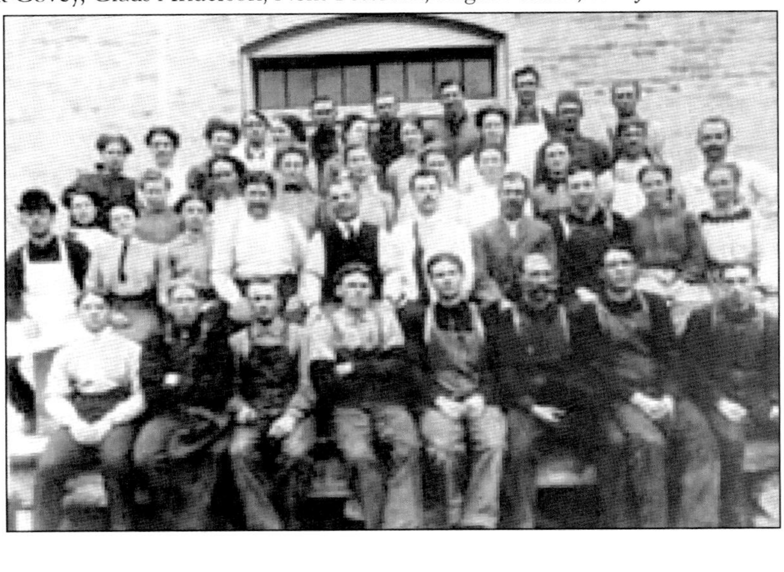

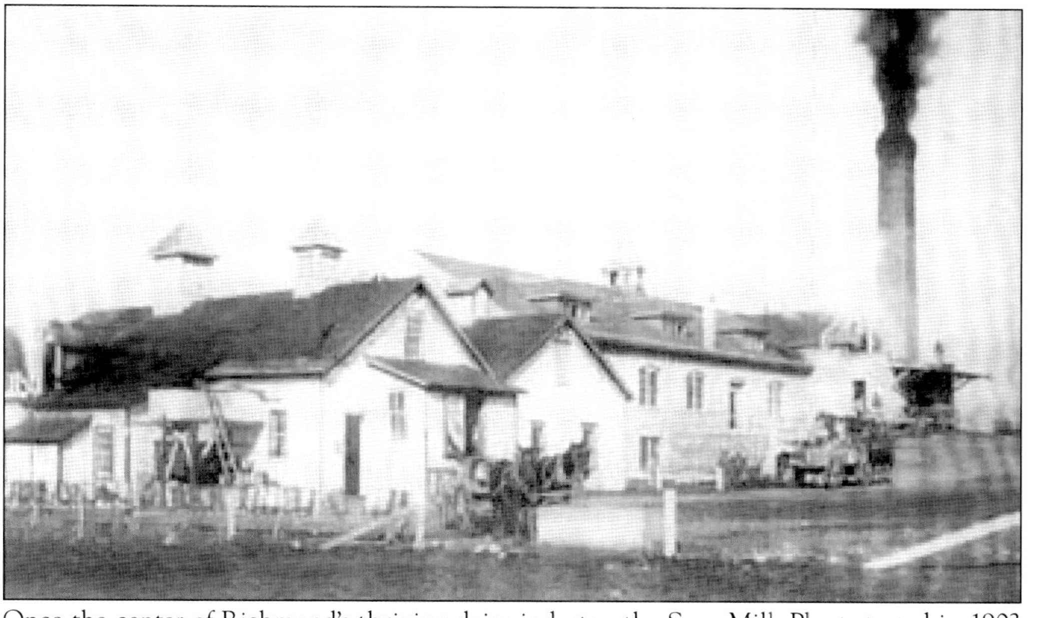

Once the center of Richmond's thriving dairy industry, the Sego Milk Plant started in 1903 under the name Utah Condensed Milk Company. Notice the milk cans hanging on the fence to dry. Before the big milk tanker trucks, the farmers would send their milk to the plant each day in these cans, which would be emptied, washed, and returned. By 1933, milk was being collected for condensing from nearly 3,000 farms daily.

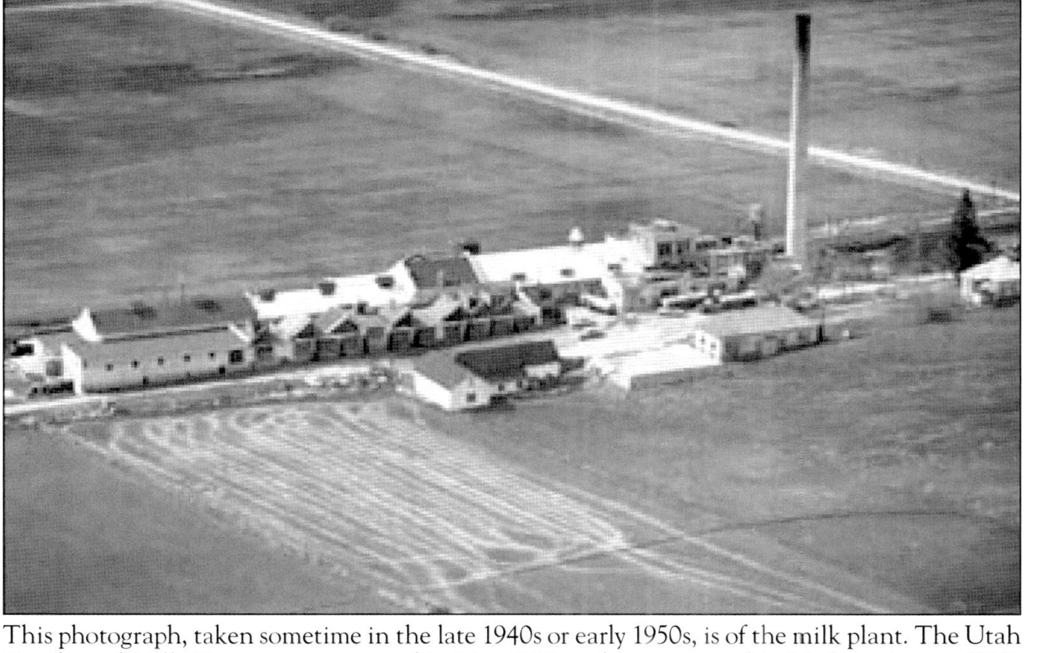

This photograph, taken sometime in the late 1940s or early 1950s, is of the milk plant. The Utah Condensed Milk Company was started in May 1903 and incorporated in Utah in August 1903. The Richmond plant was the third to be erected west of the Mississippi River and was by far the largest. (Courtesy of Hal Rumel.)

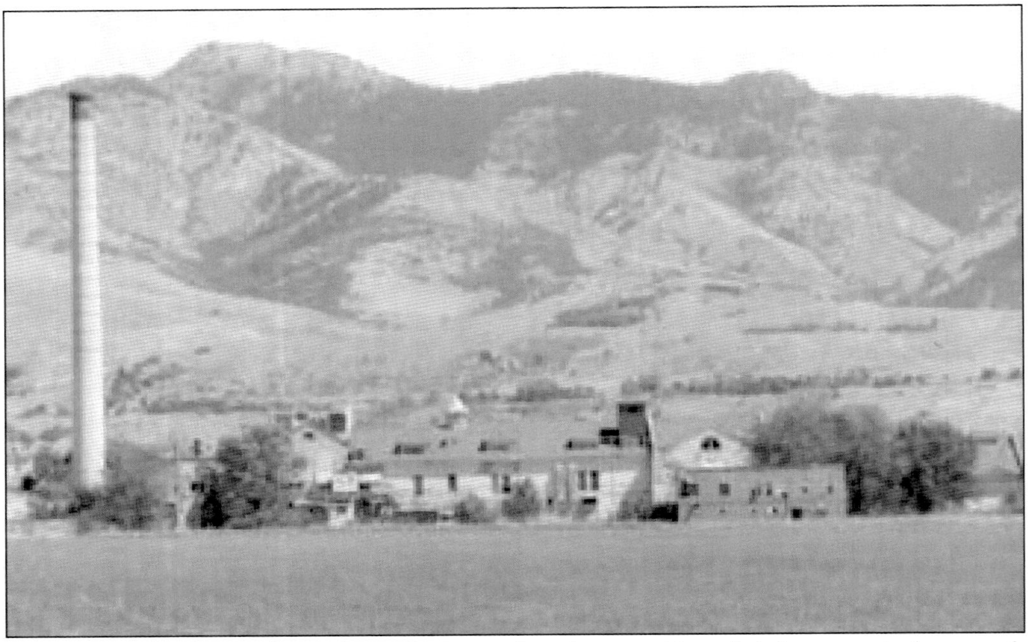

The Sego Milk Plant still stands on the west edge of town, although it is uncertain how much longer it will remain. It has been abandoned for many years and is in a state of serious disrepair. Many consider it to be an accident waiting to happen or at the very least, a fire hazard. It will be a sad day for many when the iconic smokestack finally comes down. (Courtesy of Kathy Jones.)

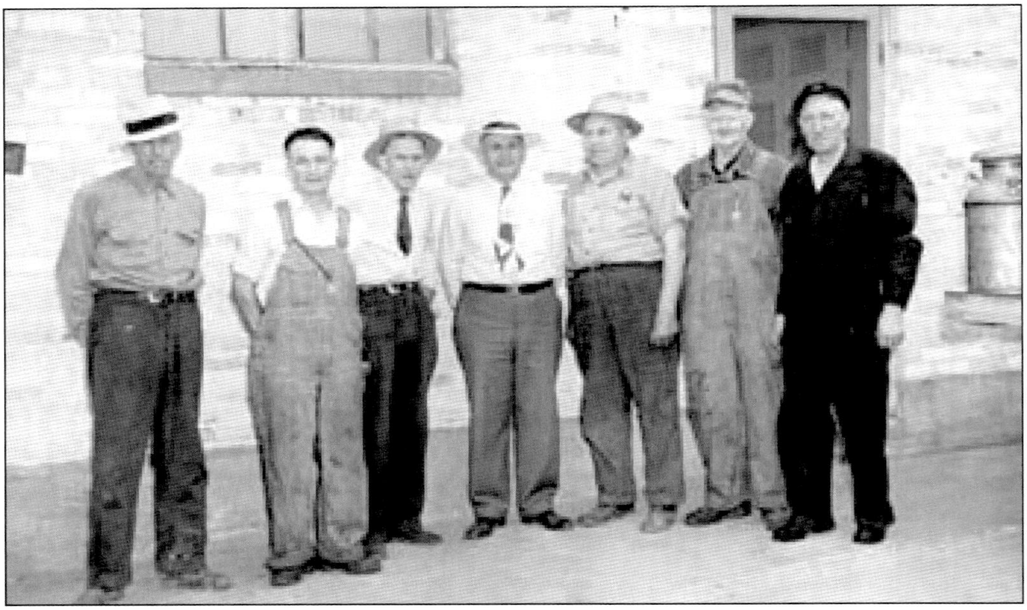

From left to right, Ivan Christensen, Glen Allen, Ernest Johnson, A.L. Kircher, J.R. Johnson, James Steed, and George Egan are pictured at the Sego Milk Plant in 1950. At this time, the plant was producing and shipping more than 38 million cans of evaporated milk annually. The milk plant's name was changed several times over the years. It was also known as Pet Milk, Hi-land Dairy, and Western General Dairy.

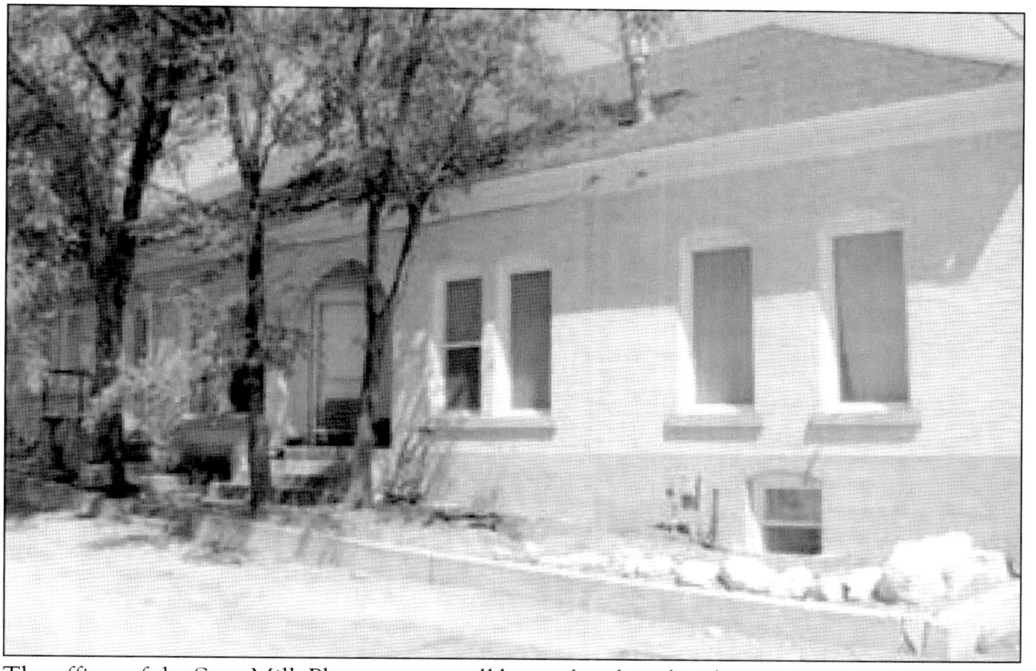

The offices of the Sego Milk Plant were not all located within the plant. Some were in a separate building just to the east of the main plant. The office building still stands today. It was unused for many years following the closure of the plant but has since undergone some renovations, and the offices are now rented out as apartments. (Courtesy of Kathy Jones.)

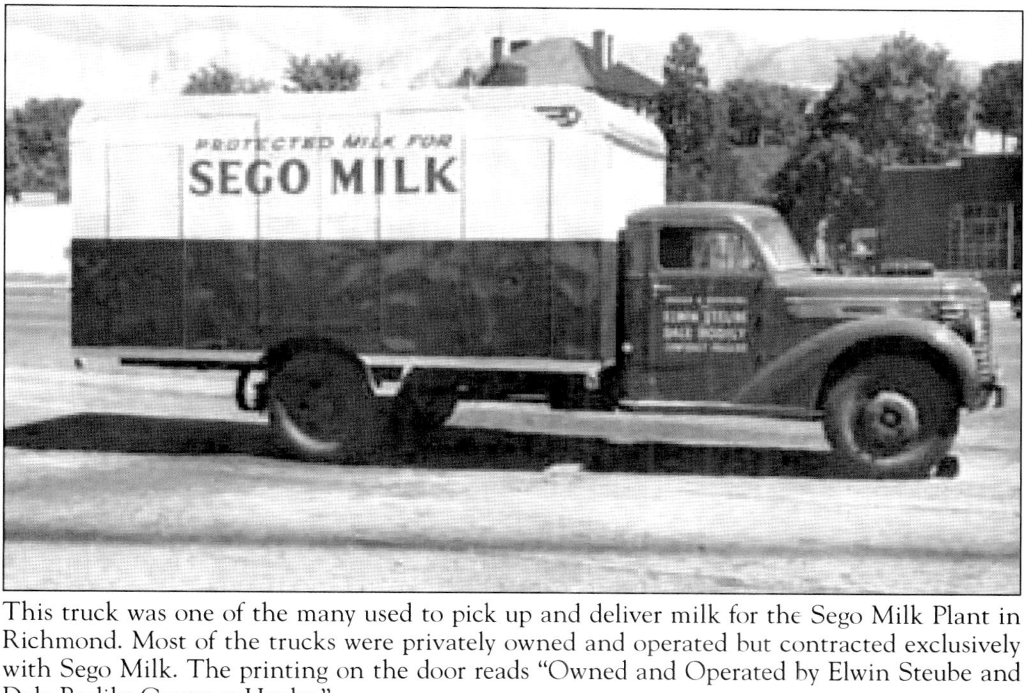

This truck was one of the many used to pick up and deliver milk for the Sego Milk Plant in Richmond. Most of the trucks were privately owned and operated but contracted exclusively with Sego Milk. The printing on the door reads "Owned and Operated by Elwin Steube and Dale Bodily, Contract Hauler."

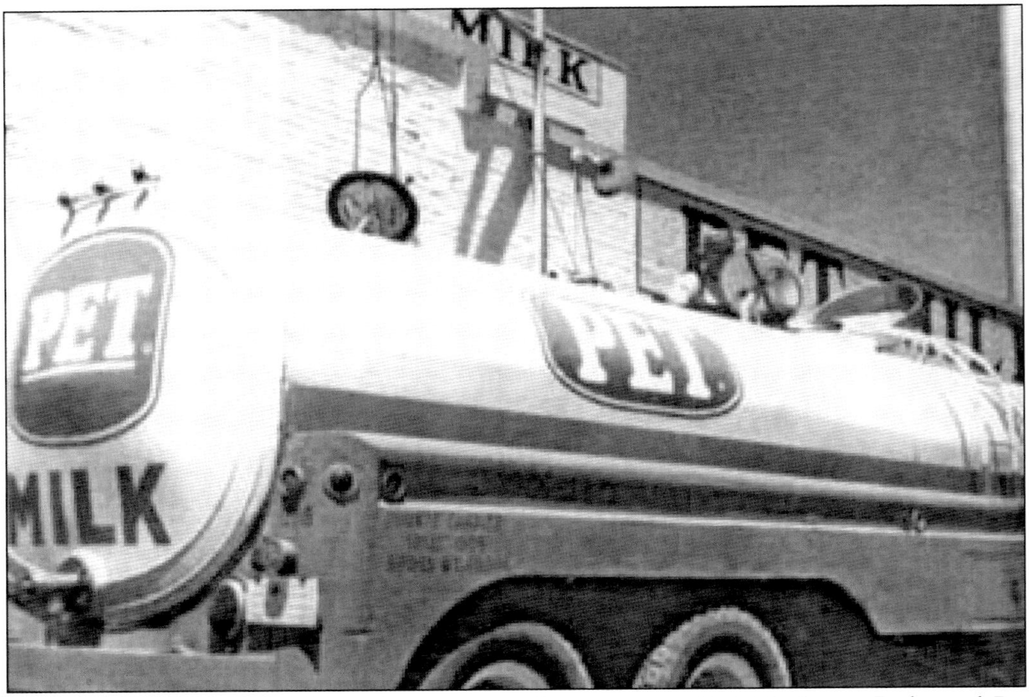

Pictured is the back of a Pet Milk tanker truck unloading milk at the Pet Milk Plant in Richmond. Pet Milk was once known as Sego Milk. Before that it was the Utah Condensed Milk Company, which started in 1903. It was later known as Hi-land Dairy and finally as Western General Dairy.

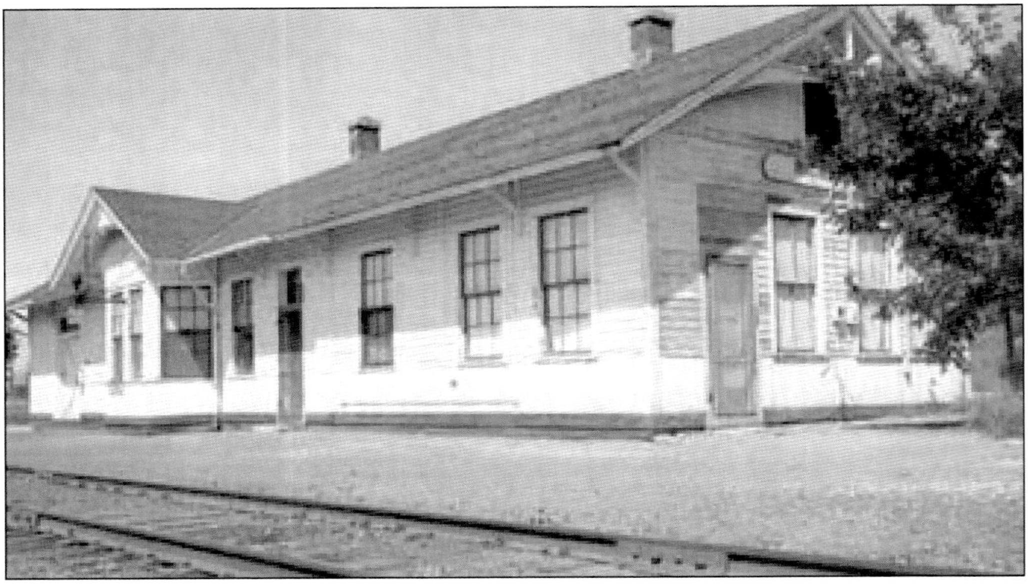

The Union Pacific Railroad depot in Richmond was also an agent house. Bill and Virginia Fleming and three of their children occupied this railroad home and depot from April 1953 to September 1965. The Flemings built a new home at 94 North State Street, leaving the depot with many good memories and looking forward to a good night's rest without the click-clack of passing trains. (Courtesy of Virginia Fleming.)

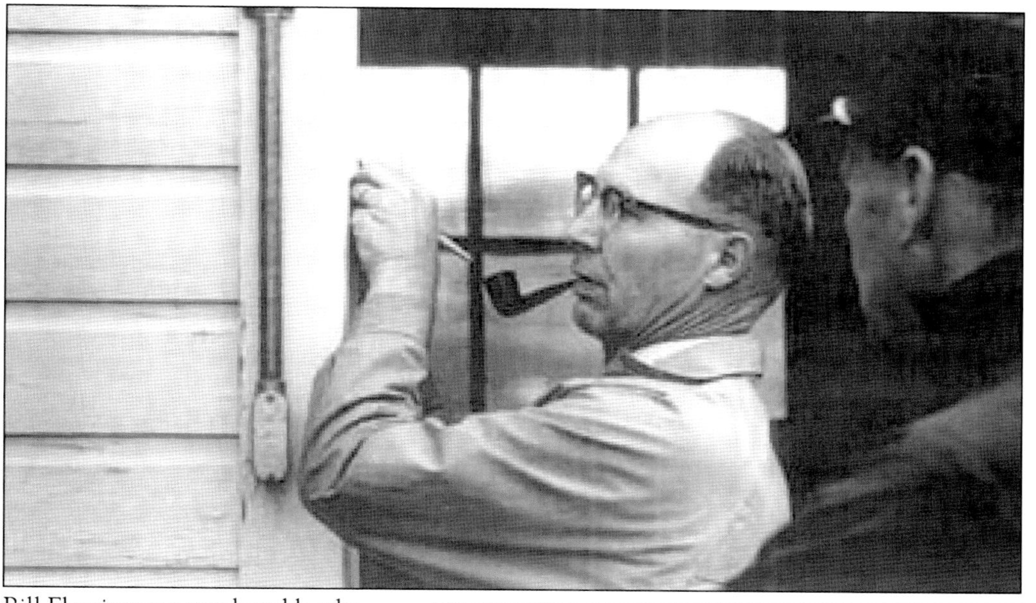

Bill Fleming was employed by the Union Pacific Railroad in Richmond from April 1953 to September 1969. Bill would check in each morning by 7:00 to take the orders, which came from Salt Lake. When Bill first started, he took the orders by telegram; later, they were taken by telephone. Bill would also get the orders from Sego Milk, and later Pet Milk, which provided a lot of business for the depot. It is recorded that there was $80,000 in business each month from the milk plant. Every fall, the "beet run" gave a lot of business to the railroad through the loading and delivering of beets. Trains were the main transportation for a long time. The trucking industry eventually took over, and the railroad was used less. The Union Pacific Railroad in Richmond closed down in 1973, and the sound of the train whistle is now a rarity. (Both courtesy of Virginia Fleming.)

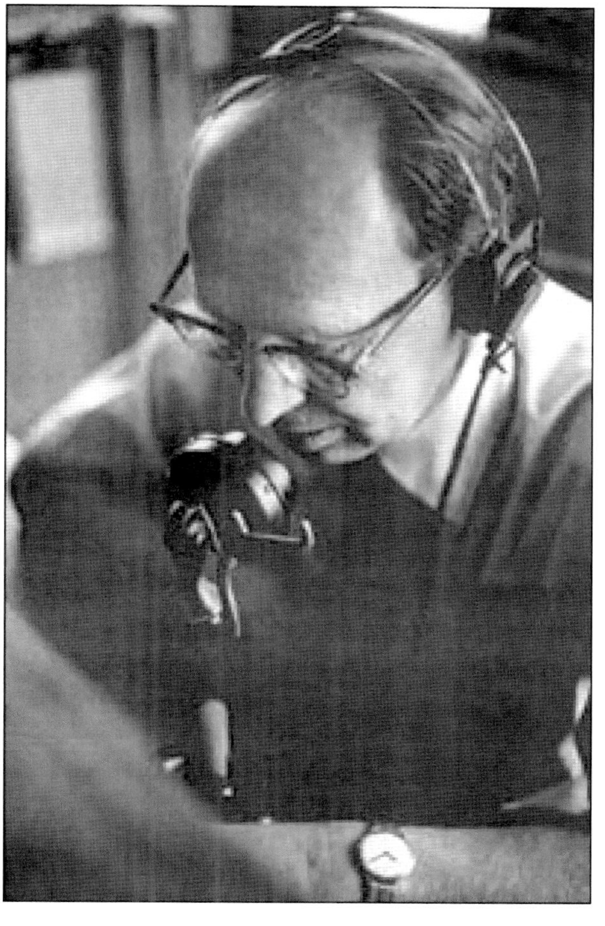

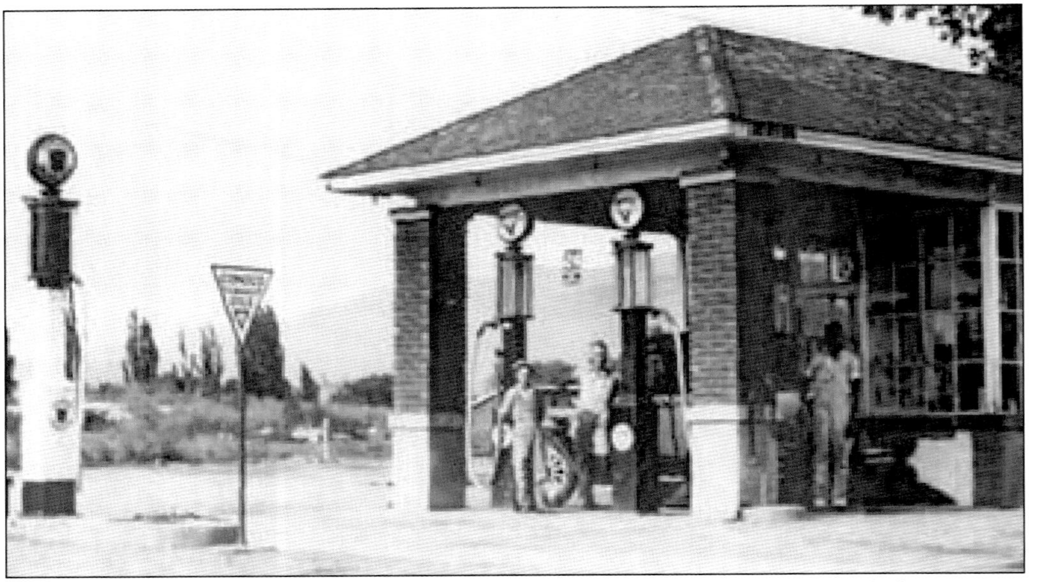

By 1925, Plant Auto required expansion. Henry Thomas Plant Jr. built and opened Plant Service Station across the street from his car shop. The service station was eventually expanded, as well. Plant Service Station catered to local patrons and travelers passing through, as well as commercial accounts, including the Sego Milk truck fleet. The property was formerly part of the original Richmond Fort. Henry's son Ross H. Plant joined him in the business upon his return from military service in World War II.

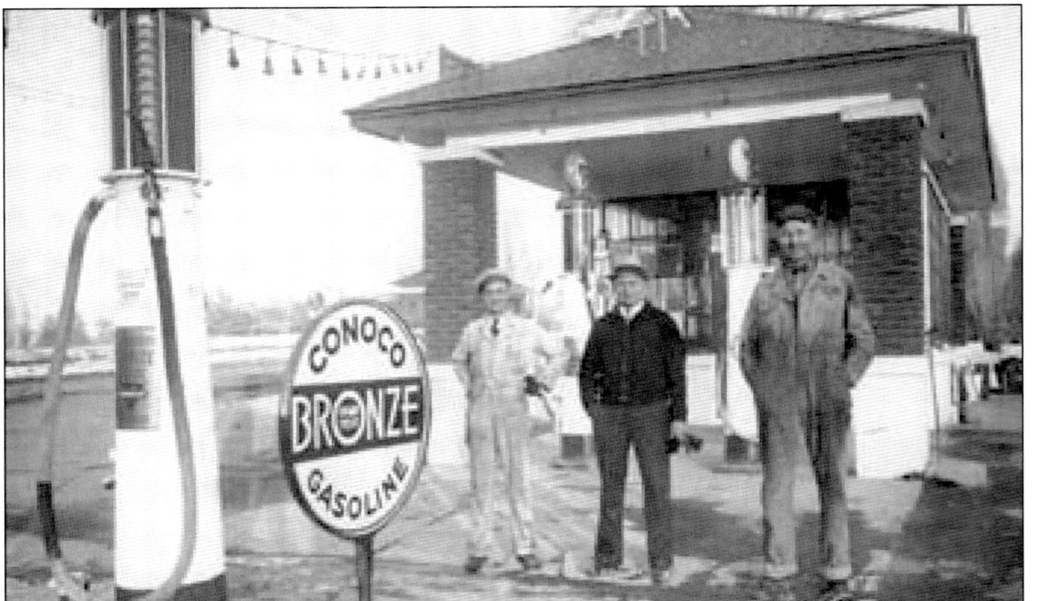

Plant Service Station was located on the corner of Main Street and Highway 91. Henry Thomas Plant Jr. (center) was the owner of the gas station. He employed Dean Albiston (left) and George Ecklund (right). Dean was the service station attendant, and George was the master mechanic. The station opened for business on July 1, 1925. (Courtesy of Favell Plant.)

Three

FAITH OF OUR FATHERS

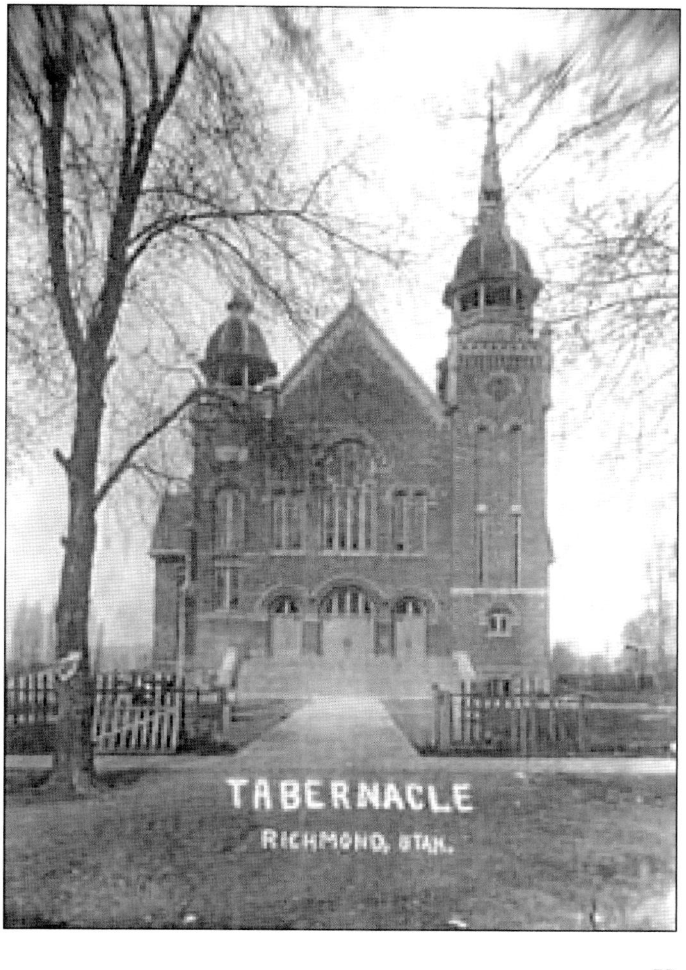

The Benson Stake Tabernacle was begun in 1903 under the direction of Church of Jesus Christ of Latter-day Saints apostle Marriner W. Merrill. It stood on the corner of 100 West Main Street, where the current stake center stands. Upon Merrill's death in 1906, the building was still incomplete, but in honor of his dedication to the building, his funeral was held there, even though there was no glass in the windows. Being February, it was cold.

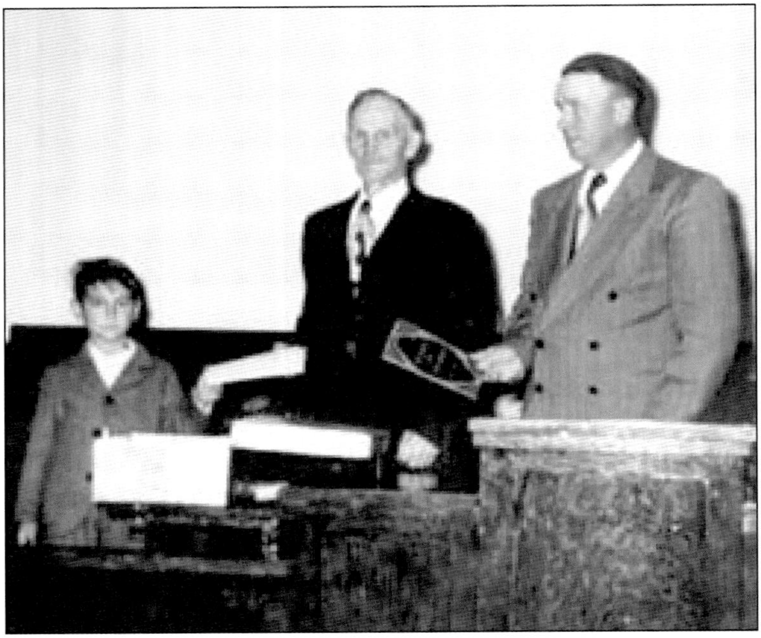

In 1949, the Richmond Sunday School made a time capsule that was to be opened in 50 years. The box contained pictures, books, and other memorabilia. Pictured here are Bruce Hoppie (age 8), William Hendricks Lewis (age 92), and Sunday School superintendent J.E. Erickson as they add items to the box. The box and its contents are now displayed in the Richmond Relic Hall.

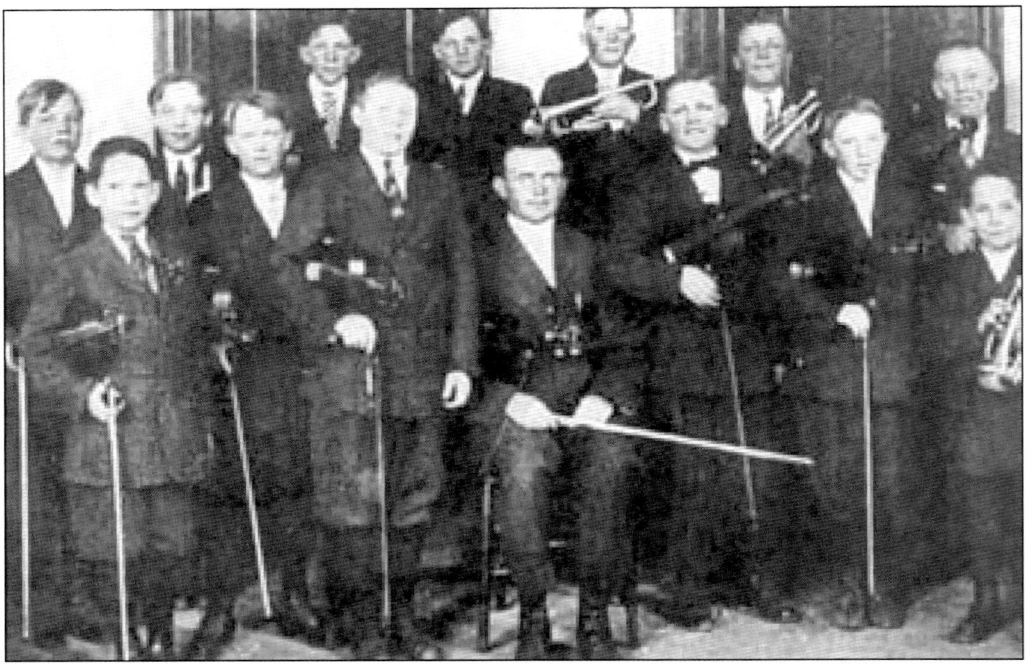

The boys in this 1915 photograph are unidentified, but they are members of the Richmond Deacon's Band. Music and drama groups were common in all small towns at the time. These boys were most likely members of the Richmond Ward of the Church of Jesus Christ of Latter-day Saints.

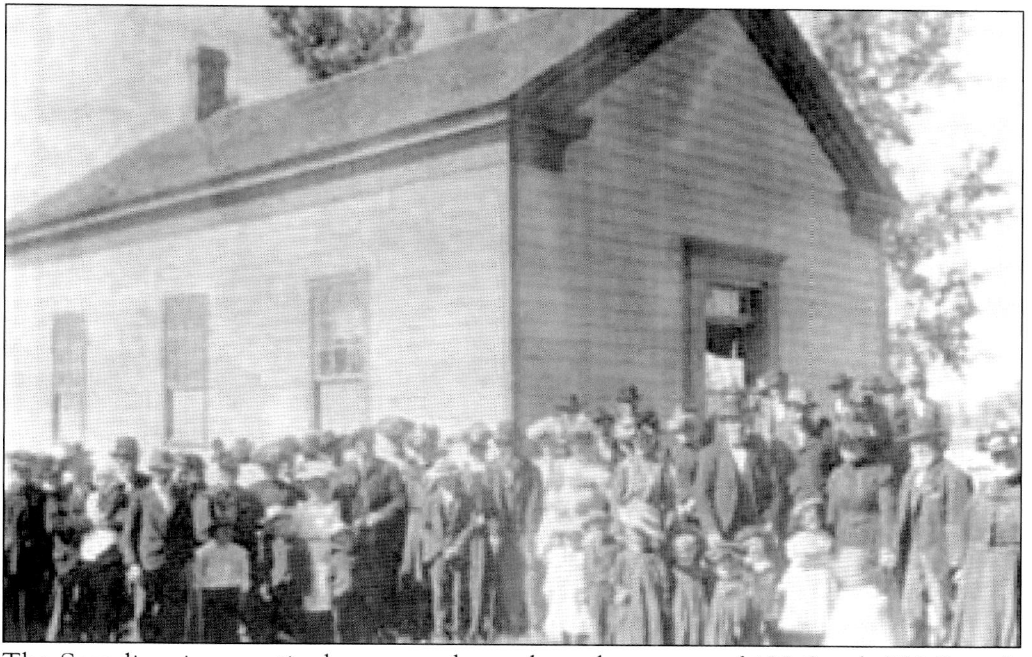

The Scandinavian meetinghouse was located on the corner of 100 South 200 East. It was common in the early days for groups of immigrants who spoke the same language to band together and run their own church meetings and schools. Richmond was home to a large number of Scandinavian immigrants.

An unidentified Richmond family is pictured on their way to church on a typical Sunday morning. Local streets were often plagued by ankle-deep mud from October to June. The bearded man in the background is thought to be a well-known Cache Valley character who went by the name of Peg-Leg Smith.

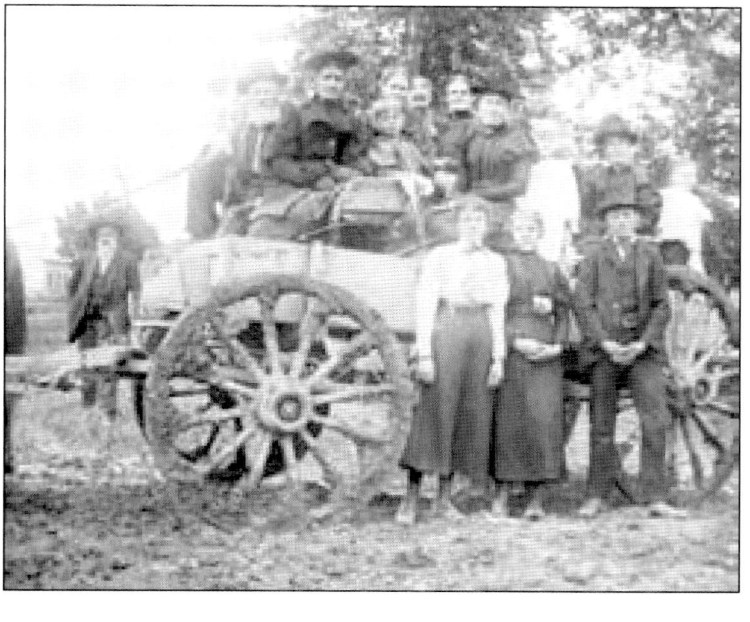

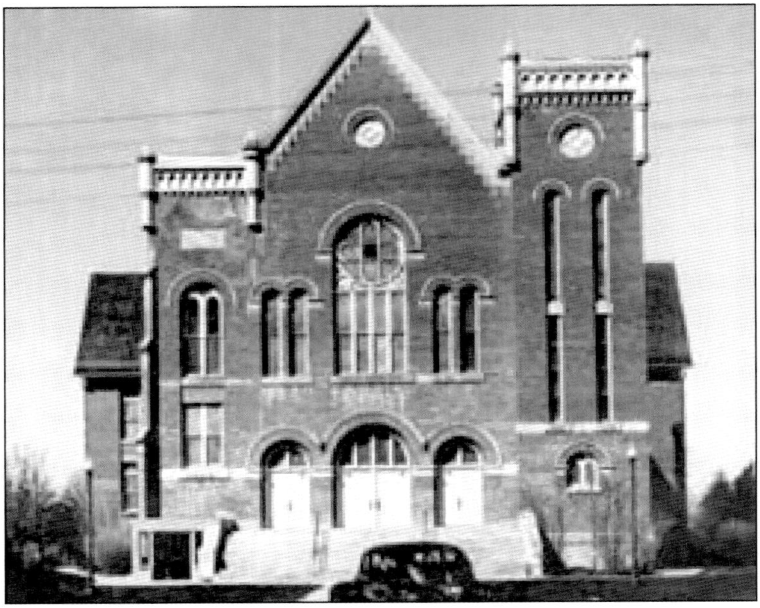

The original construction of the Benson Stake Tabernacle included two tall spires that rose up from each of the square towers, the north tower being much taller and more ornate than the south tower. They stood for many years before being removed. It has been said they were damaged in the same windstorm that tore the roof off of the Red Brick School in April 1909.

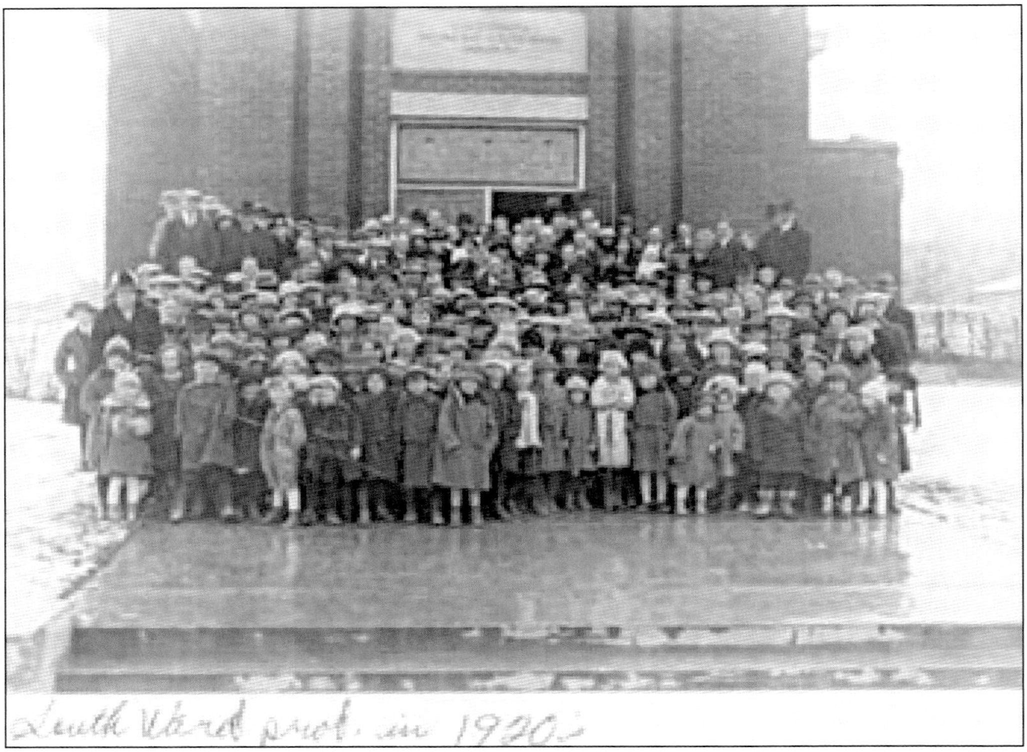

The Richmond South Ward members are pictured here in the 1920s in front of the South Ward meetinghouse. The church was finished in 1923 and was located at 335 South State Street. It was demolished after the 1962 earthquake. The cement marker from above the door was uncovered in recent years during excavations on the property. It is displayed in the front yard of the Spackman home, which now sits on the site.

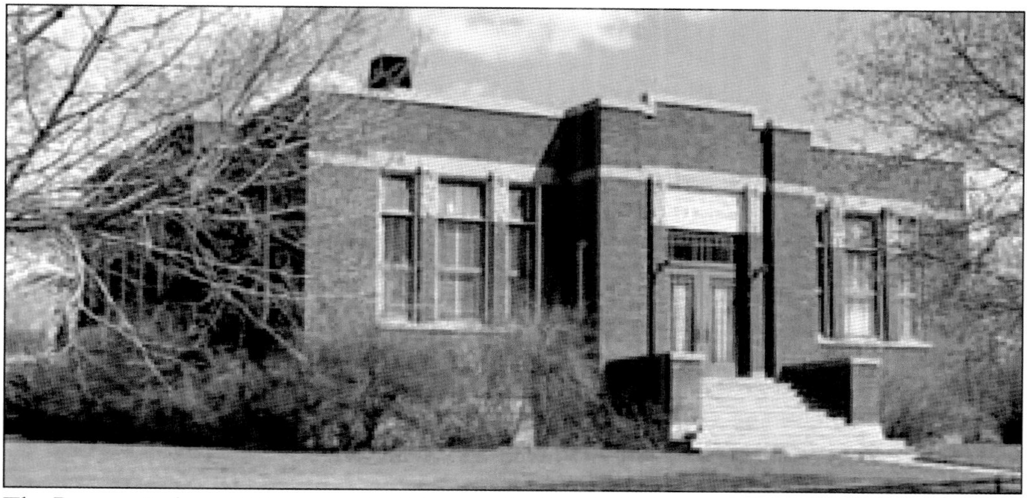

The Benson Stake LDS Seminary Building on the North Cache High School campus is pictured in 1949. It was described as "an institution which fosters clean, wholesome, and high ideals . . . operated with the belief that spiritual development is as important to the welfare of an individual as social, physical, and scientific development."

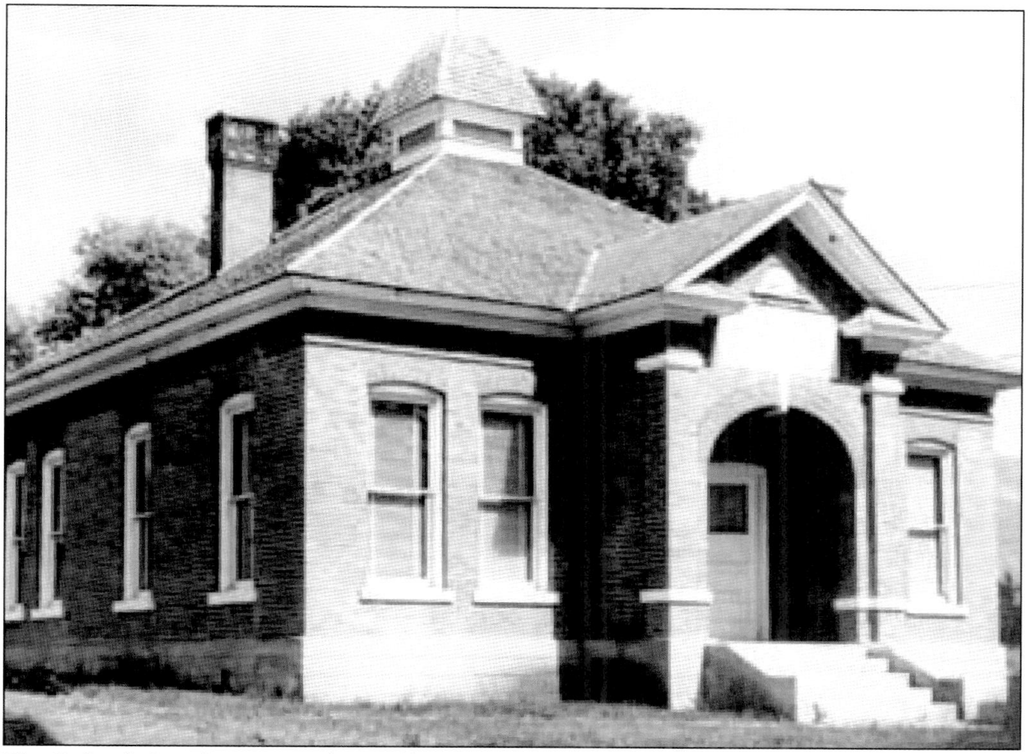

The Bishop's Storehouse, or tithing office, was erected in 1907 by a local builder named Wallace K. Burnham. It is one of 28 well-preserved tithing buildings still in Utah. It also served as an office for the stake presidency and as a meeting place for the high council. The building was bought by the Daughters of Utah Pioneers for $500 in 1959. In 1968, it was deeded to Richmond City, which allows the James and Drusilla Hendricks Camp to run it as a museum.

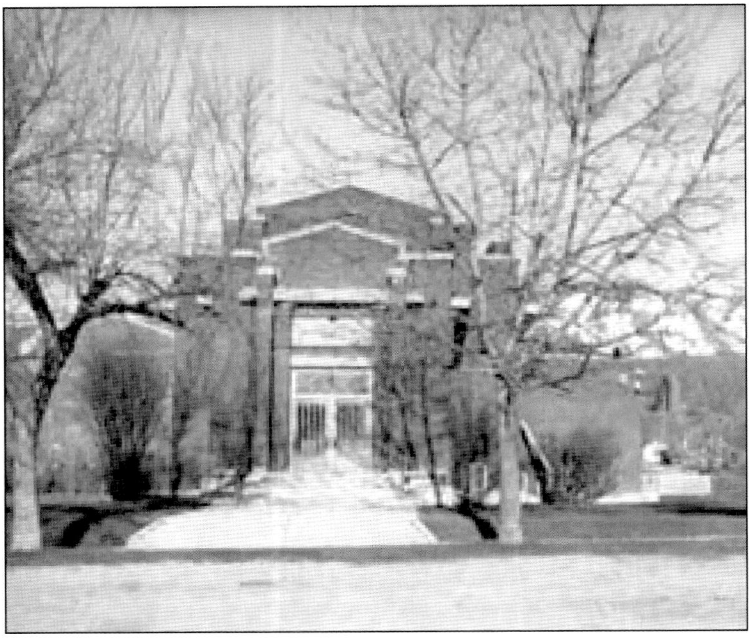

The Richmond South Ward chapel was finished in 1923. This building was located at 335 South State Street. The first bishop was James L. McCarrey, with Howard M. Egan as first counselor and Carl J. Carlson as second counselor. LaFayette Hendricks served as ward clerk. The cost of the building was as follows: ground, $400; building, $25,071.92; and furniture and fixtures, $5,838.57. This totaled $31,310.49.

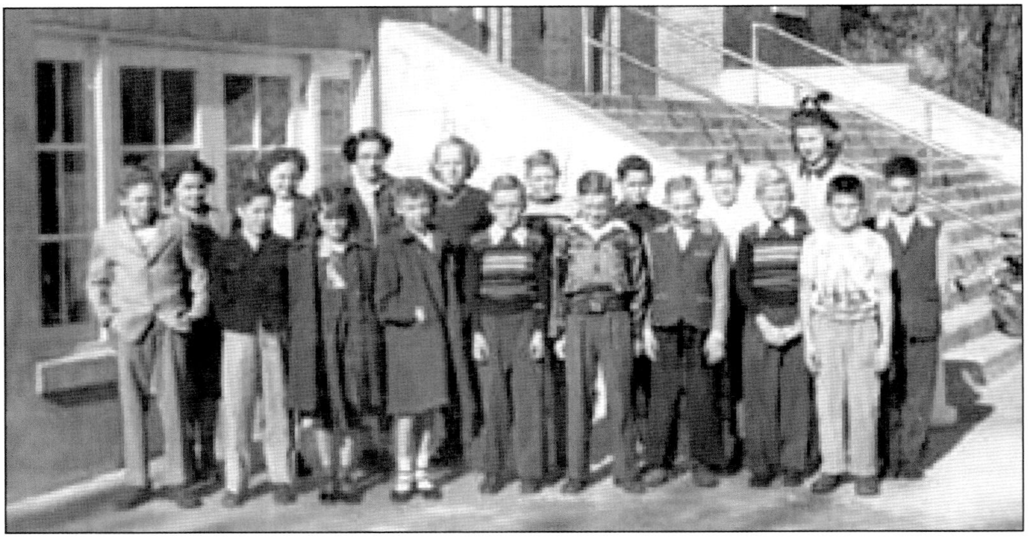

The Second Intermediate Sunday School class of 1947 are pictured. Included in this image are, from left to right, (first row) Gary Spackman, Vaughan Peart, Nancy Carlson, Sharon Albiston, Lee Skidmore, Larry Farnes, Neldon Hawkins, Lynn Skidmore, R.B. Nelson, and Milen Housley; (second row) Mary Lou Duce, Merriss Hendricks, Helen Albiston, Rose Marie Bullen, Steven Larson, Ronnie Lewis, Eldon Humphries, and Zelle Erickson (teacher).

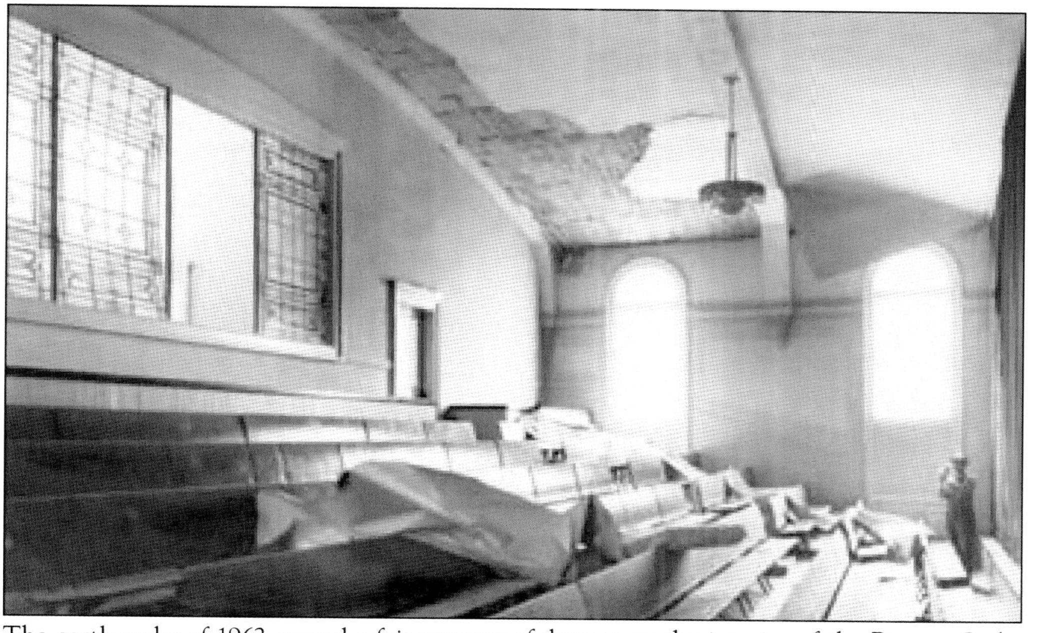

The earthquake of 1962 caused a fair amount of damage to the interior of the Benson Stake Tabernacle; however, much of it was merely cosmetic. Note the bowing of the middle stained glass window. Much of the damage was repairable, but because of some shifting of the rear wall, the decision was made to condemn it and tear it down.

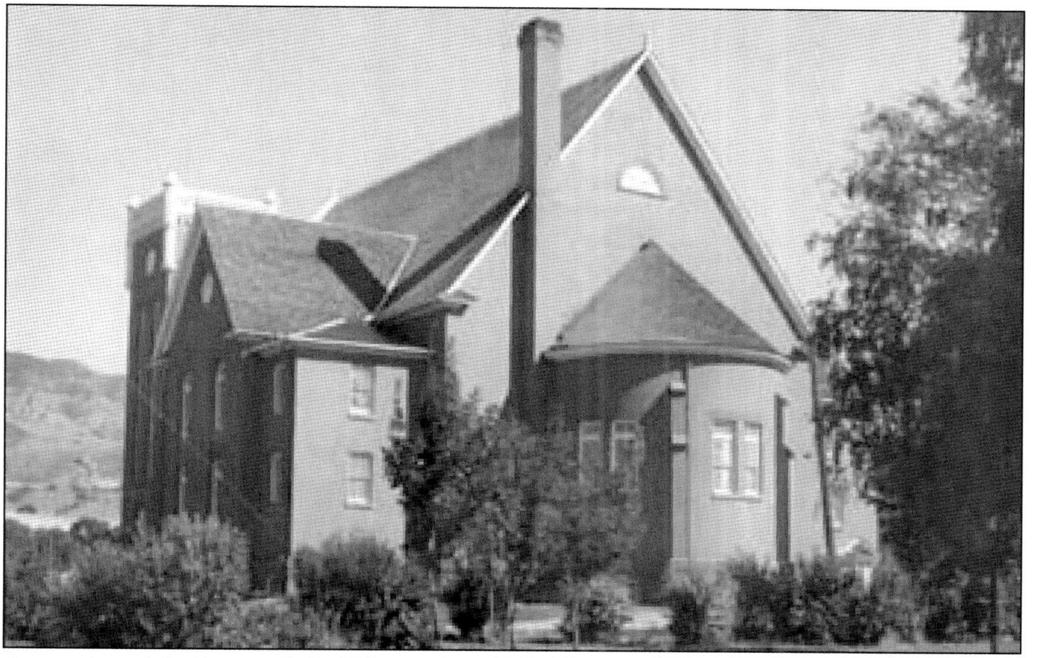

A rear view of the Benson Stake Tabernacle in 1962 following the earthquake is pictured. Note the cracks in the chimney and wall. The government disaster relief program would not pay to repair the building, but it would pay to replace it. Hence, the decision was made to demolish the tabernacle and replace it with a modern building. The town still laments the loss of this beautiful church.

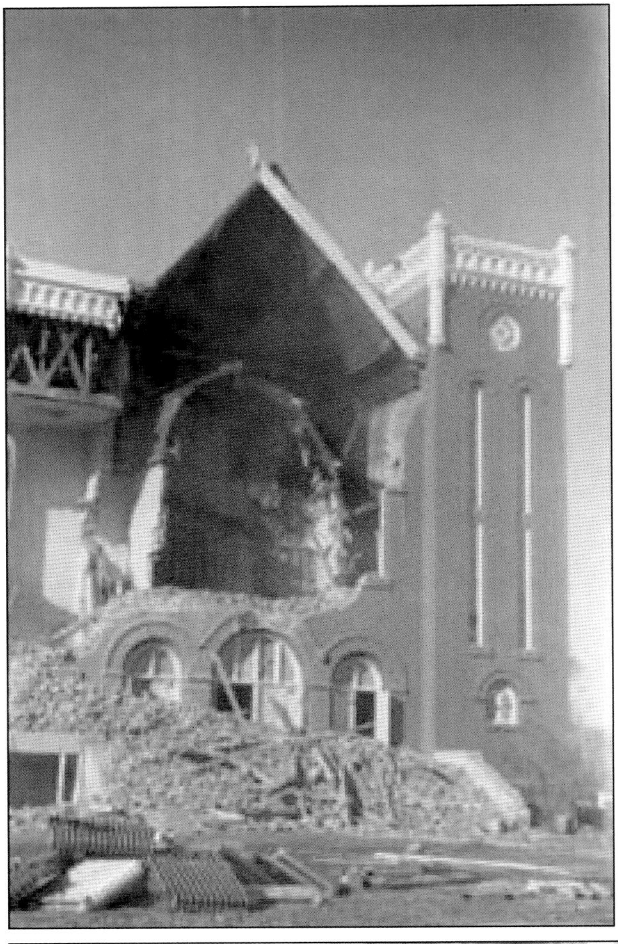

Following the 1962 earthquake, the Benson Stake Tabernacle was demolished to make way for a modern stake center. Very little was salvaged from the original building. The solid oak pews were piled up and burned. The pulpit was saved and is displayed in the Relic Hall. Some light fixtures were saved and used years later in the restoration of the Relief Society Building.

This is a primary class of eight-year-olds from the Richmond Ward in 1949. Pictured are, from left to right, Marilyn Housley, Marilyn Humphries, Diane Hodson, Kathryn Traveller, Sally Brown, Bruce Hoppie, Billie Bair, Ted Wheeler, and Edith Plant (teacher). This photograph was included in a time capsule that the ward sealed in 1949 and was opened in 1999.

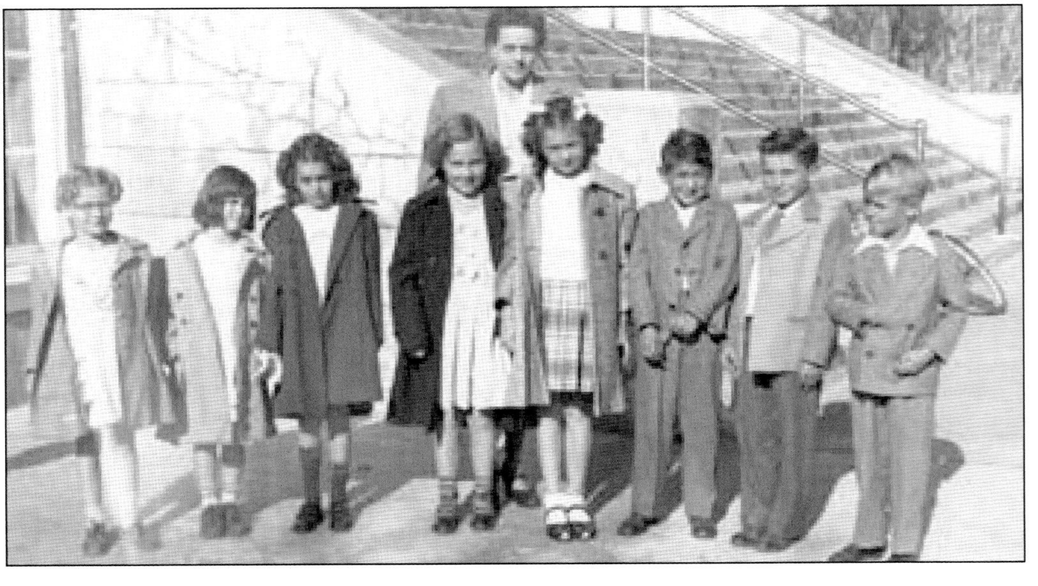

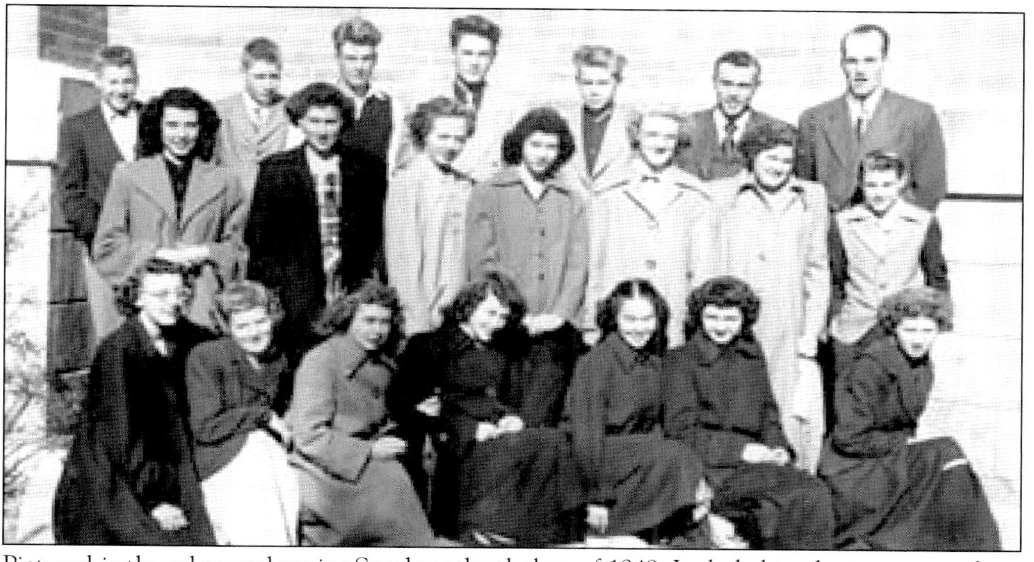

Pictured is the advanced senior Sunday school class of 1949. Included in the image are, from left to right, (first row) Marie Monson, Anna Mae Hill, LuAnn Traveller, Louise Ericksen, Beth Stoddard, Ann Jean Bair, and Mary Lou Hawkins; (second row) Molly Ann Last, Marva Hawkins, Carol Nelson, Arva Housley, Velda Mae Duce, Marion Anderson, Chad McGavin; (third row) Morris Hill, Marvin Olsen, Tex Johnson, Bruce Brown, Tad Traveller, William Skidmore, and Gordon Webb (teacher).

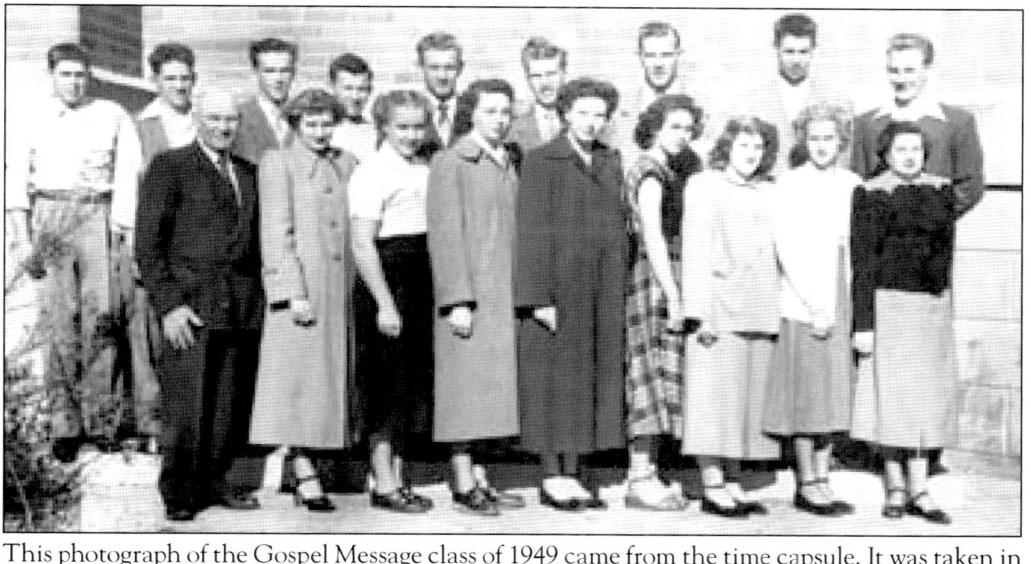

This photograph of the Gospel Message class of 1949 came from the time capsule. It was taken in front of the tabernacle. Included are, from left to right, (first row) Ray Pond (teacher), Janet Pond, Janice Christensen, Elaine Nelson, LuDean Burbank, Ilene Housley, Ruth Bair, Eloise Christensen, and Grace Hendricks; (second row) Howard Anderson, Junior Sanders, Richard Skidmore, Dee Hill, Thad Carlson, Lynn Talbot, Dell Bullen, Gary Lewis, and Keith Hamp.

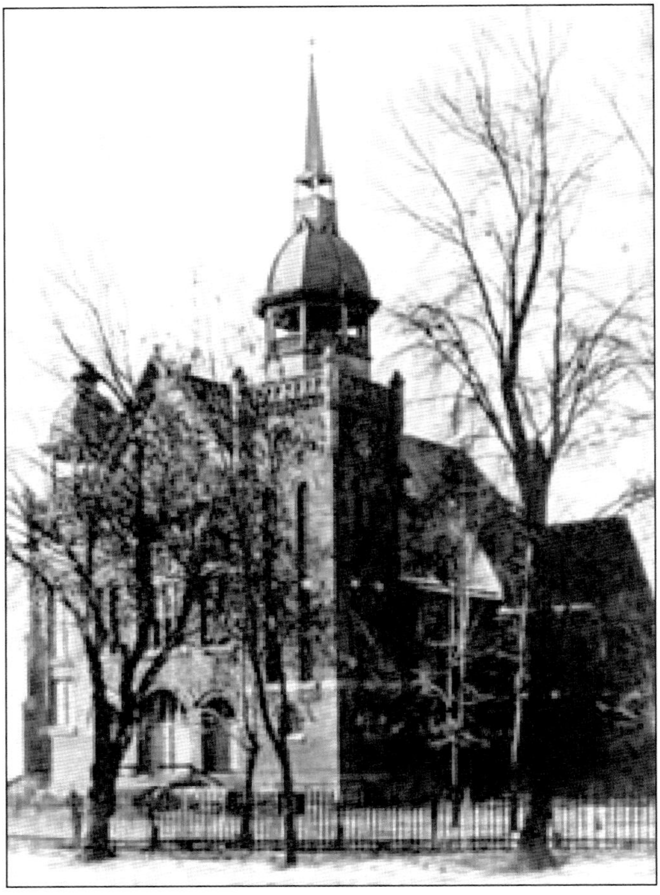

The Benson Stake Tabernacle is pictured here prior to April 1909. This is thought to be the last image taken of the tabernacle before the spires were taken down. It is said the spires were damaged in a violent windstorm in April 1909, necessitating their removal. Several other buildings in town also sustained damage at that time.

The exact date of this photograph of the Benson Stake Tabernacle is unknown, although it is believed that it was taken in May sometime in the early 1950s. Photographer Ariel Benson was said to have ridden the Ferris wheel at Black and White Days to gain a bird's-eye vantage point. There is no other way a shot could have been taken from this angle at the time. (Courtesy Ariel Benson collection.)

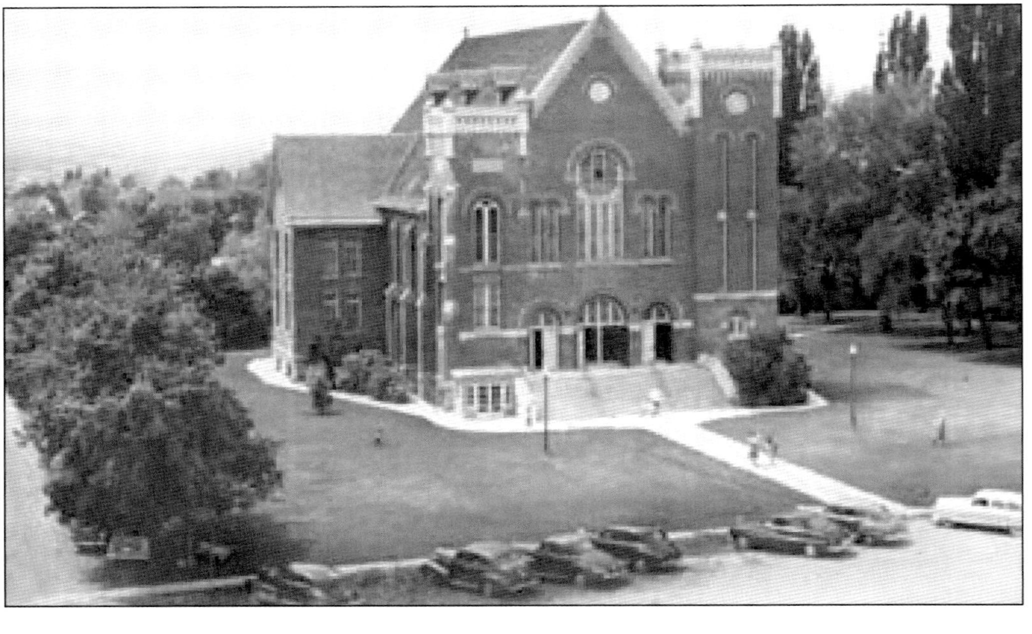

Four

Knowledge Is Power

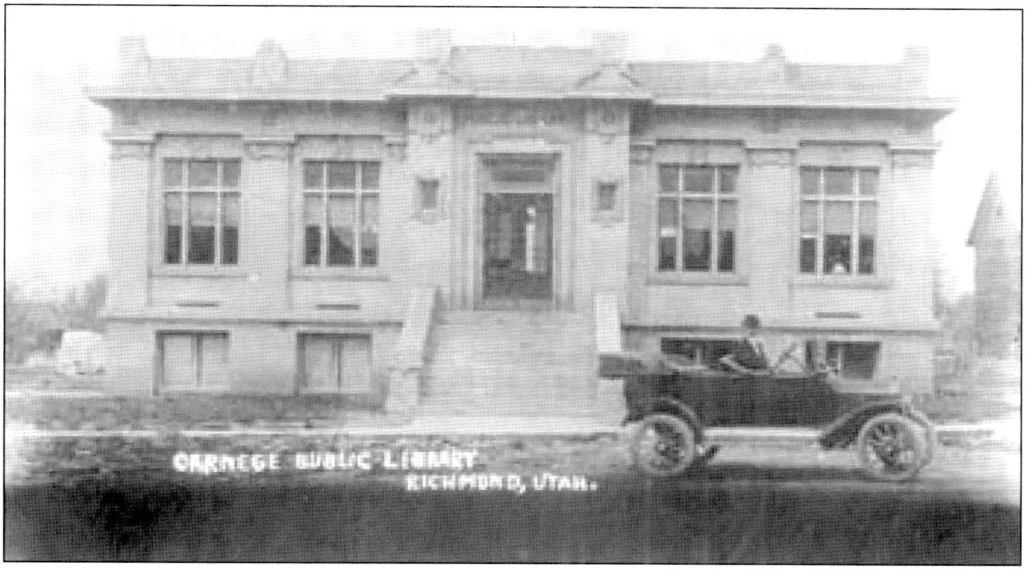

Richmond City received funding from the Carnegie Foundation to build a library in 1912. Construction began in 1913, and the building was finished and opened in 1914. Lulu Burnham was the first librarian. The library still stands on Main Street between State Street and 100 West. It is one of the very few original Carnegie libraries still in use as a library.

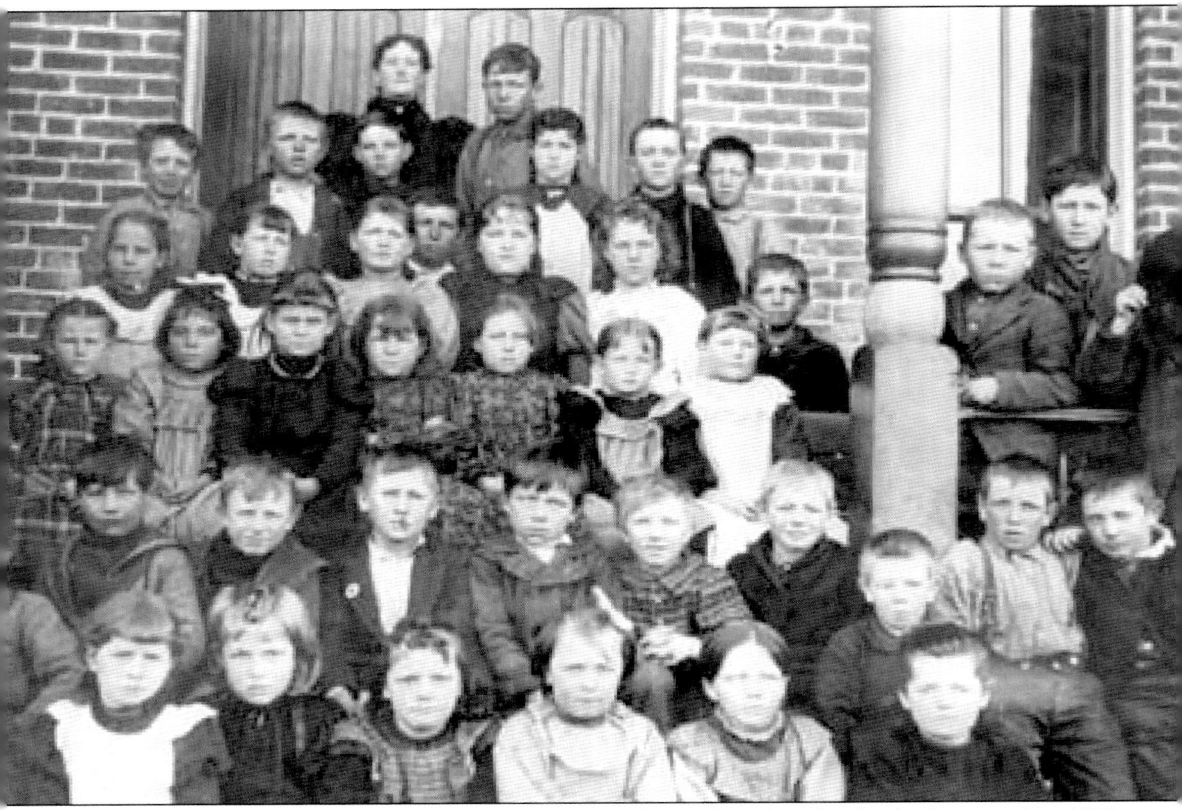

This is probably one of the first classes to attend the Red Brick School, which opened in 1893. The class likely contained children of various ages. The teacher, Linnie Telford, lived into her late 90s. Included in this image, which was taken on the front porch of the school, are, from left to right, (first row) Olive Peart, Jennie Ashment, unidentified, Justie Shepard, Ada Anderson, and Meta Christofferson; (second row) Leonard Christensen, Cecil Merrill, Lawrence Monson, Currie Hunt, Earl Skidmore, Earnest Hope, Willard Hendricks, Sergvent Frondson, unidentified, and Jack Ashment; (third row) Linda Burnham, Marian Merrill, Ione Thomson, Leone Robinson, Hazel Robinson, Mildred Merrill, and Otelia Frondson; (fourth row) Edna Burnham, Olive Hendricks, Sarah Woodland, Roy Stagg, Crilla Merrill, Lorena Feltman, Eugene Bail, Cory Allen, Arthur Hunt, and unidentified; (fifth row) two unidentified, Theo Merrill, Jennie Stoddard, Willie Bingham, and Ray Stagg; (sixth row) Linnie Telford (teacher) and Hugh Eskersly.

Pictured on the front steps of the Richmond Tabernacle are, from left to right, (first row) Fred Bateman, Mern Johnson, and Ruby Johnson; (second row) Eric Thorpe, Oral Ballam, unidentified, Elizabeth Eskelson, Flora Allen, and Leona McCarrey. They were teachers and staff from Richmond Park Elementary School in the early 1950s.

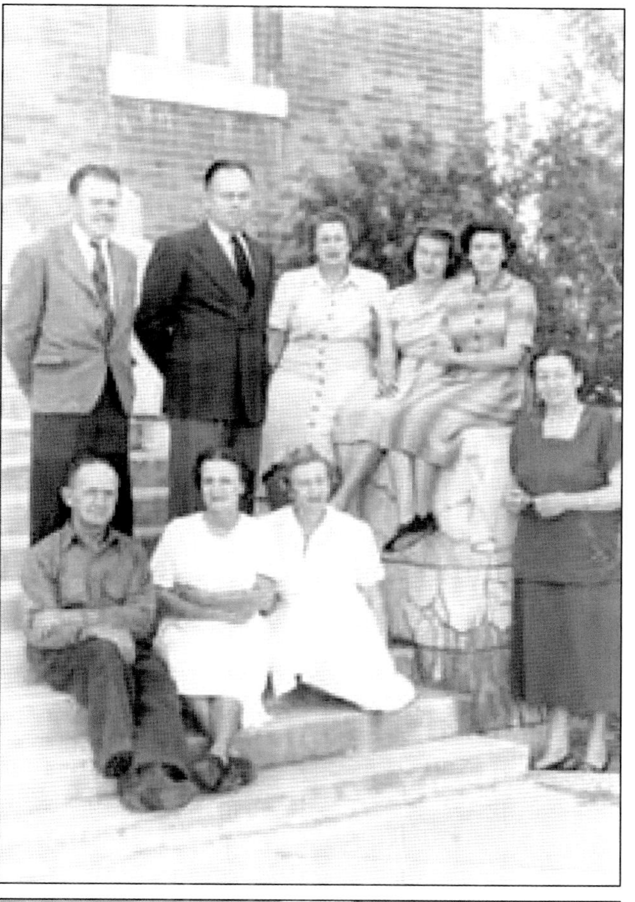

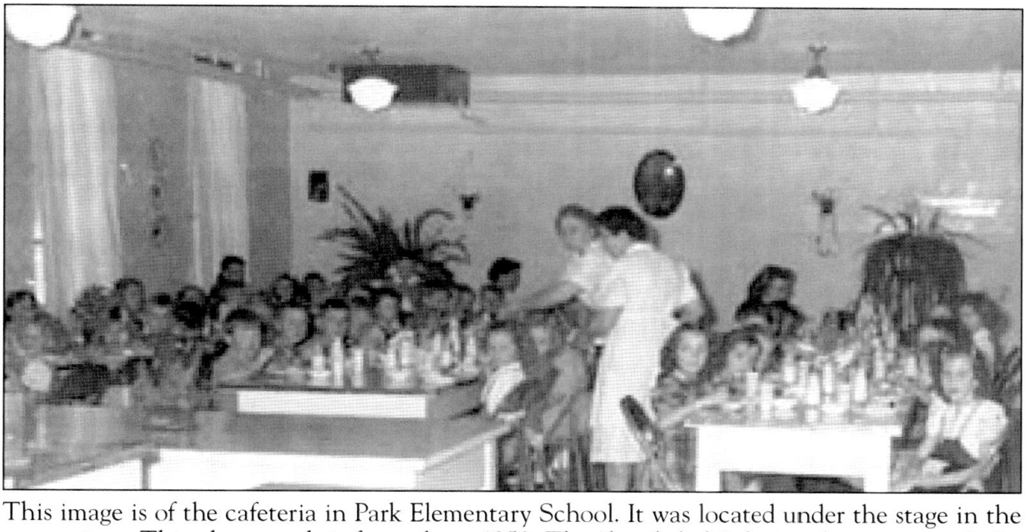

This image is of the cafeteria in Park Elementary School. It was located under the stage in the gymnasium. This photograph is from about 1950. The "lunch lady" facing the camera is Ruby Johnson. Notice the glass milk bottles and the fact that the lunch ladies are serving the children. The cafeteria is still there today, but it is now used as the school's music room.

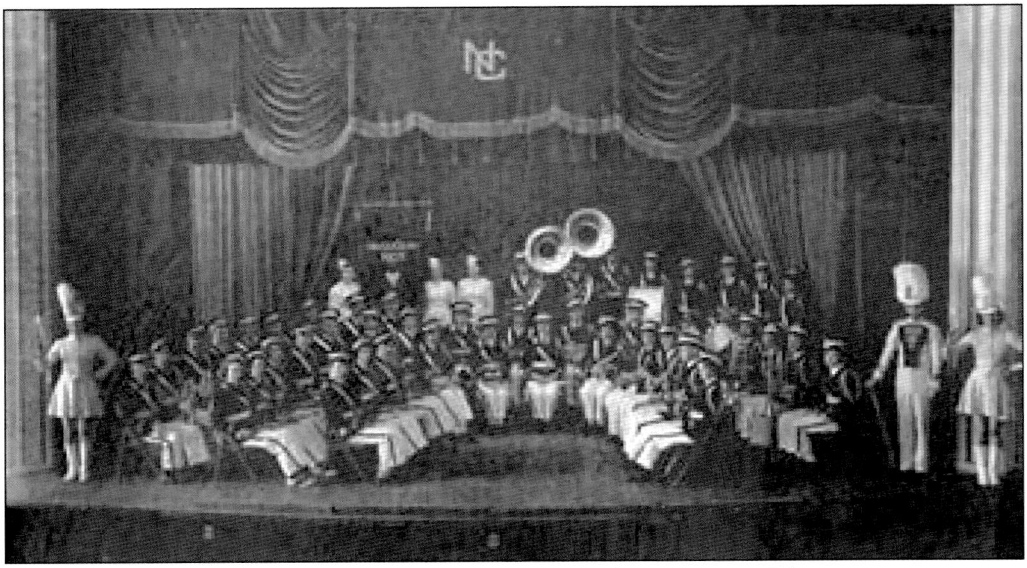

The North Cache band is shown here on its amazing auditorium stage. The stage curtains were all beautiful crushed velvet in maroon and had heavy gold fringe. It was a thrill to hear the band strike up the school song at rallies and games. North Cache would not have been complete without the band to add color and pep to the various school activities.

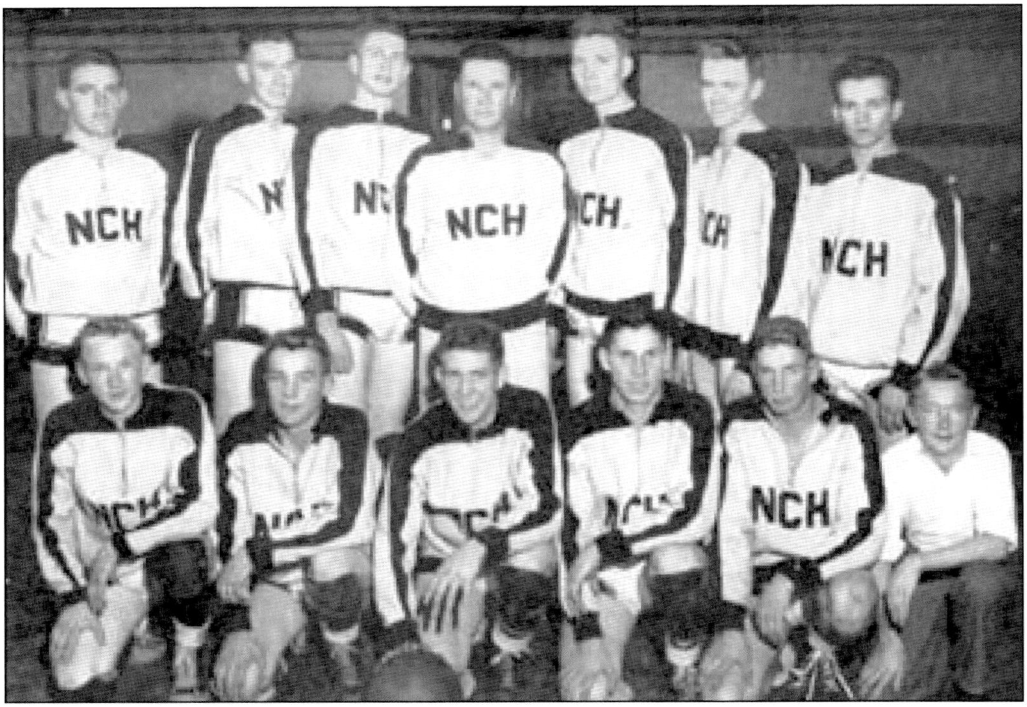

The year 1946 saw the North Cache High School Bulldogs take the state championship in basketball. Pictured are, from left to right, (first row) Cleon Hodges, Jay Griffin, Jay Van Noy, Leon Webb, Dean Bergenson, and Richard Bagley (manager); (second row) Bud Porter, Leon West, Nathan Done, Jay Whitman (coach), Max Christensen, Grant Ballam, and Clavel Haslem.

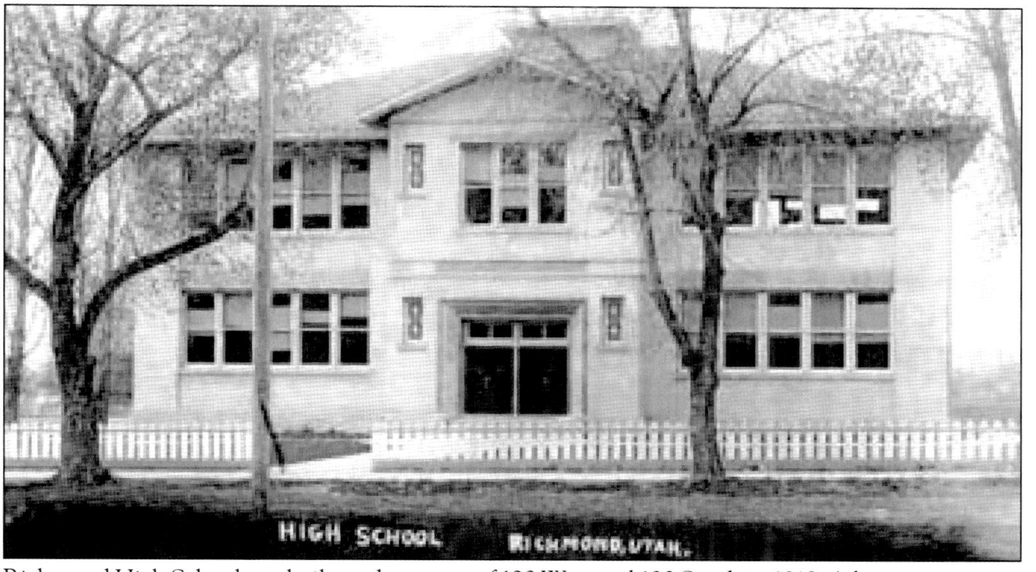

Richmond High School was built on the corner of 100 West and 100 South in 1912. A large gymnasium was added in 1935. Upon completion of North Cache High, the school was converted into an elementary school and renamed Park Elementary. Other additions were built over the years, and the original two-story structure was demolished in 1993. Many residents have fond memories of this building.

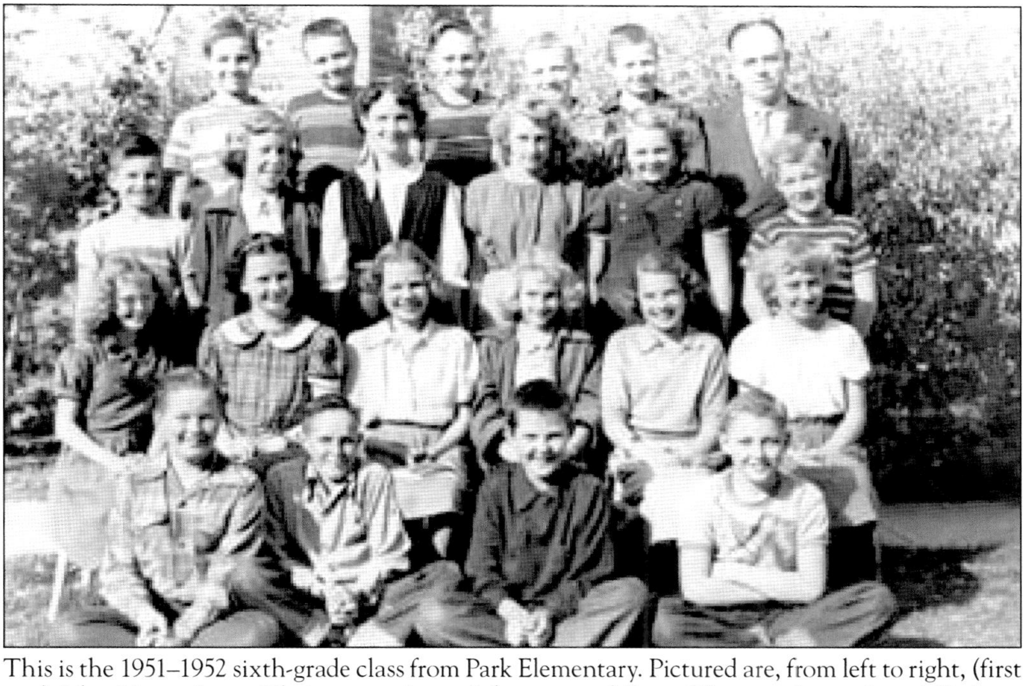

This is the 1951–1952 sixth-grade class from Park Elementary. Pictured are, from left to right, (first row) John Hayes, Lynn Christensen, Larry Johnson, and Scott Theurer; (second row) Barbara Jo Thompson, Ann Whitman, Beverley Sorenson, Ruth Ann Day, Druce Carlson, and Lorraine Purser; (third row) Clinton Housley, Ileen Bell, Elizabeth Glassford, Valeen Farnes, Deanne Smith, and David Harris; (fourth row) Merlin Humphries, Danny Drollinger, Gordon Sanders, George Duce, Greg Rigby, and Oral Ballam (teacher).

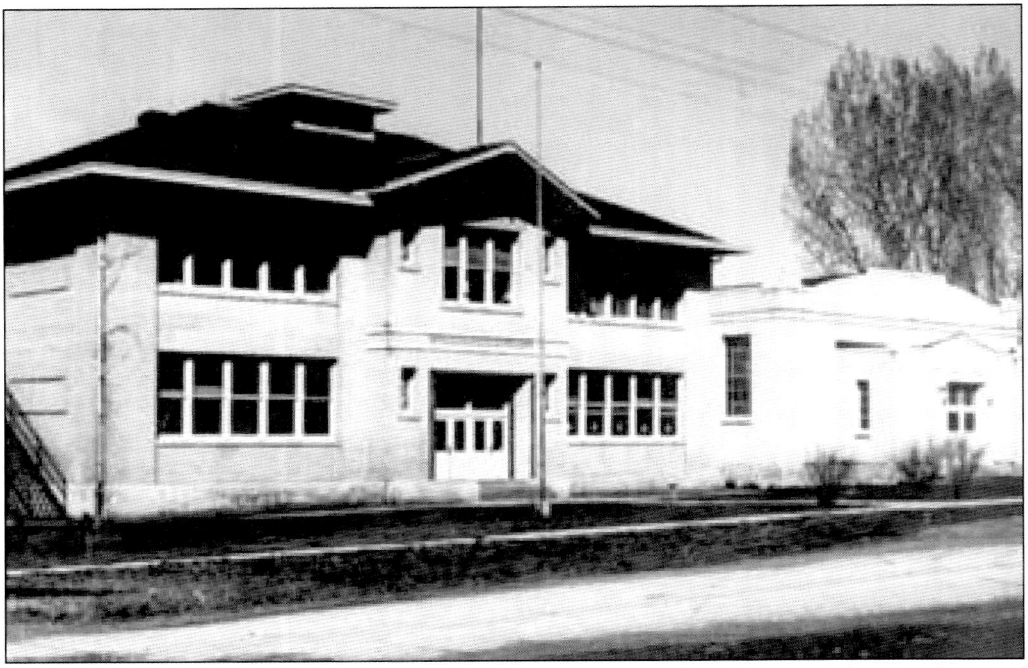

Park School, pictured above in 1948, was used as a high school from 1912 until the completion of North Cache in 1920. At that time, it was converted to an elementary school. The gymnasium was added on the north side of the school in 1935. The original two-story building was demolished in 1993, but the gymnasium is still in use. Below is a picture of Park School as it is today. Classrooms extend on both sides of the old gymnasium/auditorium. There is a modern library, computer lab, and other specialty rooms. However, students still eat lunch in the old gymnasium and attend music class in the last of the old classrooms, located under the stage.

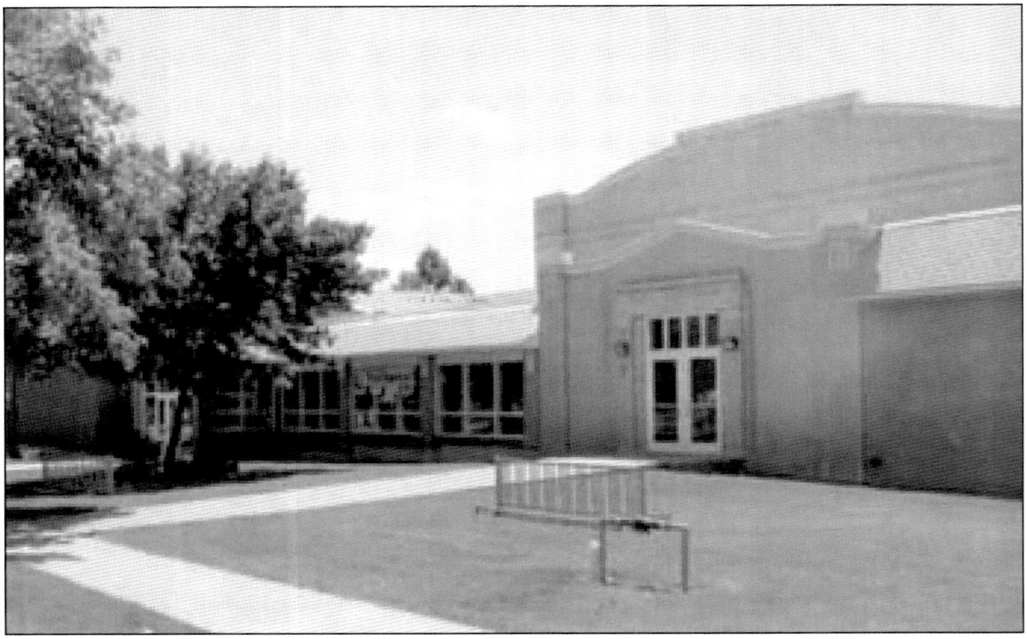

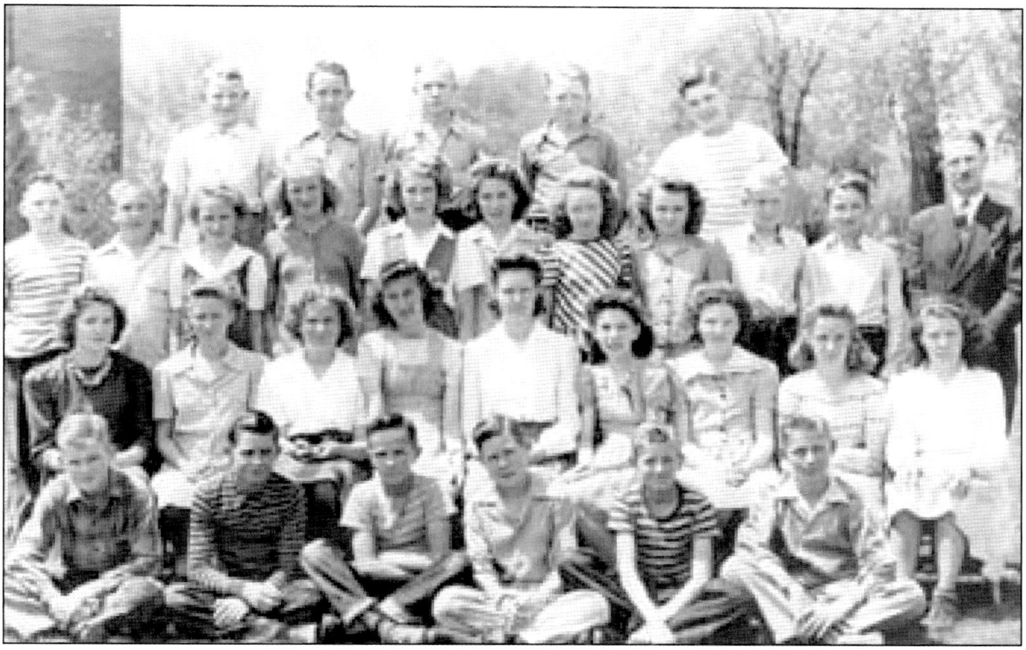

This sixth-grade class attended Park School in about 1942. Pictured are, from left to right, (first row) Merrill, LaVar Spackman, two unidentified, Richard Lewis, and Clayne Skidmore; (second row) Afton Bright, unidentified, Shirley Spackman, three unidentified, Ludean Burbank, Renae Murray, and Lillian Jonas; (third row) Earl Egan, two unidentified, Tess Carlson, two unidentified, Nancy Traveller, Joyce Whittle, Edward Johnson, Burt Erickson, and Grant Bagley (teacher); (fourth row) Richard Thompson, Dallin Bell, Lowell Andersen, Leonard Christofferson, and Dale Andrus.

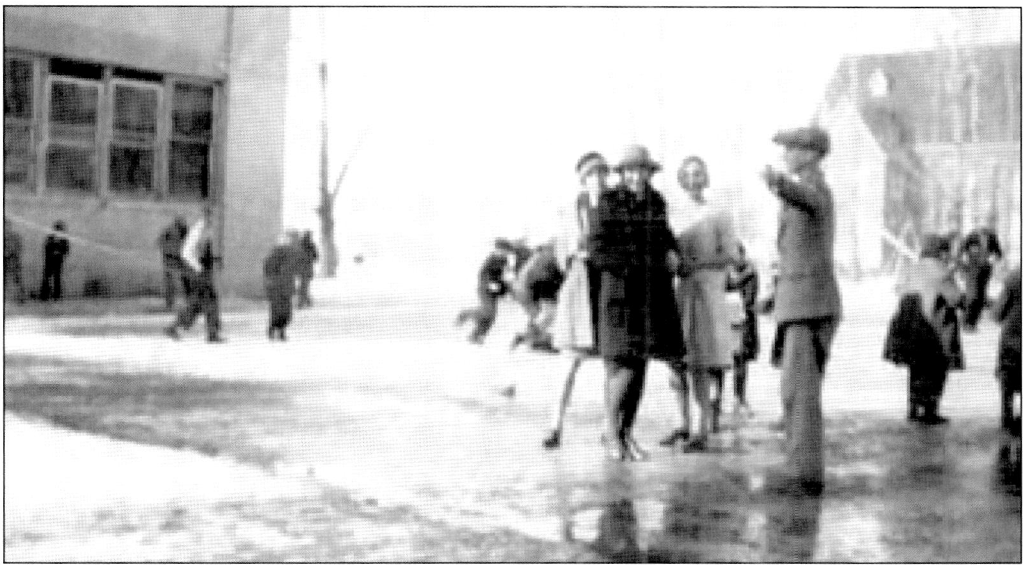

This photograph was taken in 1920 in front of Richmond High School. The school was built in 1912 and was used as a high school for only eight years. This image is relevant because it shows where the school and tabernacle stood in relation to one another. The tabernacle was demolished in 1962, following an earthquake. It was torn down in 1993. (Courtesy of Cheri Housley.)

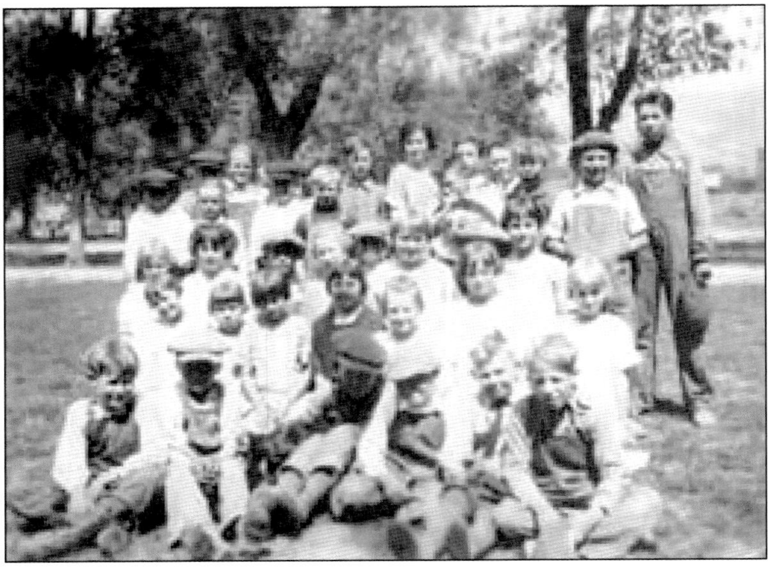

Pictured is a fourth-grade class from Richmond Park Elementary in 1924. The image was taken on the lawn of the school. The only child who has been identified is Glen Housley, who is the fifth from the right in the top row. Notice that all the boys are wearing overalls, and many of them are wearing hats.

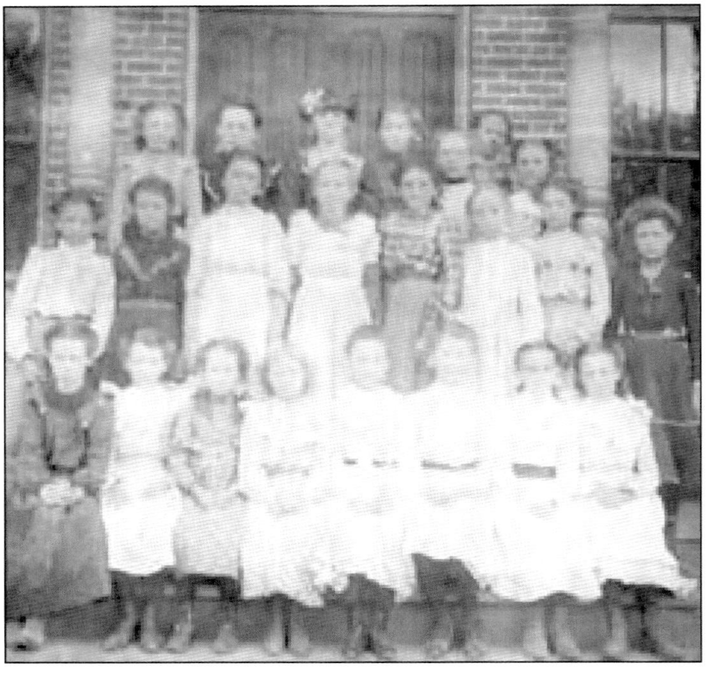

This photograph was taken around 1900 of a class on the porch of the Red Brick School. Pictured are, from left to right, (first row) Pearl Feltman, Millie Thompson, Annie Merrill, Esther Johnson, Christobel Petty, Edith Bullen, Esther Webb, and Loretta Merrill; (second row) Sarah Erickson, Mabel Stagg, Leone Thompson, Ivy Burnham, Leone Bair, Othelia Anderson, Viola Shepard, and Hazel Hendricks; (third row) Nellie Anderson, Cora Bateman, Annie Erickson, unidentified, Tennie Hendricks, Helen Larsen (teacher), and Minnie Johnson.

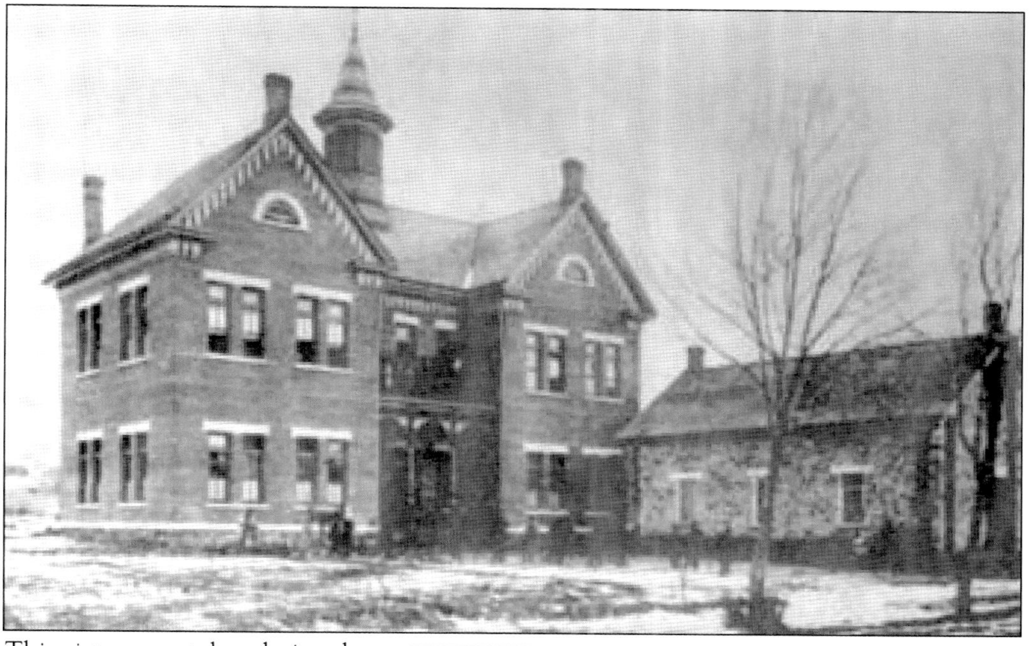

This picture was taken during the short time that both the Red Brick School and the Old Rock School were standing, about 1893. The Old Rock School was torn down shortly after the Red Brick School opened. When the Red Brick School was torn down, around 1930, some of the rocks from the foundation were used to build the Daughters of Utah Pioneers marker, which still stands in the city park just east of the highway.

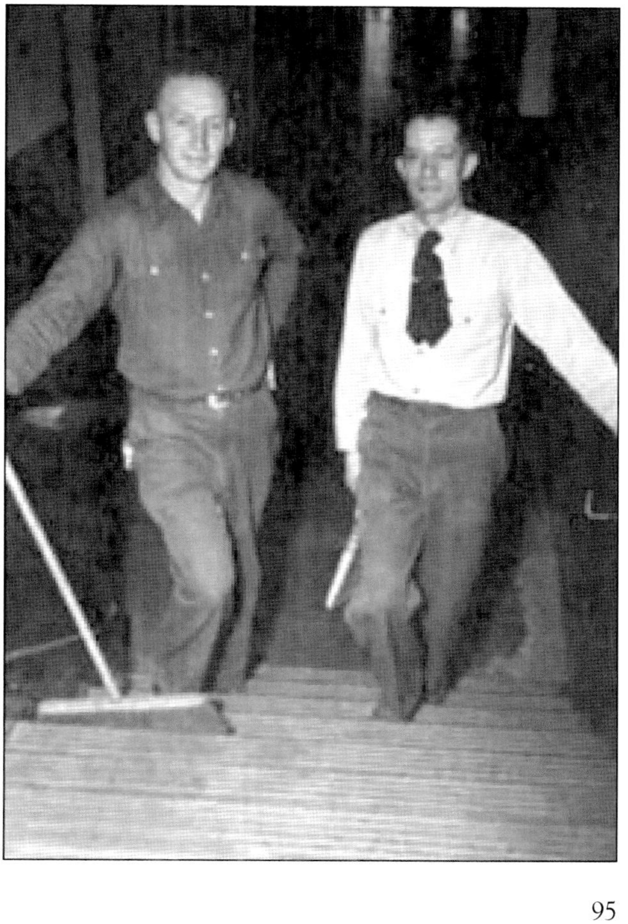

Dean Bullen and Charles Peart, both from Richmond, are pictured standing at the bottom of one of the many staircases at North Cache High School. Dean and Charles were both custodians at North Cache in 1950. Since the school had four stories, there were many stairs to climb as they attended to their duties. Charles also owned Charlie's Candy Store, which was located on Main Street in Richmond.

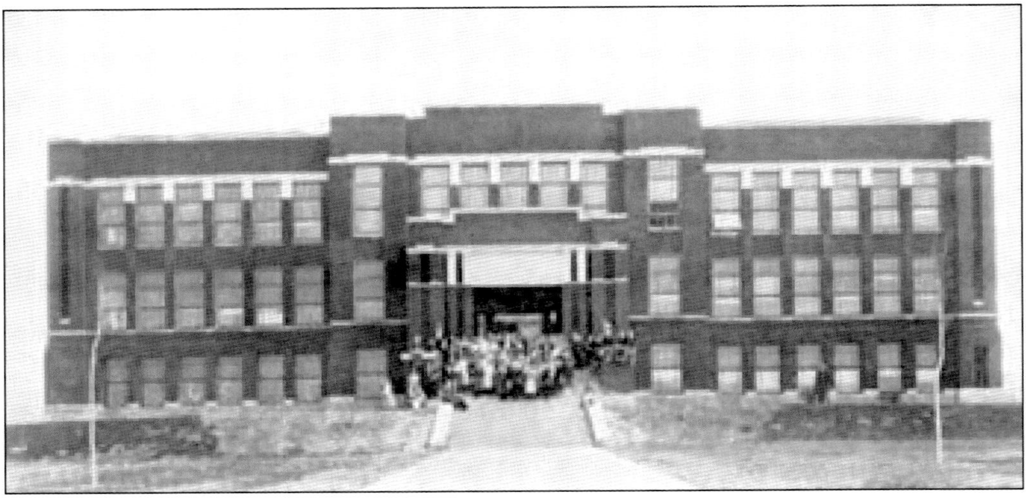

The photograph above was taken in 1923 and shows North Cache High School in its earliest days. Before that, the high school was in the old Park School. North Cache served northern Cache Valley well for many years as a high school until Sky View opened in 1964. It was then used as a junior high and, later, as a middle school. In the end, it served as a freshman center, housing only ninth-grade students. It was finally demolished in 1999, after the new North Cache School (below) was built behind it. Students from Richmond attend kindergarten through fifth grade at Park School, sixth and seventh grades at White Pine Middle School on the north end of town, and eighth and ninth grades at North Cache. Then, they head off to Sky View in Smithfield for 10th through 12th grades.

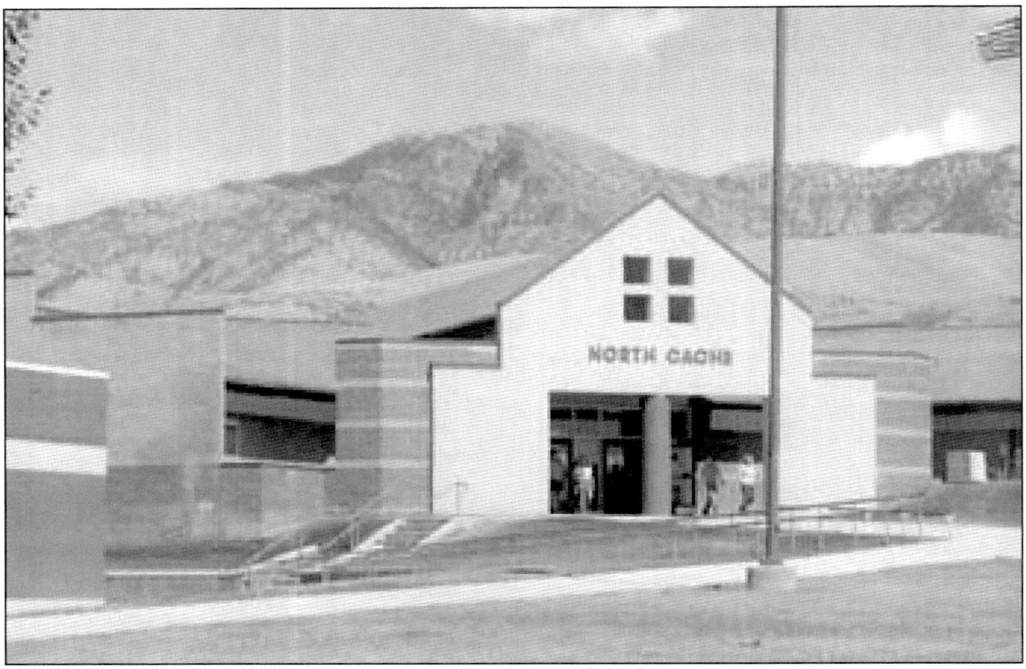

The annual Harvest Ball at North Cache High School had the theme "By the Light of the Silvery Moon" in 1949. The assembly and dance were planned accordingly, and the Future Farmers and Future Homemakers worked diligently to make it a success. The queen of the Harvest Ball was Billie Lu Doane (Bagley) and Dallin Bell was crowned King.

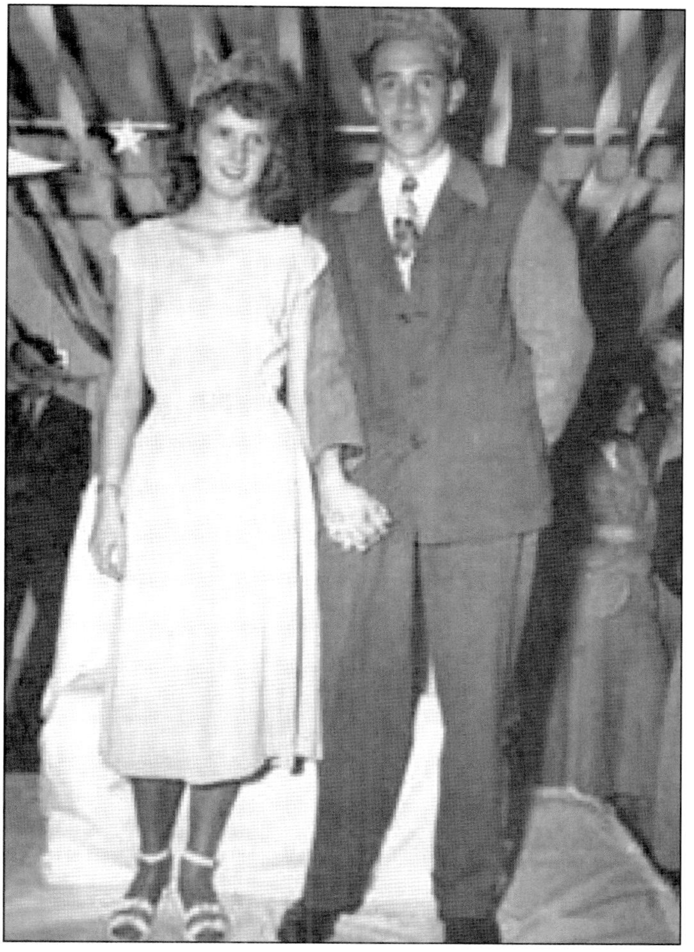

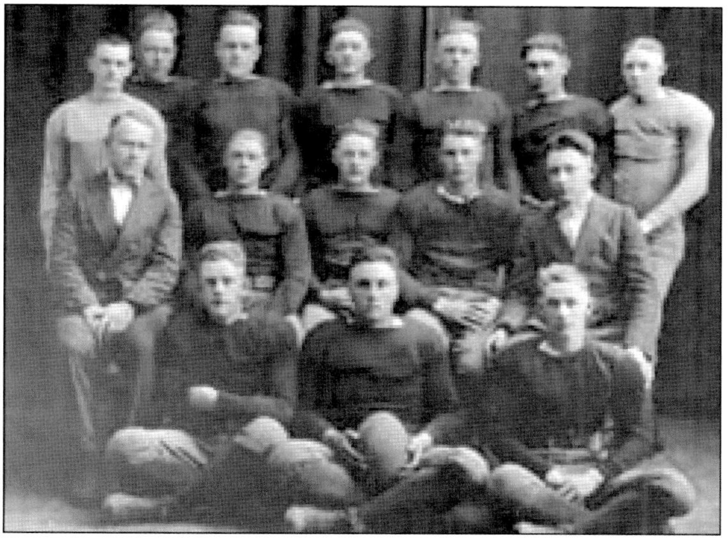

North Cache High School fielded its first football team in 1919. Pictured are, from left to right, (first row) LaVille Merrill, Herbert Adamson, Ivan Merrill; (second row) C.B. Johnson (coach), Rulon F. Thompson, Rulon Merrill, Lowell Van Noy, and Ariel Merrill; (third row) Angus Woodruff, Glen Walters, Oscar Troseth, Amos W. Bair, George Smith, Allen Hendricks, and Silas Andersen.

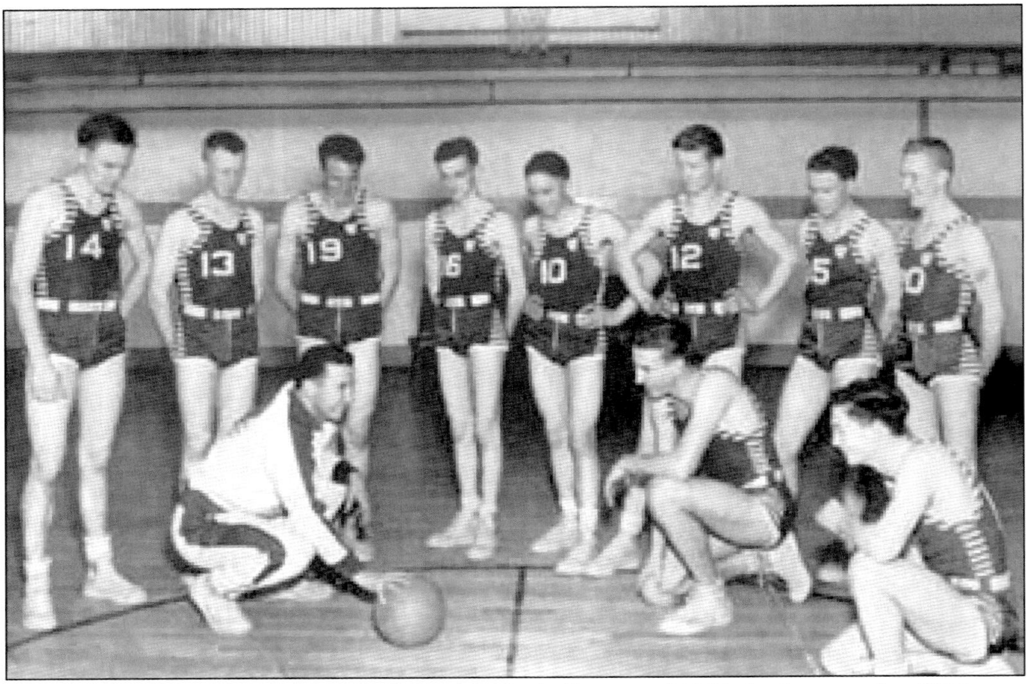

Pictured is the North Cache High School basketball team of 1940. In front are Jay Whitman (coach), Howard Hansen, and team captain Dean Andrew (right). Standing are, from left to right, Charles Low, Cannon Parkinson, Ray Hayes, Robert Toolson, Kenneth Elwood, Max Rich, Clark Ellerman, and Dick Griffin. The team took the region championship in a playoff game with Ogden High. The final score was North Cache 26, Ogden 24.

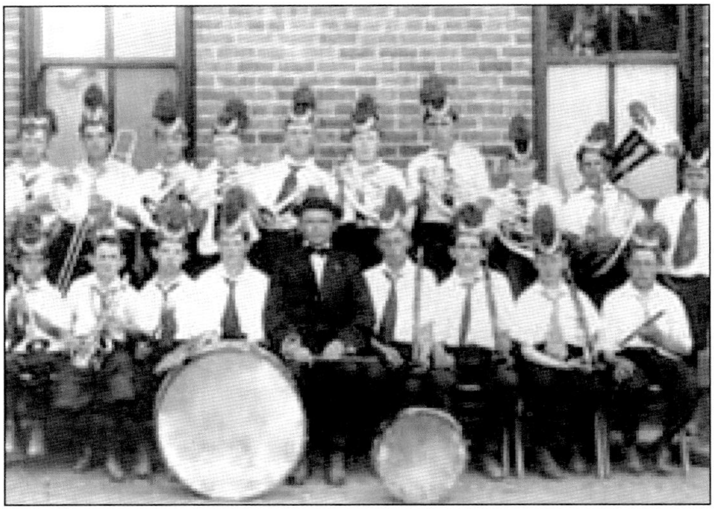

Music has always been an important part of life in Richmond. Pictured here is Richmond High School's first band. The bandleader was John A. Omansen (center, front). The photograph was taken on the south side of the Red Brick School, which was across the street from what is now Park Elementary on 100 West, between Main Street and 100 South. The image was taken in approximately 1916.

Five

A Little of This, a Little of That

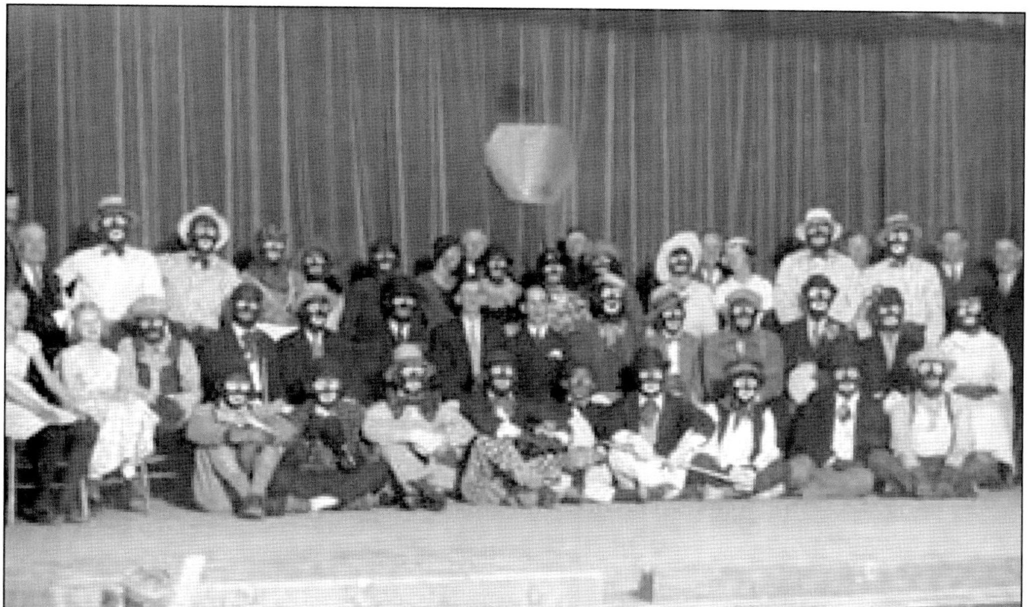

Richmond has been home to a variety of dramatic clubs over the years. Plays of all kinds have been performed in the local schools and churches, at the Opera House, and more recently, in the Community Building auditorium. The performance pictured above is believed to have taken place in the Community Building in the 1940s and would not be condoned today.

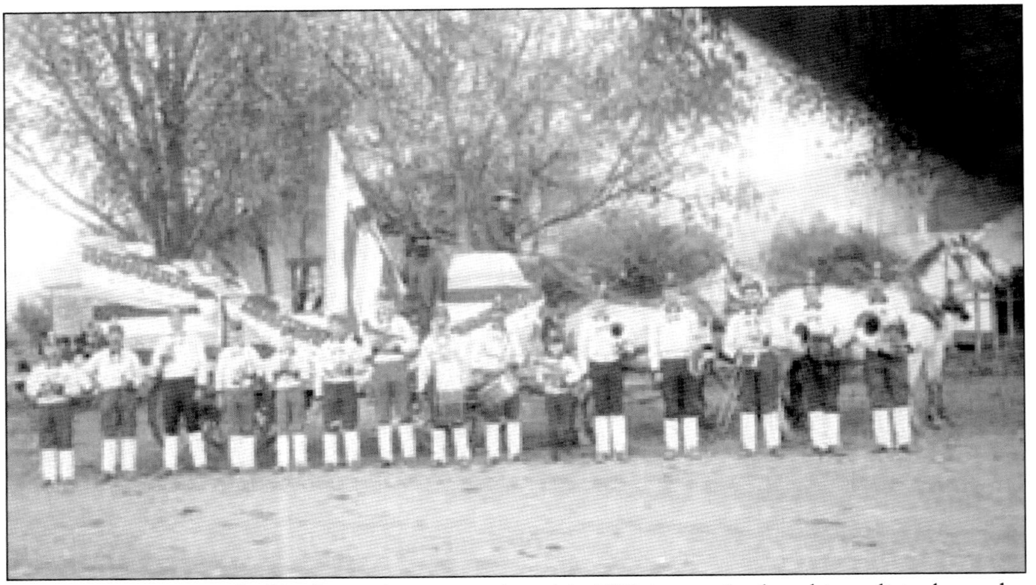

The Republican Band of Richmond is pictured in this 1891 image. It played in political parades from Richmond to Ogden. The lights on their hats enabled them to play at night. They were the largest band north of Salt Lake City. Included in this photograph are, from right to left, Francis Whitehead (bandleader), John Anderson, Mick Johnson, Frank Whitehead, Freddy Merrill, Jim Smith, Brigham Hyer, Will Smith, Will Horn, John Whitehead, Riley Bair, Jim Davenport, Willie Merrill, Frank Burnham, Ed Peck, Homer Bair (driver), and LeeAnder Peart (holding the flag).

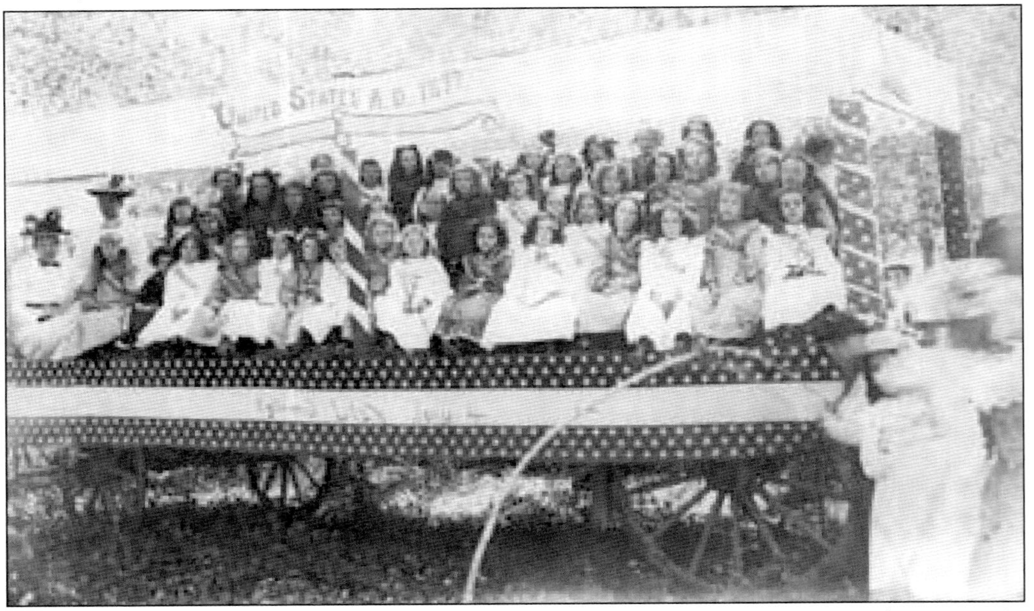

Pictured is a float from a Richmond Independence Day parade that was held on July 4, 1899. At that time, there were 45 states in the union; Utah was the newest, having achieved statehood in 1896. All 45 states were represented, with each girl on the float wearing a sash with the name of a state on it. This photograph was found recently between the walls of an older home in town that was undergoing some remodeling work. (Courtesy of Ted Johnson.)

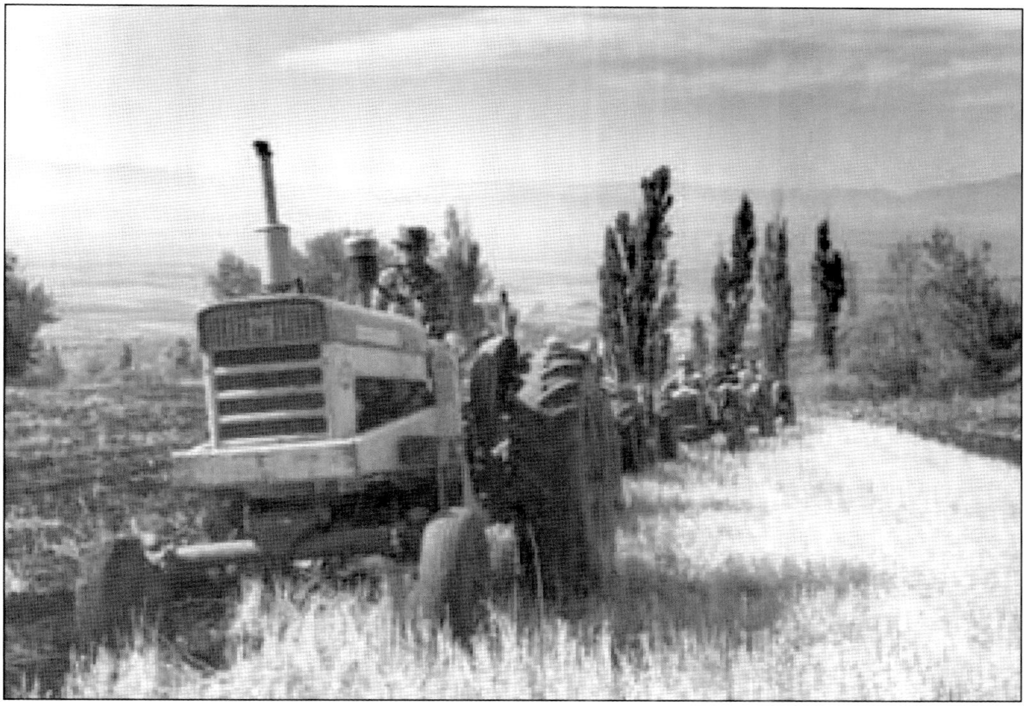

Pictured here is the High Priest group from a local Church of Jesus Christ of Latter-day Saints ward. They are plowing Dean Smith's field. The Smith family tells the story that Eddie Smith had been very sick with kidney failure. His parents, Dean and Aldean, were spending a lot of time with him. The church group stepped in to help with the farming, and with many tractors, it did not take long. Garr Christensen is on the lead tractor.

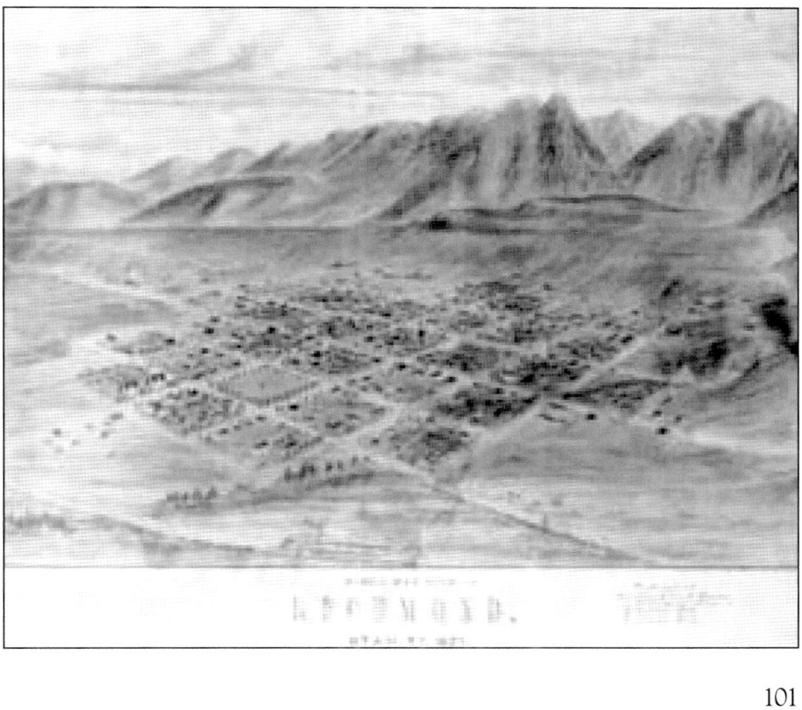

Pictured is a copy of a map of the Richmond Territory from 1875. The current Highway 91 runs on 200 West today, but in 1875, the main road through the area ran down State Street, which is why the space between the sidewalks on each side seems so wide today.

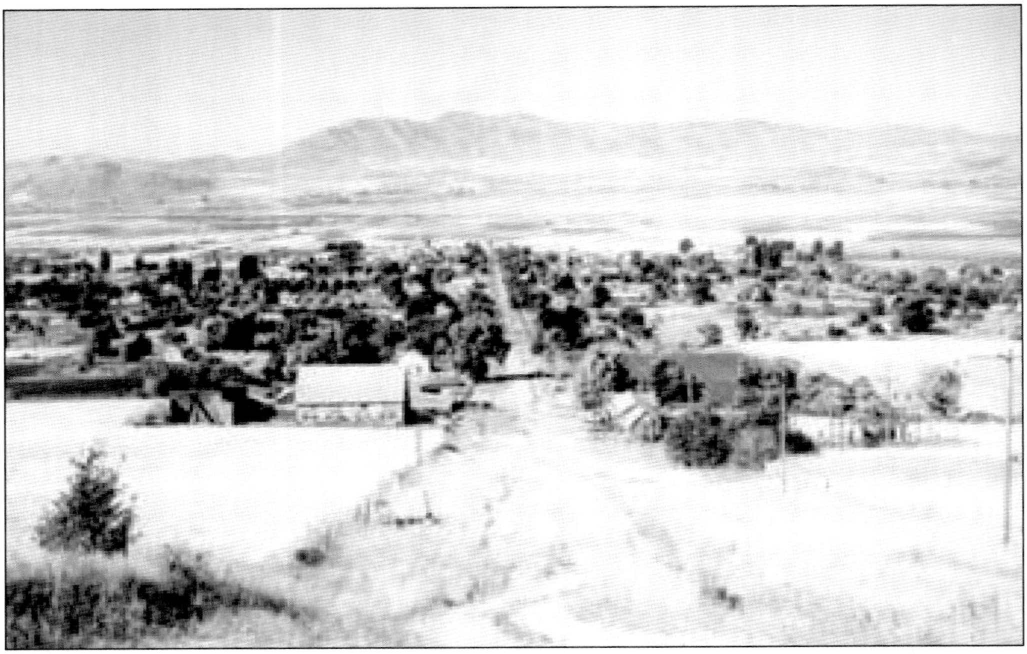

The photograph above, taken in the 1960s, provides a good view of Richmond from the vantage point of about 400 East Main Street. The changes that have taken place in the last 50 years are evident in the photograph below, which was taken in 2010 from almost the same spot. The trees are bigger now, obscuring many of the houses, so it is hard to tell which remain. Christensen's barn is much the same, as is the smokestack at the old milk plant. It is interesting to note that much of East Main Street was still dirt in the 1960s. As much as people complain today about growth in Cache Valley, the valley floor beyond Richmond has seen surprisingly little change. (Above, courtesy of Cheri Housley; below, courtesy of Kathy Jones.)

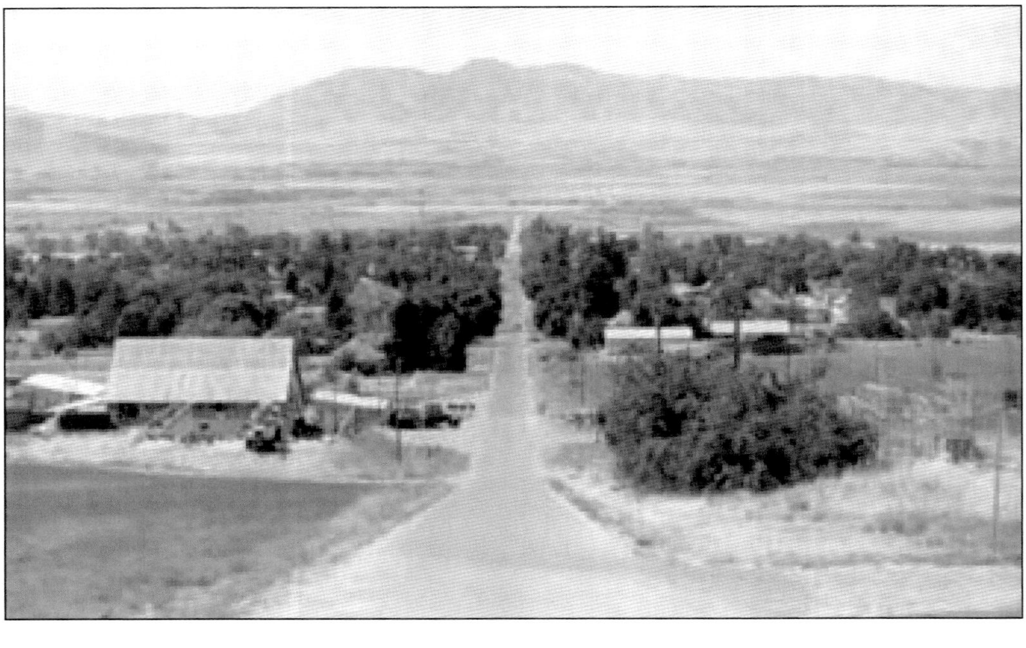

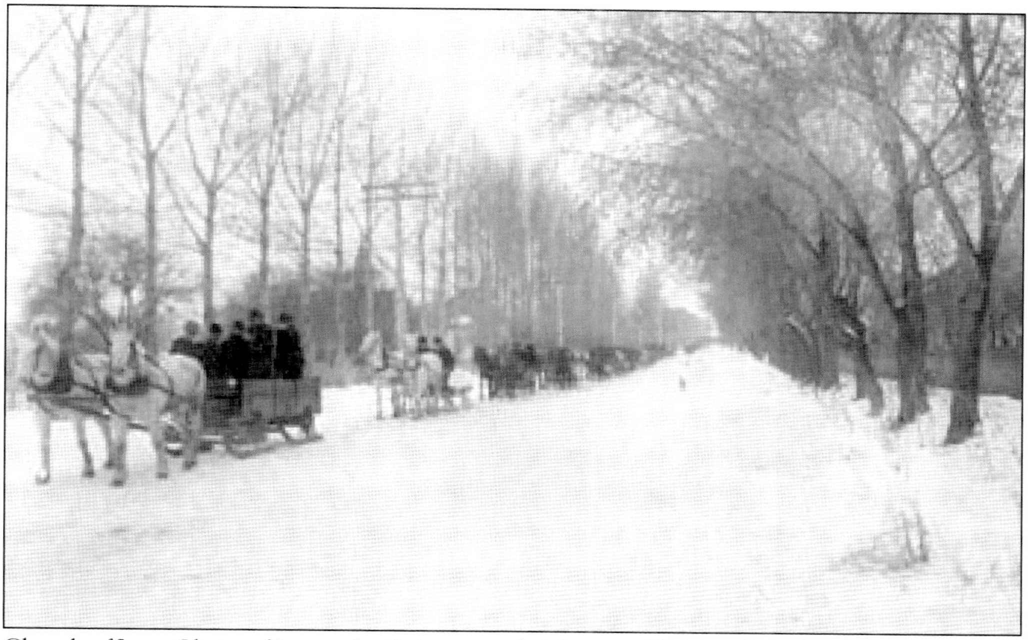

Church of Jesus Christ of Latter-day Saints apostle Marriner W. Merrill died February 6, 1906, at his home in Logan, Utah. His funeral was the first meeting held in the nearly complete Benson Stake Tabernacle in Richmond. There was no glass in the windows yet, and it is said that the service was long and cold. Shown here is the funeral procession as it moved east along Main Street. The tabernacle is visible through the trees.

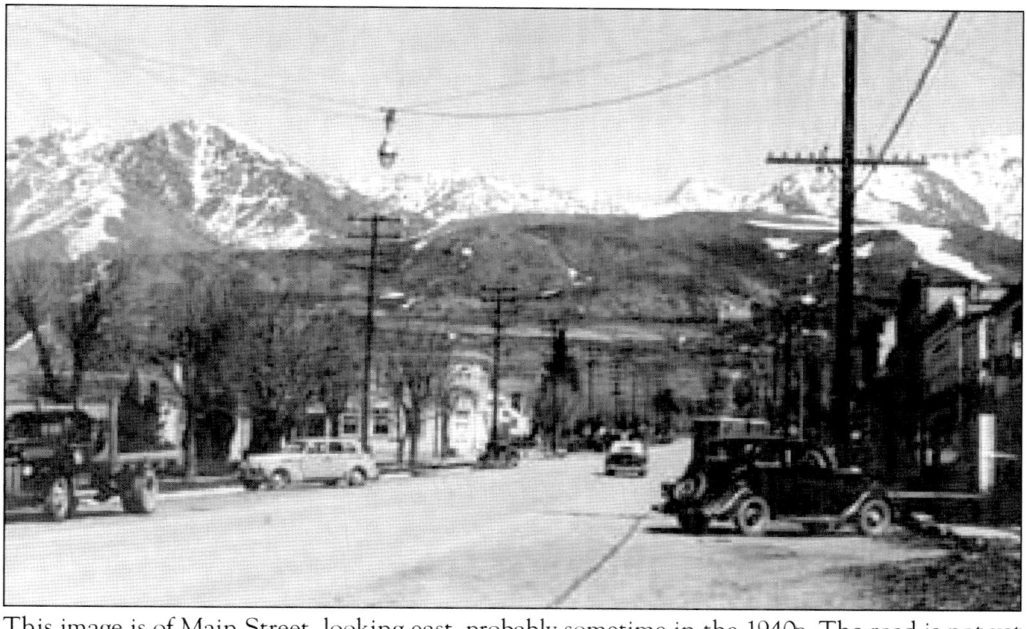

This image is of Main Street, looking east, probably sometime in the 1940s. The road is not yet paved. The streetlight hung over the middle of the street in front of the library. This would have been a typical spring day in downtown Richmond, with snow-covered Cherry Creek Peak rising above the town.

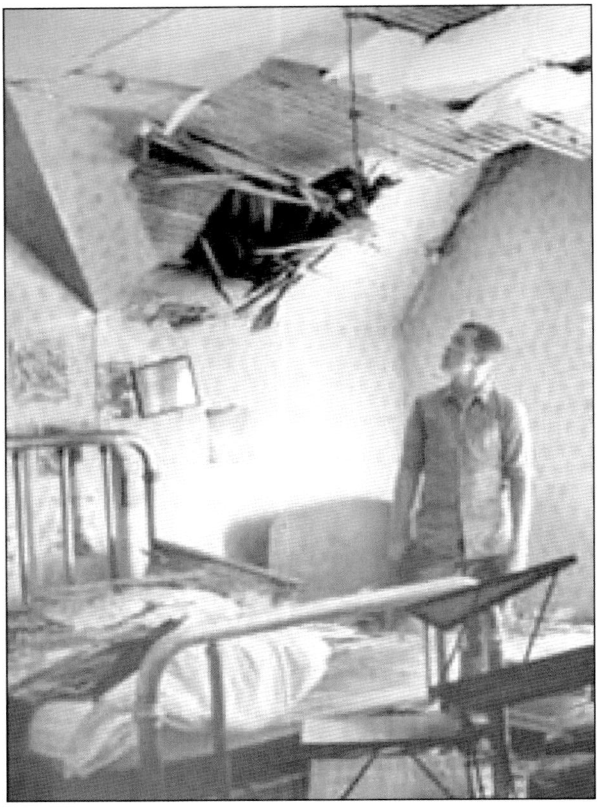

August 30, 1962, was a day that changed Richmond forever. Being very close to the epicenter of an earthquake with a magnitude of 6.1 on the Richter Scale, the town sustained major damage. Many of the older homes were damaged beyond repair and were torn down and replaced with modern dwellings. Amazingly, no major injuries were reported.

Many of the town's residences were damaged in the earthquake of 1962. Richmond was the closest town to the epicenter and took the brunt of the damage, although many towns reported having been affected. This house lost several bricks and must have received some interior damage, as many items have been moved out to the lawn.

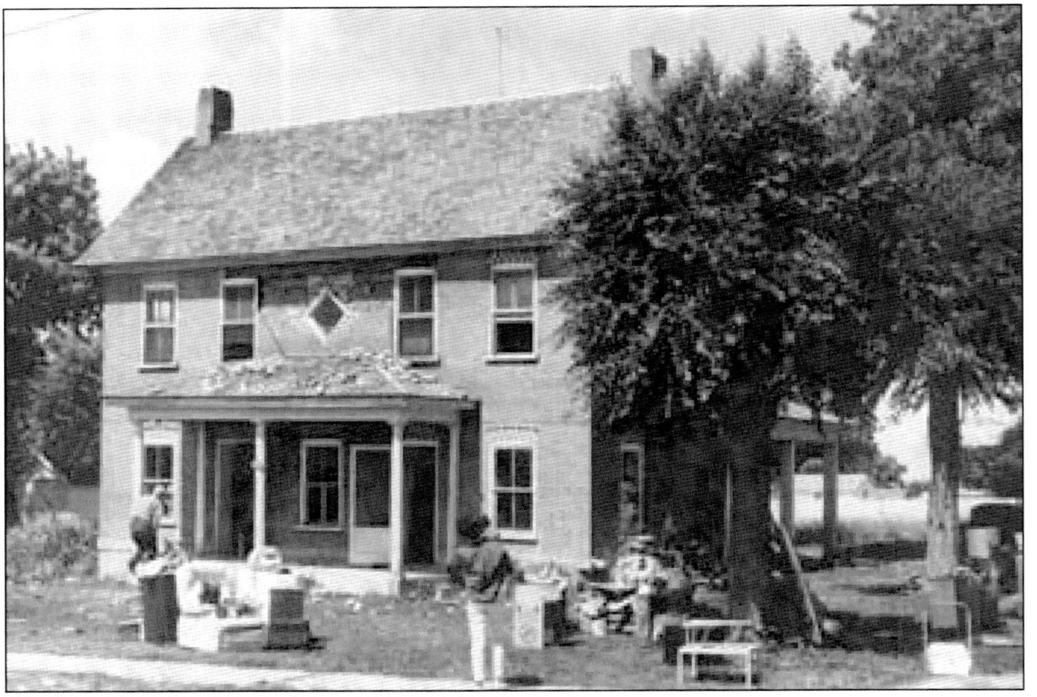

The Richmond earthquake of 1962 caused considerable damage in the town. Along with structural damage to many buildings, the contents of most houses and businesses was shaken up and tossed around. Theurer's Market on Main Street escaped major structural damage, but the merchandise did not fare so well.

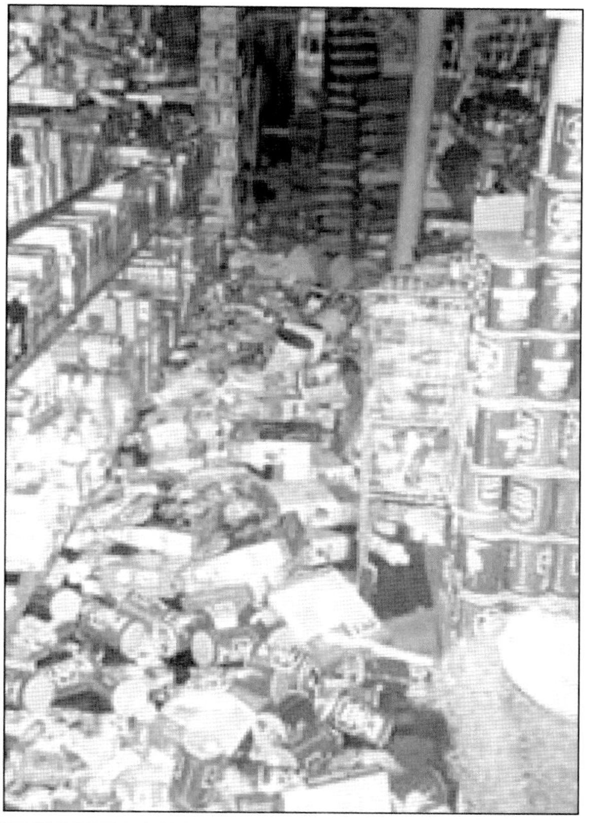

Things were shaken up at Nivison Drugs during the earthquake of 1962. August 30th started out like any other day, but then the earthquake hit. By the end of the day, most homes and businesses had a big clean-up job on their hands. Much of the inventory could not be salvaged and was discarded, leading to heavy financial losses for some business owners.

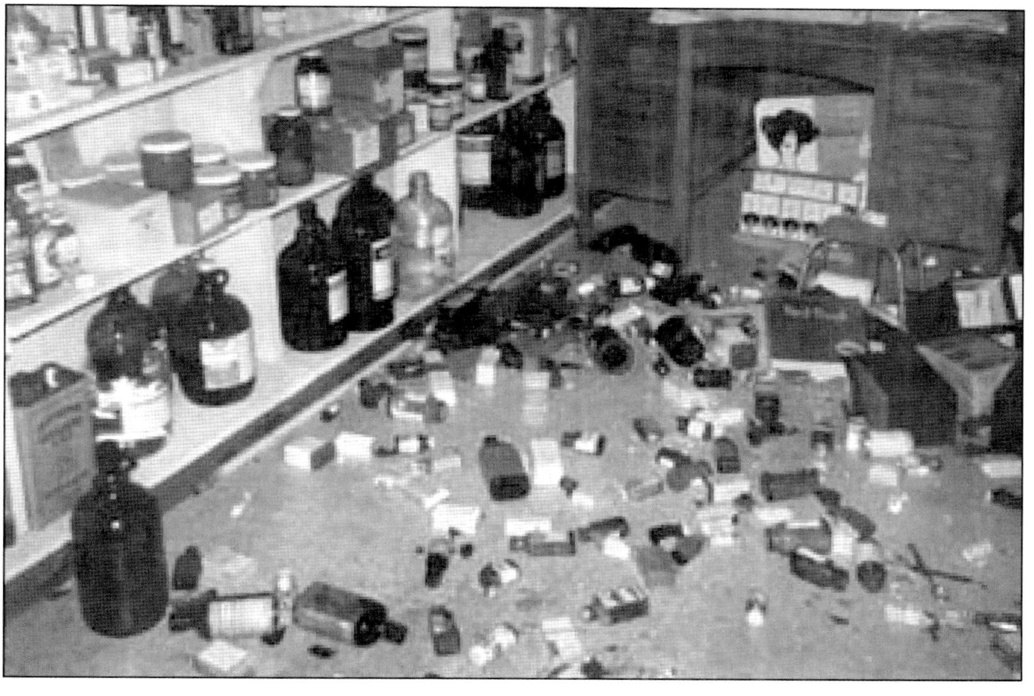

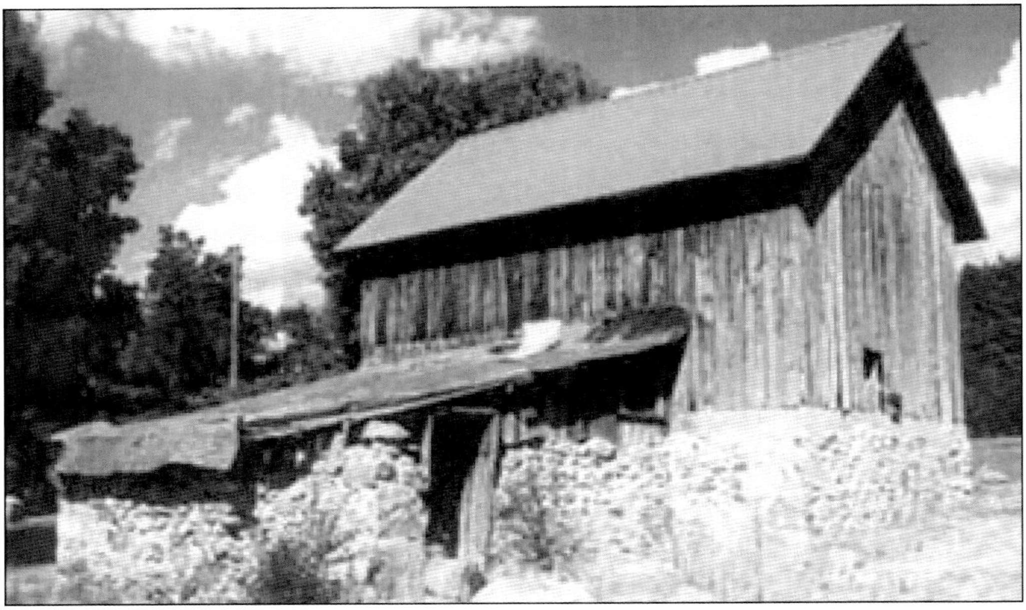

Built in the late 1800s by the sons of homesteaders Howard and Amanda Egan, this barn is located at 530 South 100 East. The wood came from a mill the Egans ran near Franklin Basin. The rocks came directly out of Richmond's notoriously rocky ground. The barn appears to have been built in two sections, with the lean-to constructed first and the taller section added sometime later. (Courtesy of Angela Nelson.)

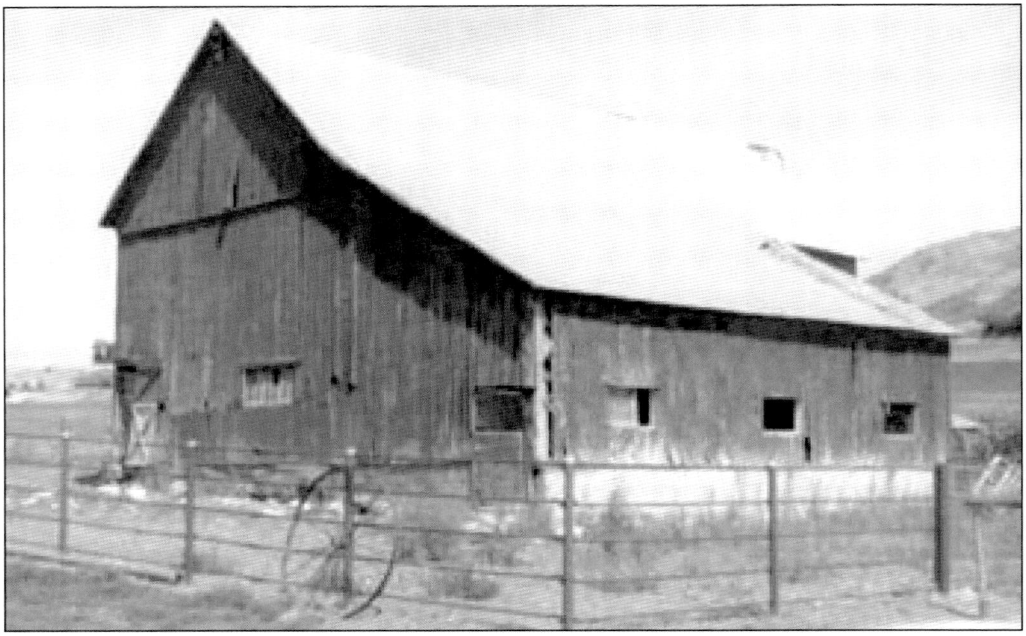

This classic English barn was built at 308 North 300 East in the early 1900s by Alma "Shorty" and Clara Spackman. Being built on a slope allowed more levels than usual, including the rare inclusion of a fruit cellar under the main floor. A lean-to addition was built on later, enlarging the usable space. (Courtesy of Kathy Jones.)

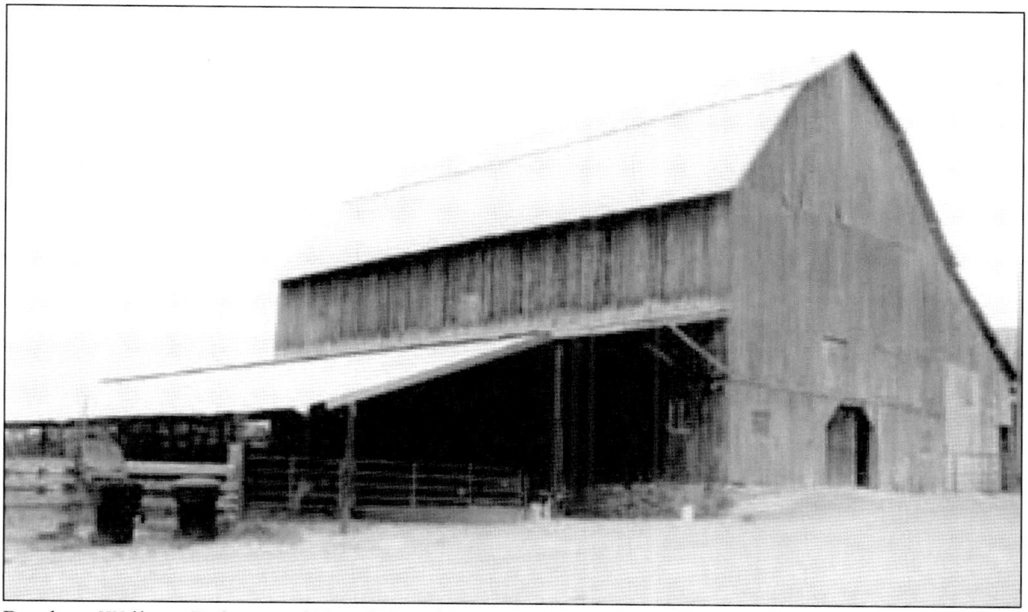

Brothers William Robert and Enoch Bartlett Tripp, new converts to the Church of Jesus Christ of Latter-day Saints, built this barn at 725 South 250 East in 1895. Stalls for horses, cows, and other animals filled the main floor, and there was a large hayloft above. Today, the barn is used by the adjoining veterinary practice to house large animals. The barn has been used for dances, basketball games, screening movies, and other activities over the years. (Courtesy of Kathy Jones.)

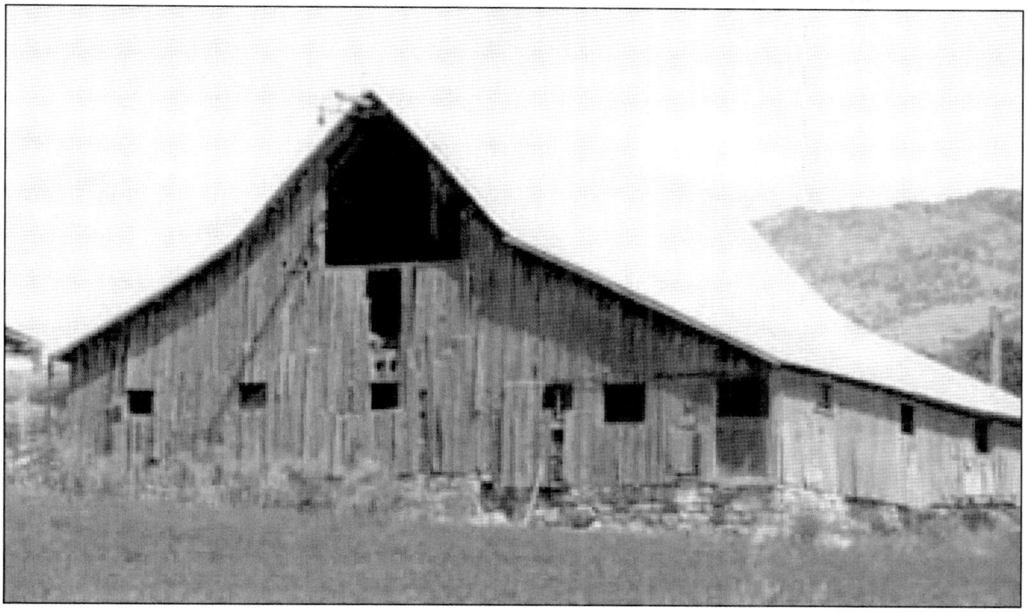

Located at 695 East 500 North, this large barn was constructed about 1900. It was built using the old method of attaching posts and beams with wooden pegs rather than with nails. Square metal nails were used to attach the siding planks. Cows were housed on each side of the barn, and the center was used for hay storage. C.I. Stoddard owned the barn until 1948, but it is not known if he built it. (Courtesy of Kathy Jones.)

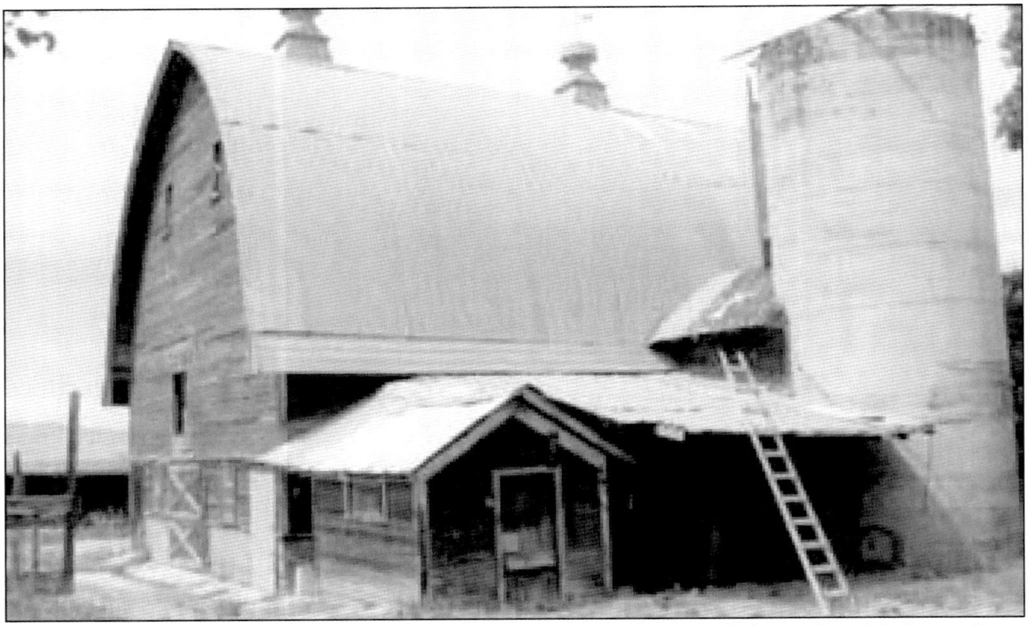

What was surely once one of Richmond's most beautiful barns belonged to Ned and Lucy Spackman. Considered to be a 20th-century "specialized" barn with an arched roof, it was built for use as a dairy barn. It is located just west of Highway 91 about a block north of the traffic light. (Courtesy of Kathy Jones.)

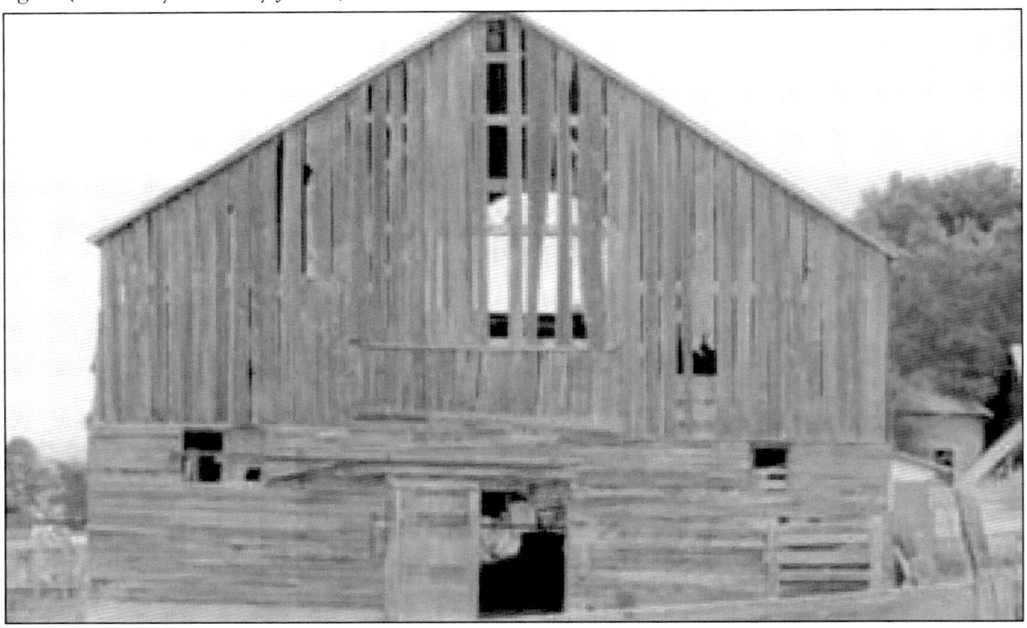

The original building site and date of this barn are not known. However, in 1940, milk hauler Edwin Smith took it apart and reconstructed it piece by piece at 576 South 100 East. Edwin's father, William, also a milk hauler for Sego Milk, owned a barn just to the south of this one. Three generations of Smiths hauled milk for Sego. This barn is currently owned by Edwin's great-grandson who uses it for storage. (Courtesy of Kathy Jones.)

This is a photograph of the John T. Caine home. It was built about 1869 on the south end of Richmond, north of Mendenhall Curve. This is a classic two-story home with a balcony that includes beautiful railings and latticework. Notice the lovely porch. If the world had more porches like this and neighbors were still treated like kin, all would be better off. Porches were truly the heart of the home.

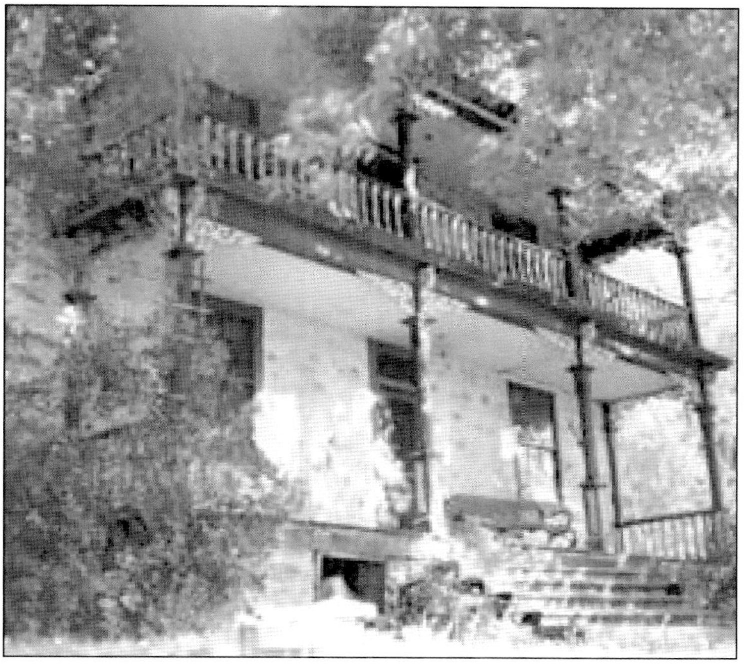

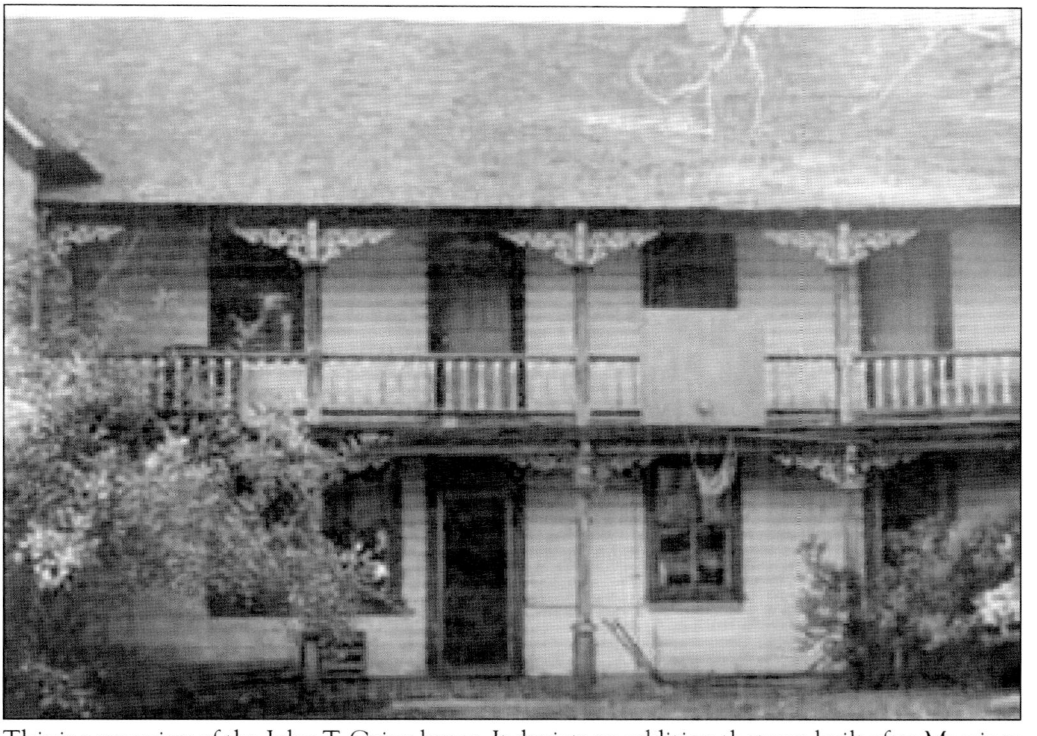

This is a rear view of the John T. Caine home. It depicts an addition that was built after Marriner W. Merrill bought the home for his fifth wife, Elna Jonsson Merrill. This home contained a secret room where Apostle Merrill could take refuge and hide from federal deputies, who hunted him for being a polygamist.

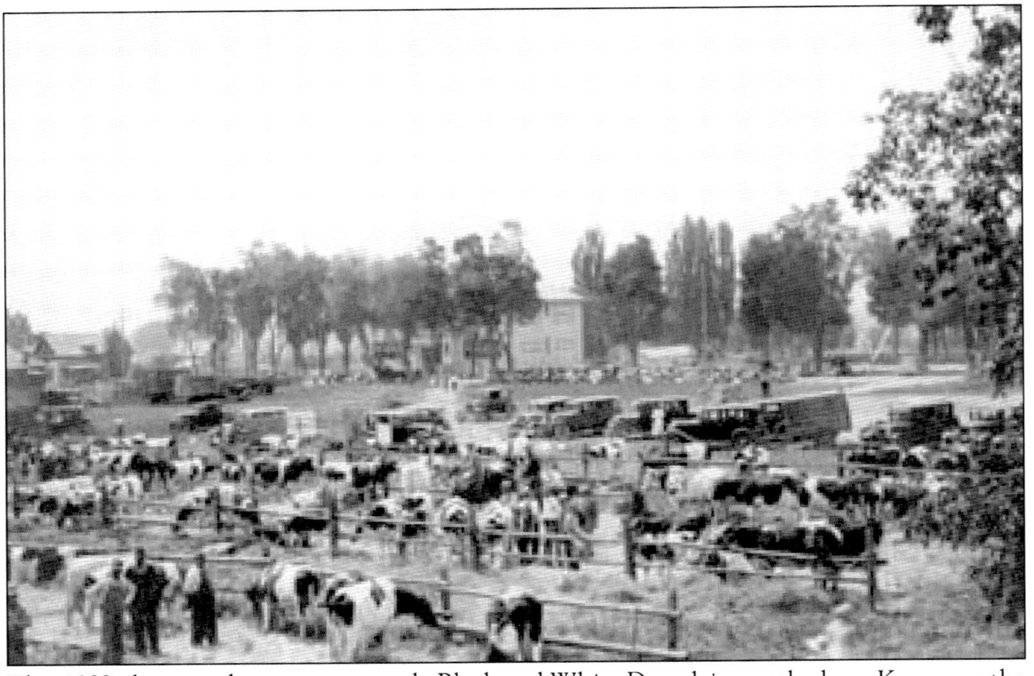

This 1933 photograph captures an early Black and White Days dairy cattle show. Known as the largest cattle show west of the Mississippi, for years Black and White Days has been attracting proud dairy farmers eager to show off their finest animals. This image was shot from the east, looking west over what are now softball and soccer fields. Notice the old Richmond Park School, which was demolished in the 1990s.

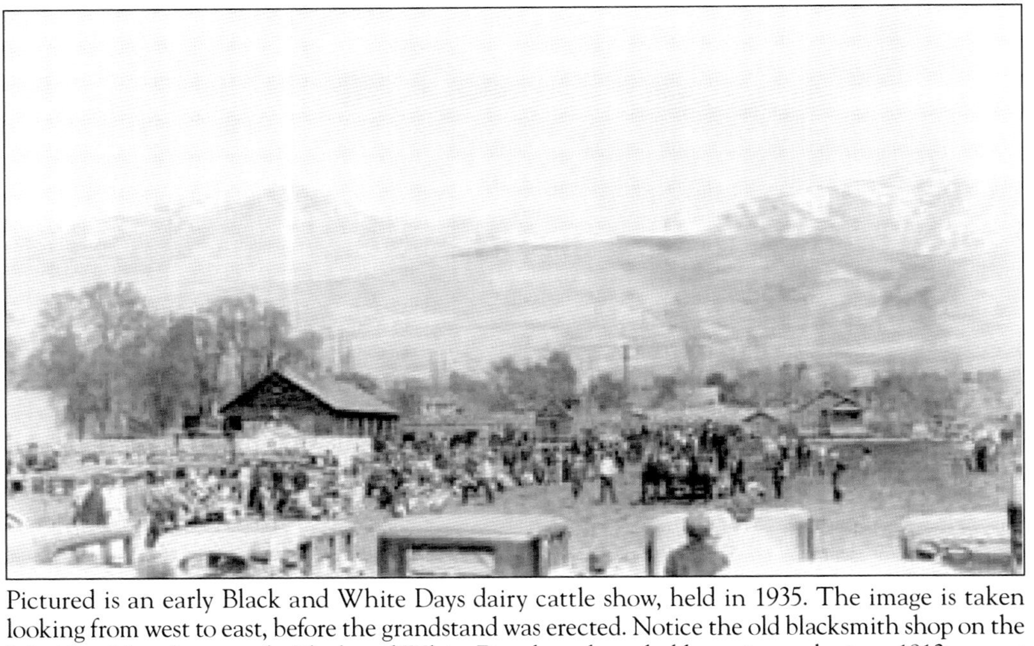

Pictured is an early Black and White Days dairy cattle show, held in 1935. The image is taken looking from west to east, before the grandstand was erected. Notice the old blacksmith shop on the left side of the photograph. Black and White Days have been held continuously since 1913, except for in 1914, when an outbreak of flu and hand, foot, and mouth disease interrupted the show.

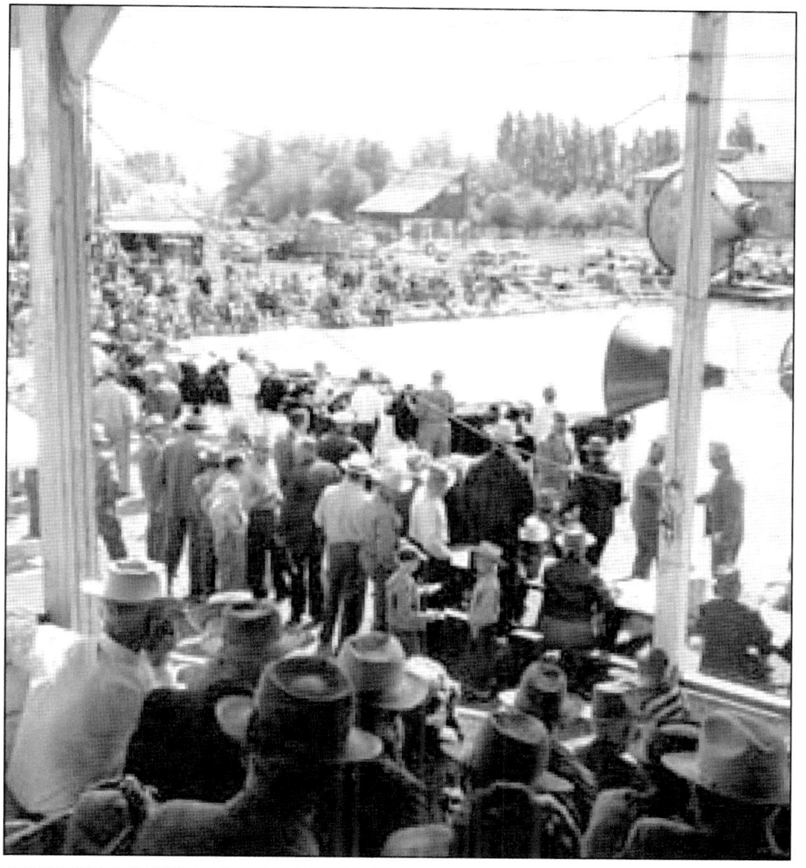

The Black and White Days dairy cattle show is pictured sometime in the 1950s. Looking from east to west, Ute's Dairy and Park School are visible in the background. The gentlemen are wearing hats and some of the girls in the crowd are wearing bobby socks. From the 1950s through the 1970s, there was usually a carnival with rides and a midway in town during the celebration.

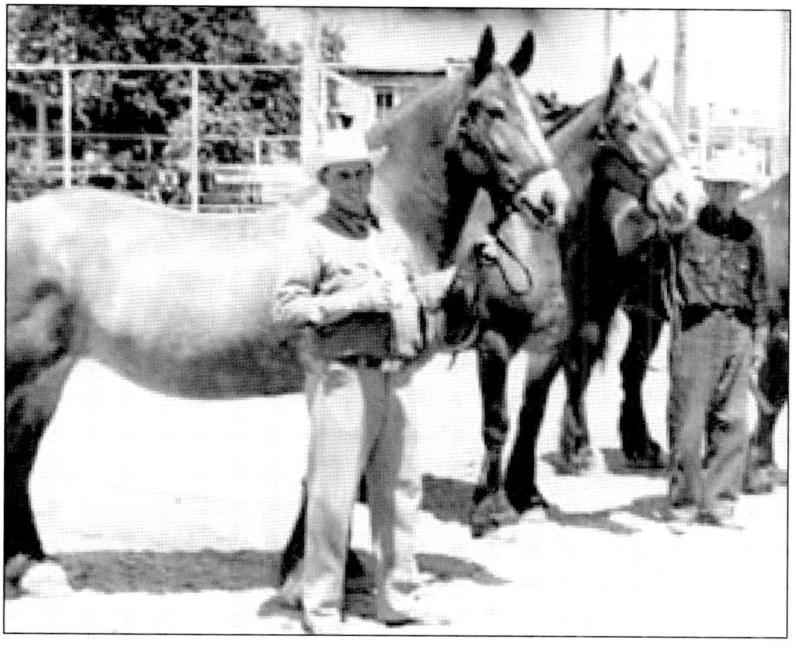

Richmond resident and dairy farmer Leon Webb won first prize at the horse show portion of Black and White Days on May 20, 1955. The show is held annually during the third week of May. The dairy cattle part of the celebration is widely touted as the largest west of the Mississippi River.

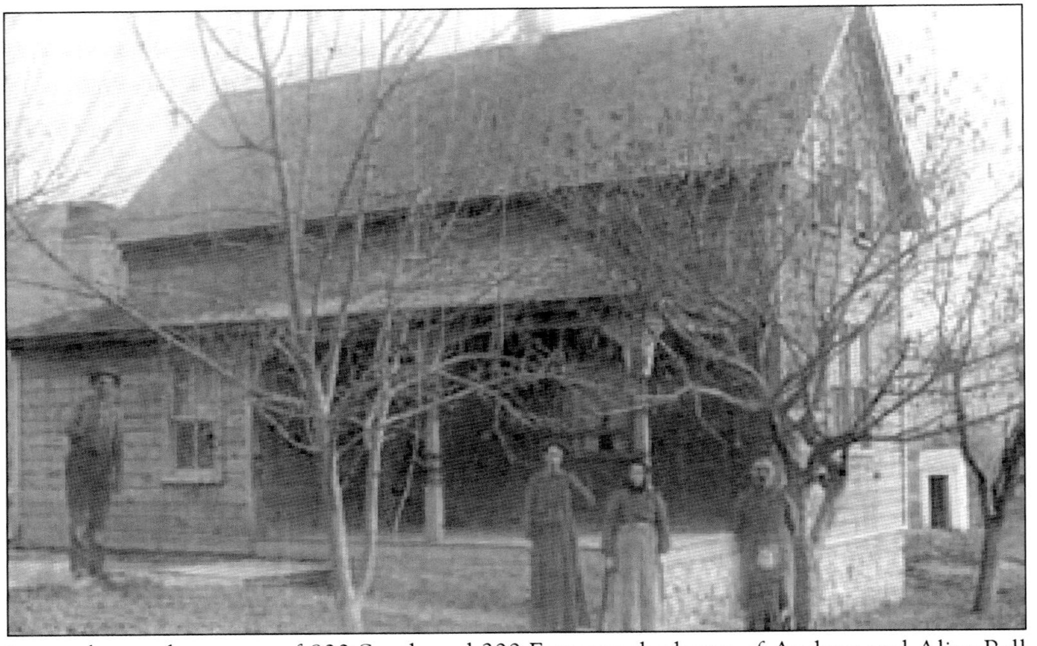

Located near the corner of 800 South and 300 East was the home of Andrew and Alice Bell Feltman. They lived there with their children: Nettie, Anne, Lorena, Pearl, and Matt. Typical of this era, the home has a rock foundation and there is an outhouse in the backyard. Many subzero midnight runs were undoubtedly made to that little building. (Courtesy of Judy Tripp.)

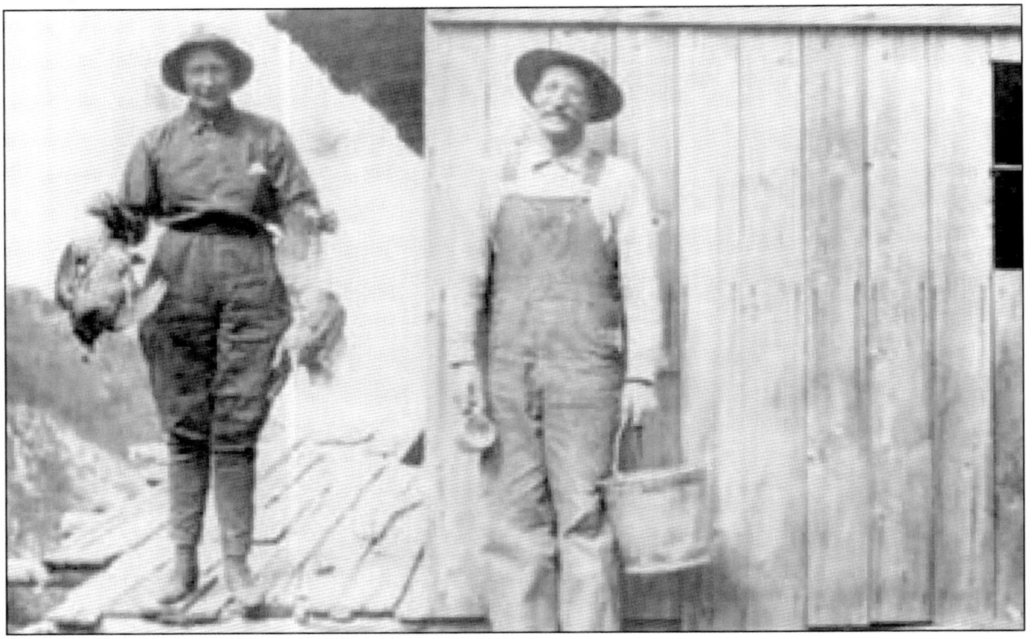

Pictured are H.M. "Bud" Egan and his daughter Lou outside the shack at the Egan Mine. The Egan Mine was located in the right-hand fork of City Creek Canyon. Edna Egan, wife of Horace "Doc" Egan, claimed that they never got enough out of the mine to do anything with, just enough to keep them coming back.

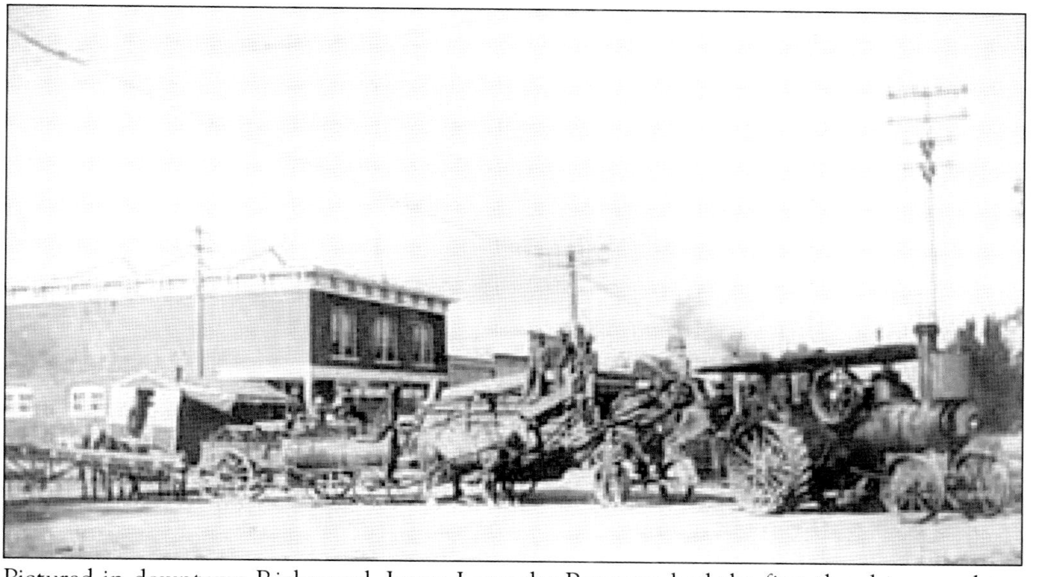

Pictured in downtown Richmond, James Lavender Bateman had the first threshing machine in the valley. James would haul the thresher throughout the area, hiring out himself and his machine to do custom threshing all week. He would bring the machine home on weekends. It was an amazing piece of equipment that certainly made the harvest season easier.

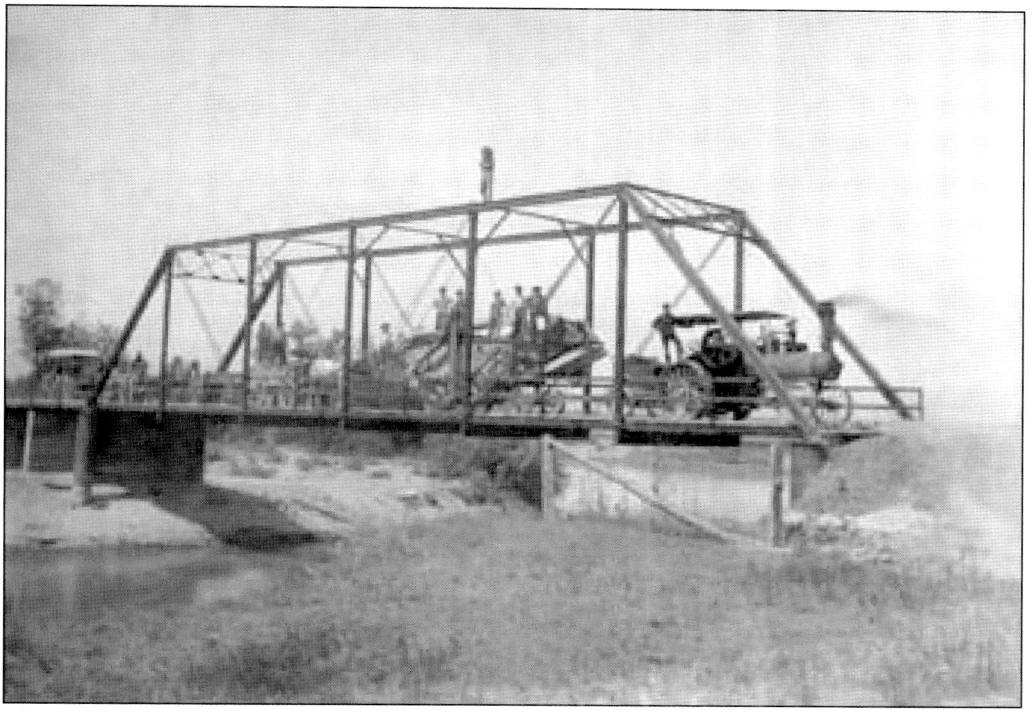

This image, taken in the 1920s on the Bear River Bridge west of Richmond, includes James Lavender Bateman's threshing machine. Fred Bateman (right) is standing on the steam engine, and James is standing on the front of the separator. James suffered a stroke that left him bedridden the last five years of his life. He died March 16, 1933. (Courtesy of Zelda Stoddard.)

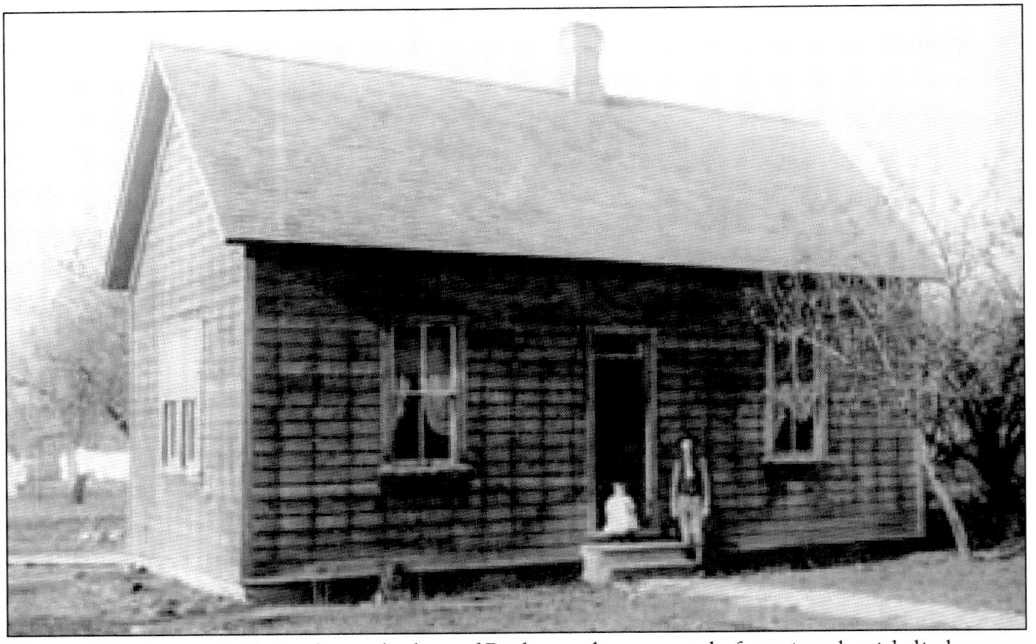

Many of the homes built in the early days of Richmond were purely functional, with little or no thought put into decorative touches. The identities of the man and child pictured are unknown, but the house presents a good example of basic construction. Paint was too expensive for many, and even the ingredients for whitewash were hard to come by. Landscaping did not become commonplace until much later.

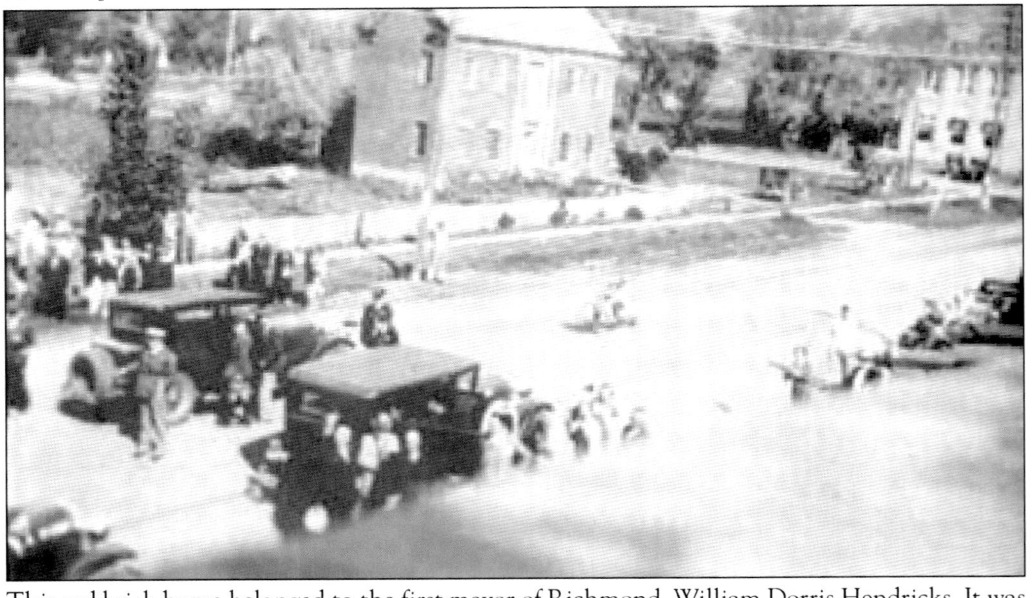

This red brick home belonged to the first mayor of Richmond, William Dorris Hendricks. It was located on the northwest corner of Main and State Streets, where the city office building now stands. The occasion of this photograph was the visit of John Nance Garner, who was running for the office of vice president of the United States in 1932. He won and served under Franklin Delano Roosevelt.

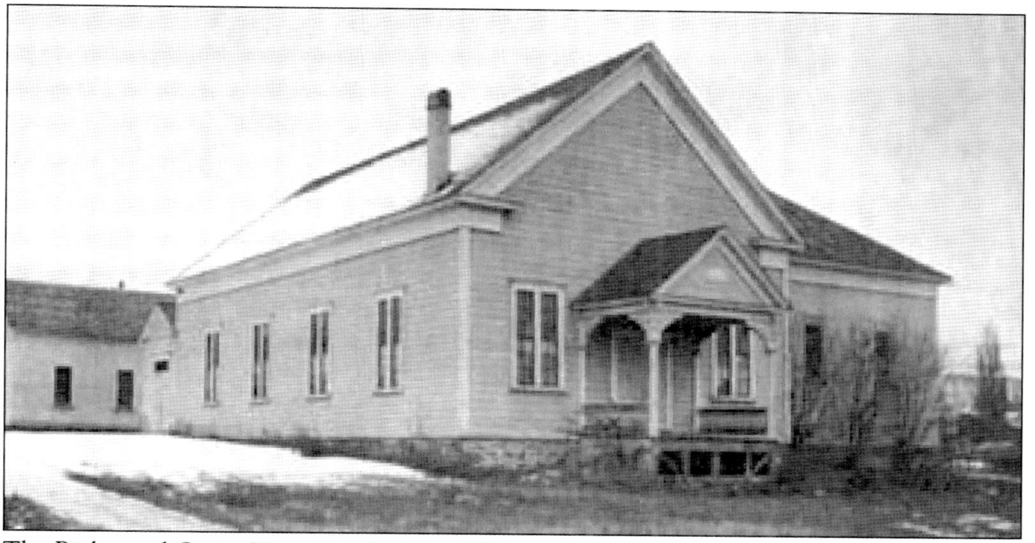

The Richmond Opera House was built in 1883 on the corner of Main Street and State Street, where the post office now stands. It was the site of many cultural and social events, including plays, concerts, dances, church meetings, professional wrestling matches, and lectures, including one by Helen Keller. August Schow, a local cabinetmaker and undertaker, stored coffins under the stage. The Relief Society Building, which still stands, can be seen in the background.

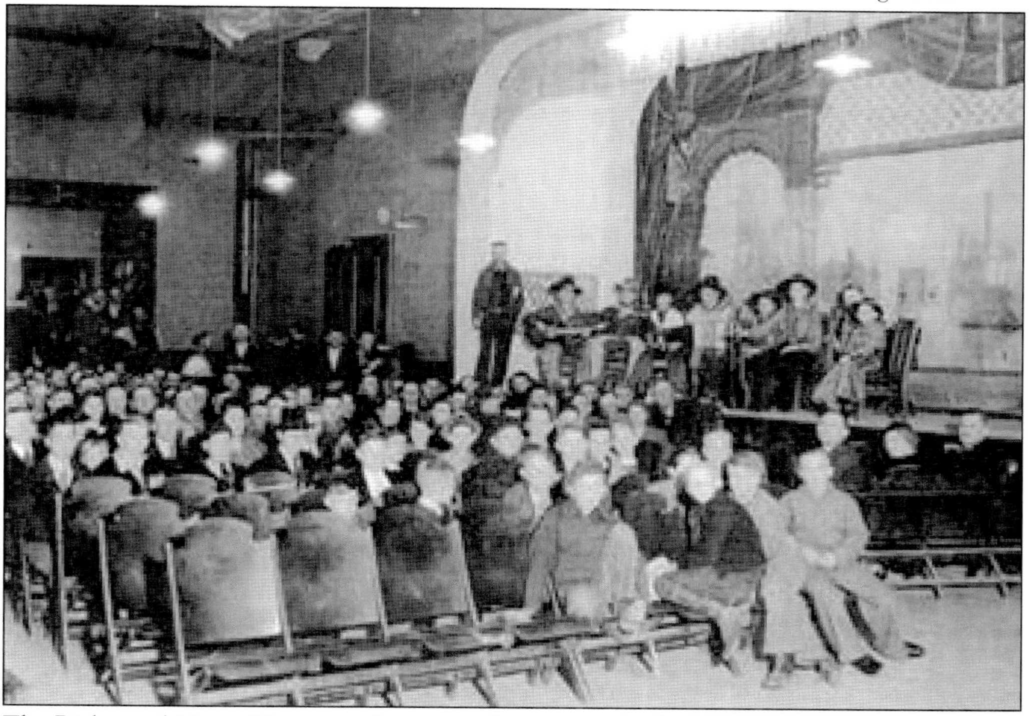

The Richmond Opera House was known as the center of cultural events in Richmond. It was built in 1883 and stood until the 1940s. This is a photograph of one such cultural event, taken in about 1910. A Western band is on the stage. People of all ages enjoyed the opera house. Some of the seats were salvaged and can be seen today in the Historic Relief Society Building.

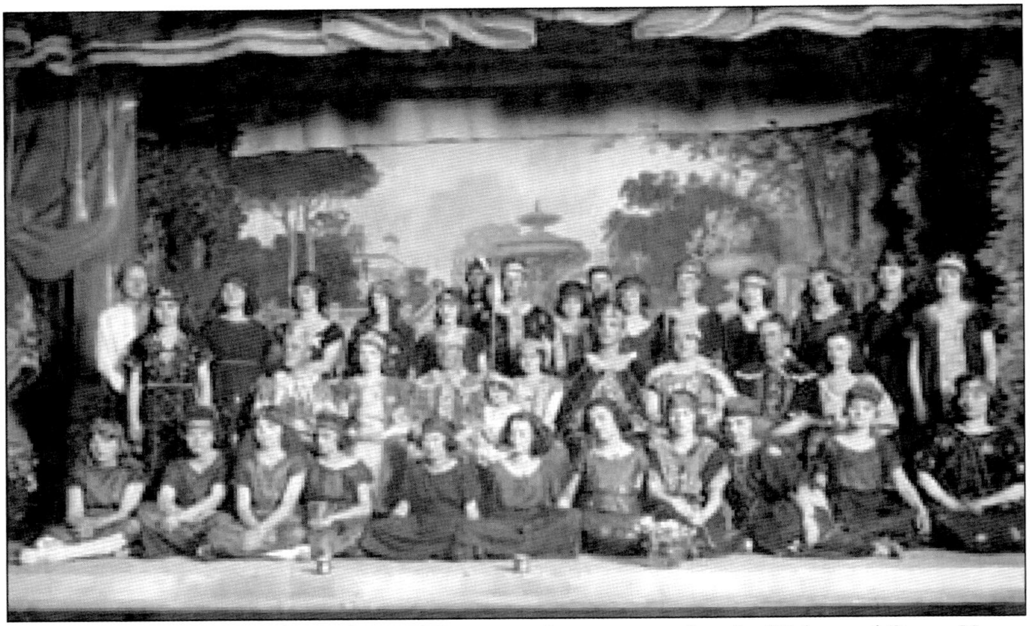

Pictured are the cast members of one of the many plays presented at the Richmond Opera House by local theatrical societies. This particular play was performed in October 1921. The opera house was also used for dances, roller-skating, professional wrestling matches, and lectures. Helen Keller once spoke there while on a cross-country tour.

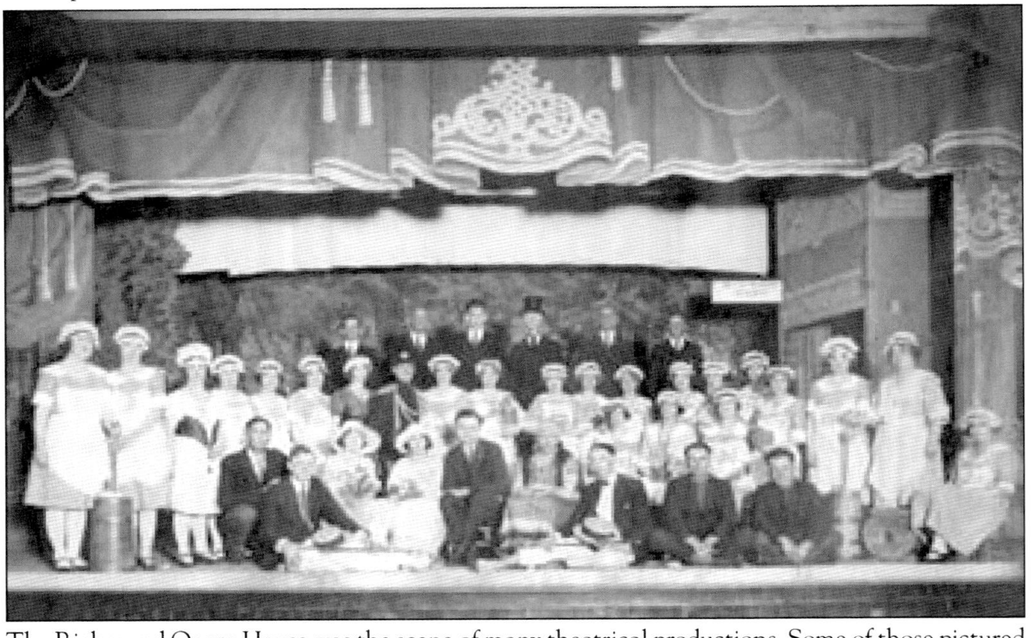

The Richmond Opera House was the scene of many theatrical productions. Some of those pictured are Lee Peterborg, Clara Anderson, Alfreda Olson, Virginia Hendricks, Clara Johnson, Iris Norris, Ruby Johnson, Elizabeth Webb Hendricks, Agnes Erickson Bair, Venice Hope Rasmussen, Esther Anderson Homer, Nell Webb, Evelyn Thompson Webb, Fred Clark, Alny Olsen, Mary Wilmont Smith, Jim Christopherson, and Orval Christensen.

This is the Woodland home at 39 South State. Pictured are, from left to right, Ezra Woodland, Nielsine "Sena" Dorthea Thompson Woodland, and Sarah Woodland. Sena met her husband, Alfred Woodland, in Richmond. She spoke no English, and he spoke no Danish. Love has a language all its own, and Sena and Alfred were married in 1876. They went on to have 10 children and a happy life.

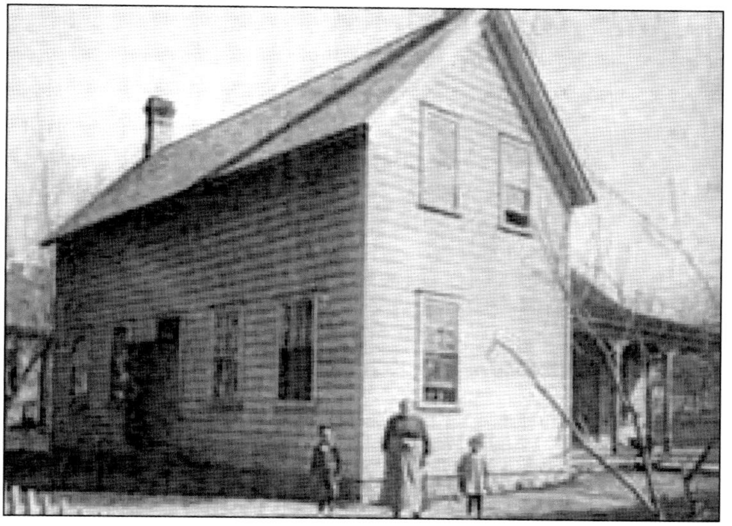

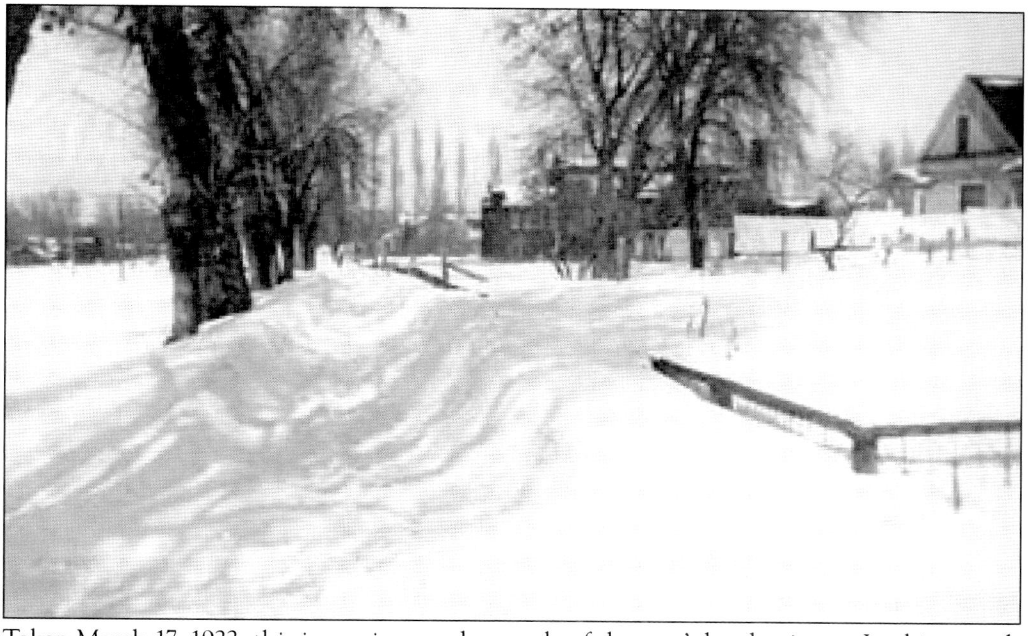

Taken March 17, 1922, this image is a good example of the area's harsh winters. Looking north from the corner of State Street and 400 South, the Richmond South Ward Church of Jesus Christ of Latter-day Saints Building can be seen behind the trees. Visible on the right is a portion of Lorenzo Murray's house, complete with laundry on the clothesline. Note how the snow covers the top of the fence, which measures its depth at three feet. (Courtesy of Cheri Housley.)

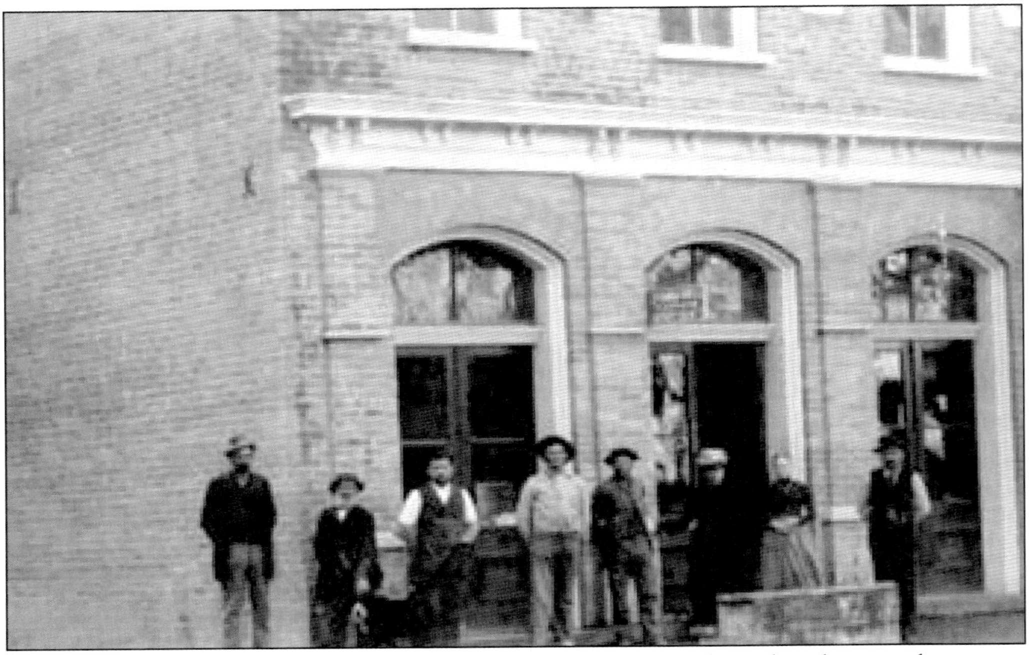

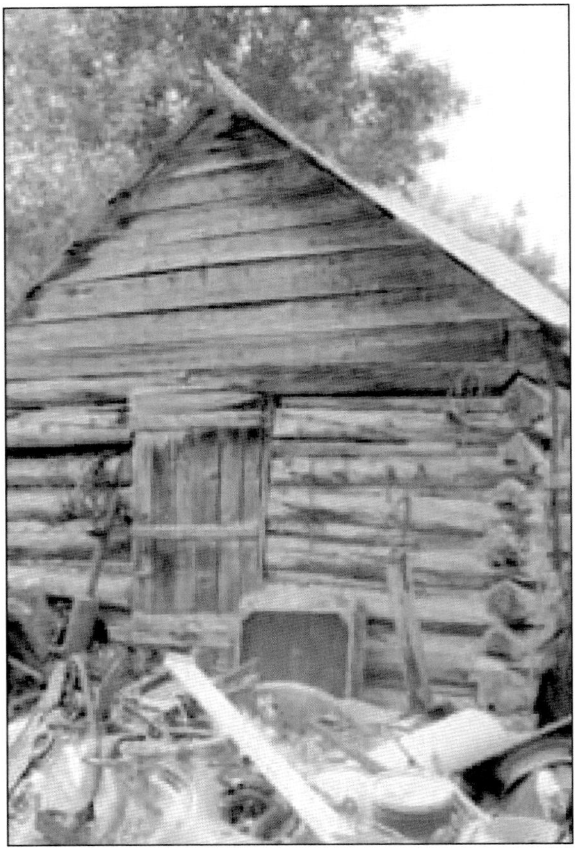

The people in this photograph are unidentified but are assumed to be Richmond residents. They are pictured standing in front of the Richmond Cooperative Mercantile on the corner of Main Street and State Street around 1878. Note the "Public Telephone Station" sign. Home telephones were a rarity at that time. People would often line up to wait their turn on the telephone.

Pictured is John Bair's log home that was in the Brower Springs settlement. It stands at 145 West 200 South. John was one of the founding fathers of Richmond and was very active in establishing and organizing the town. This is likely the oldest remaining building in Richmond.

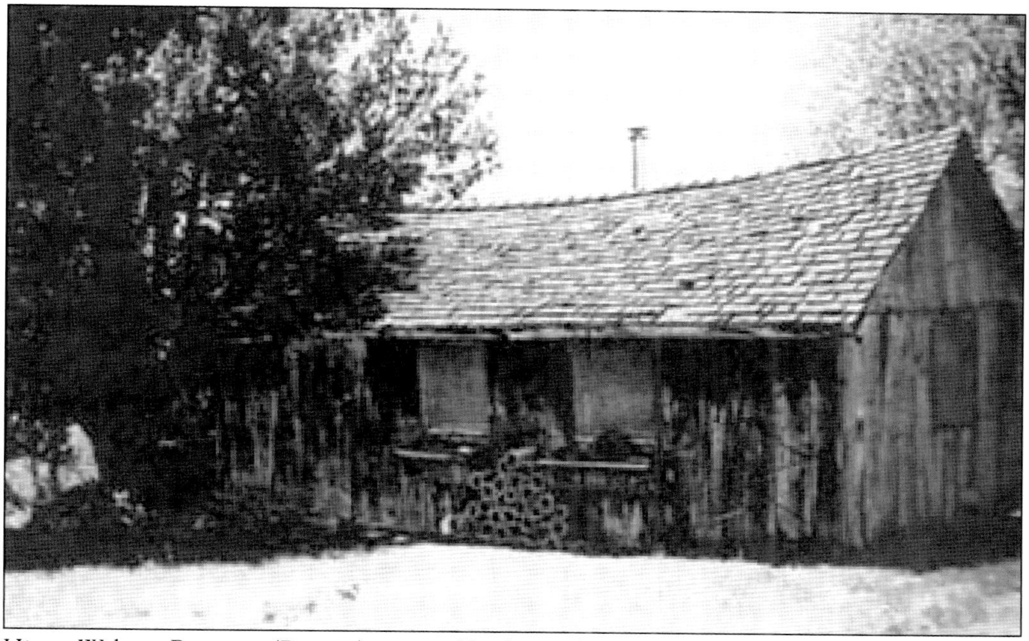

Hiram Webster Bowman (Boman) operated both a molasses mill and a sawmill on Cherry Creek, northeast of Richmond. He built this home on the property and fenced it with a wall made from rocks gathered in the field. Parts of the wall remain today. The house still stands and has been fairly well maintained. (Courtesy of Delores Buttars.)

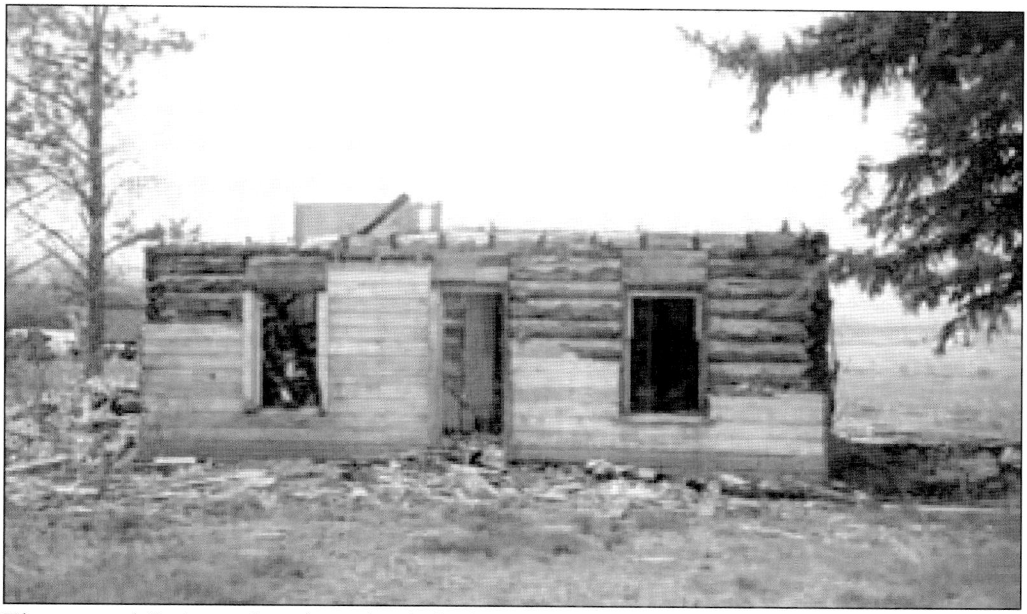

The original Richmond settlers of 1859 built a small settlement at Brower Springs, west of the current highway. Brigham Young visited in 1860 and advised them to build a fort to the east for better protection from the Indians. The settlers complied, abandoning their original homes. This cabin, demolished in 1998, stood on the corner of 400 West 200 South; it is believed to have been one of the original buildings of the first settlement.

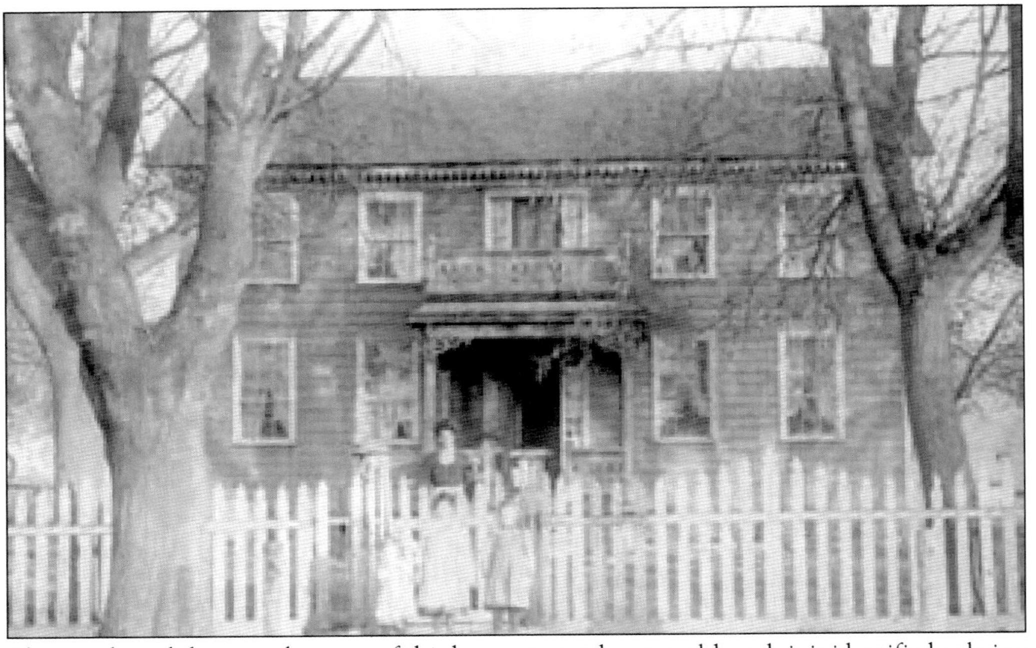

The people and the exact location of this home are not known, although it is identified as being on State Street. Houses of this type were common in Richmond. Even though times were hard, extra care was put into make this home appealing. The gingerbread trim on the roof and balcony and the curlicues on the porch show a pride in ownership.

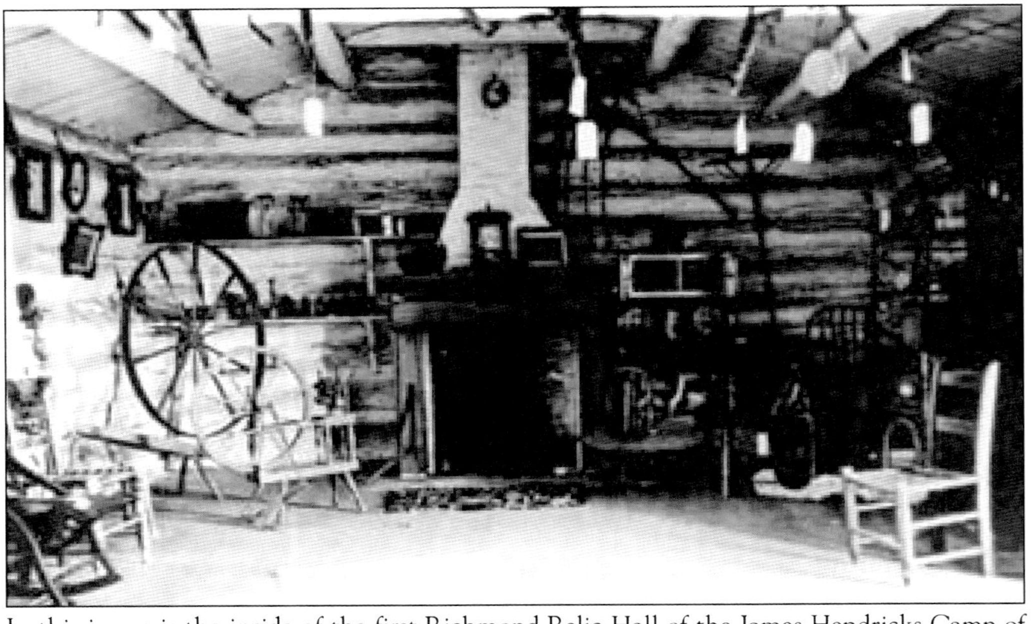

In this image is the inside of the first Richmond Relic Hall of the James Hendricks Camp of the Daughters of Utah Pioneers. The first meeting was held September 17, 1909, with Capt. Harriet Hogan Fisher presiding. Richmond had the first formal relic hall in the state. Items that are donated to the relic hall become the property of the International Daughters of Utah Pioneers organization.

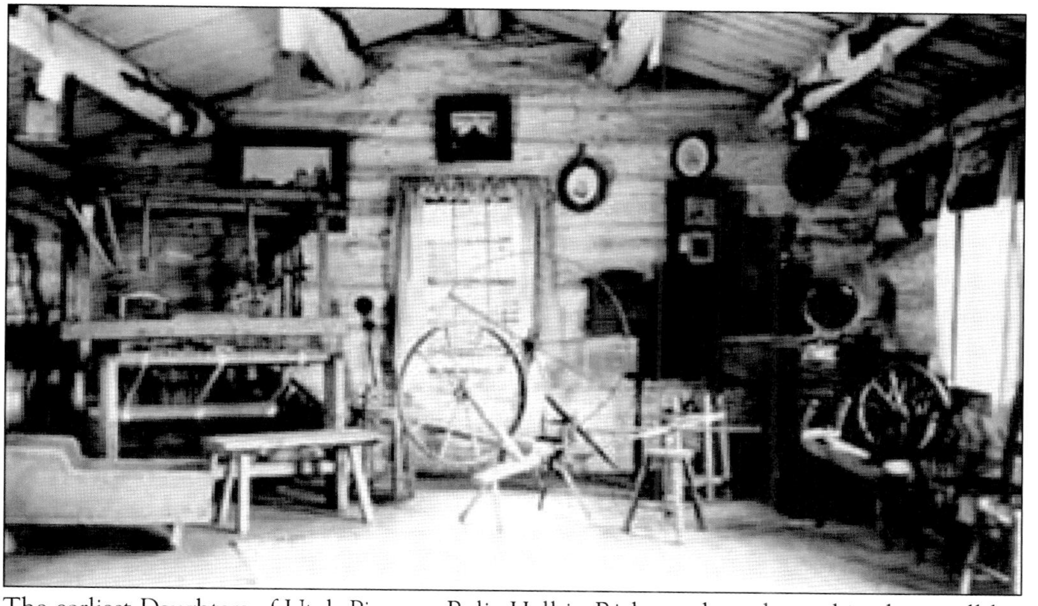

The earliest Daughters of Utah Pioneers Relic Hall in Richmond was housed in this small log cabin. As the collection grew over the years, the cabin was deemed too small, and in 1920, the collection was moved to the Relief Society Building, where it stayed until being moved to its current home in 1959. The collection is still growing, and relevant pioneer-era items are gladly accepted for display.

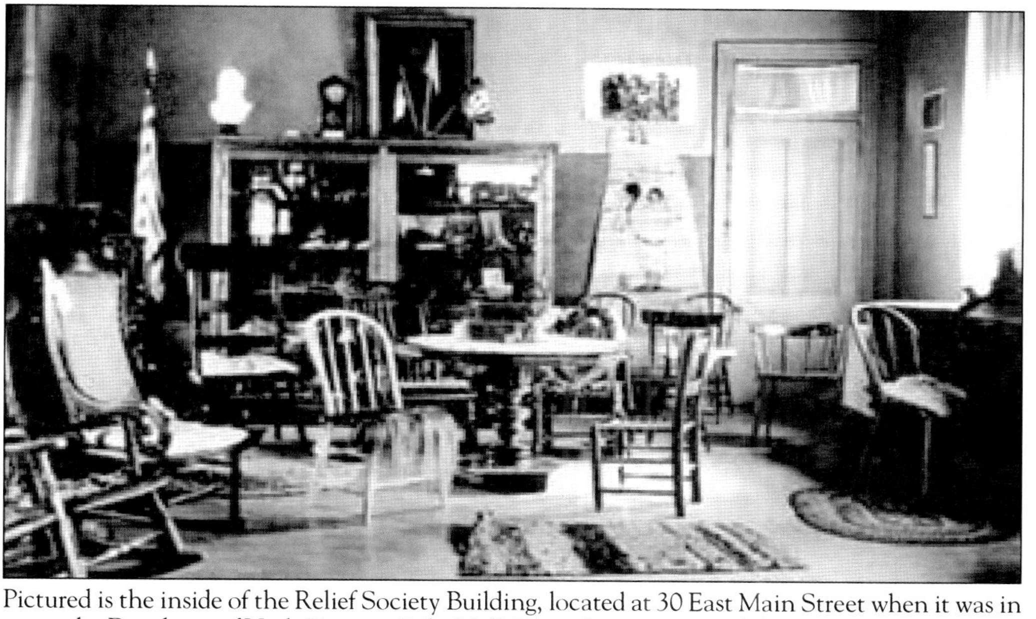

Pictured is the inside of the Relief Society Building, located at 30 East Main Street when it was in use as the Daughters of Utah Pioneers Relic Hall. The relics were moved there on January 25, 1920, and kept on display until January 1959, when Richmond City bought the old Bishop's Storehouse, which became the new James Hendricks's Daughters of Utah Pioneers Camp Relic Hall.

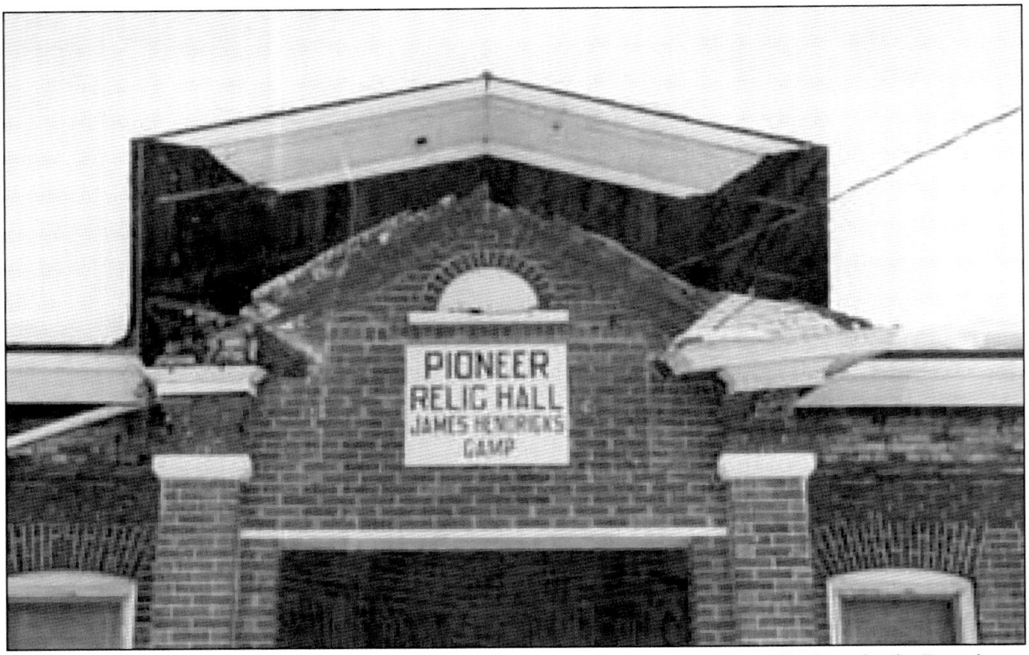

The winter of 1984 was a hard one. Damage was done to the James and Drusilla Hendricks Daughters of Utah Pioneers Relic Hall. The roof caved in to the attic, but to everyone's amazement, there was no damage done to the inside of the building or to the relics. The Lion's Club donated its time to rebuild the roof and did some remodeling inside at the same time. Members put paneling over the old lath and plaster walls, put carpet over the hardwood floors, and installed an acoustical tile ceiling. The relic hall is a well-loved and oft-visited place. Many local school classes make an annual field trip to see the wide range of items housed within its walls.

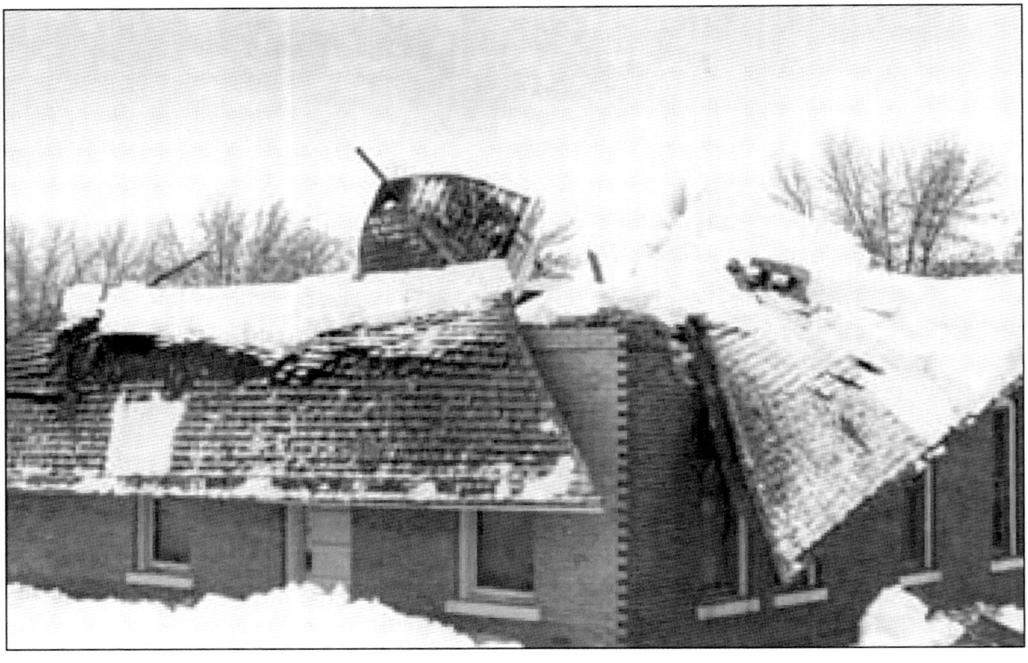

Six

Preserving Our Heritage

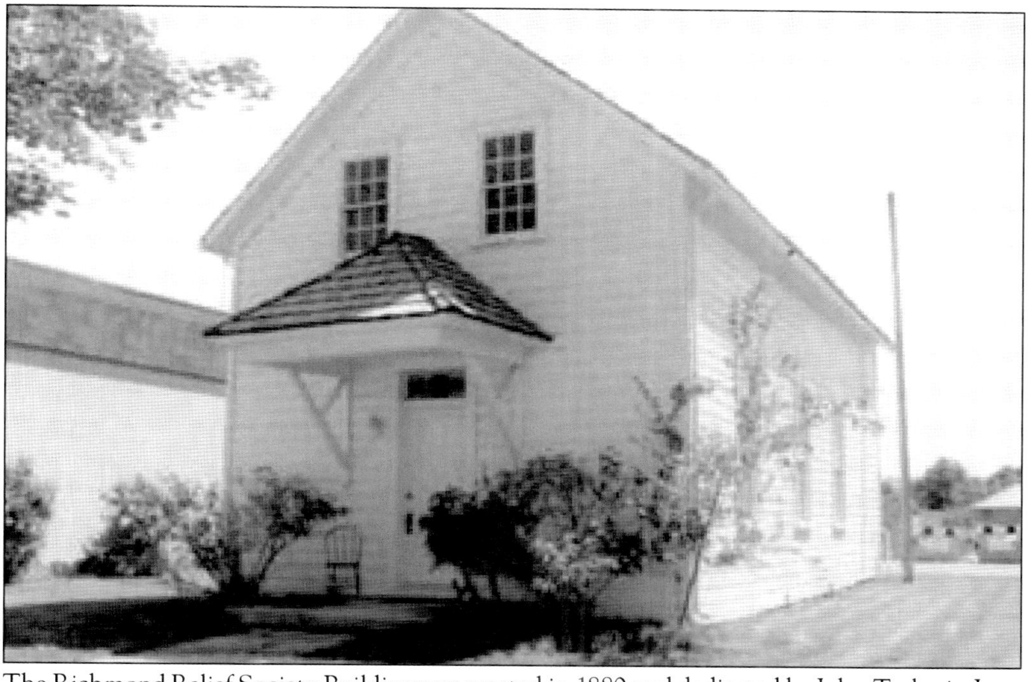

The Richmond Relief Society Building was erected in 1880 and dedicated by John Taylor in June 1882. It is a two-story frame structure measuring 21 feet by 41 feet. The building is located at 30 East Main and sits on its original rock foundation. A committee was appointed to raise money for the structure. Instrumental were Mary Jane Hendricks, Francis Traveller, Lydia Burnham, and Almira J. Merrill. Another committee of women undertook the restoration in the 1990s.

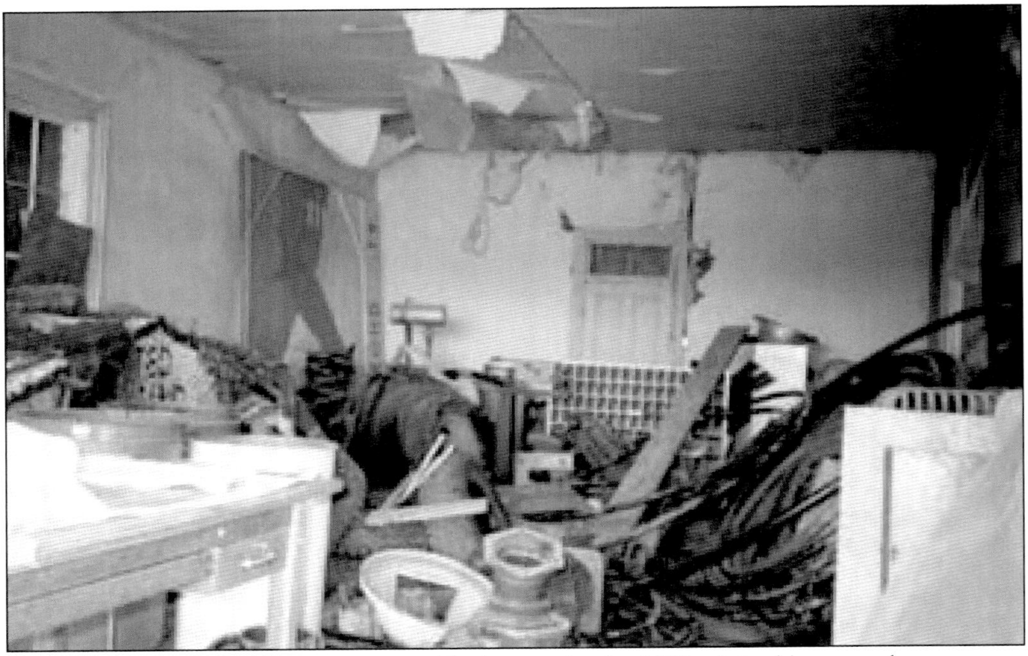

The Relief Society Building was in terrible disarray by the 1990s. It had been used as a storage shed for years. The front door is the original, but the transom has since been replaced with stained glass. A hole was cut in the back wall and a garage door was installed for the convenience of storing large items. That door has been removed and the wall rebuilt. Notice the old boxes from the post office, which were used when it was housed in the city office building. Back in those days, boxes did not have doors with locks. People never thought about taking mail that was not theirs. Times have surely changed.

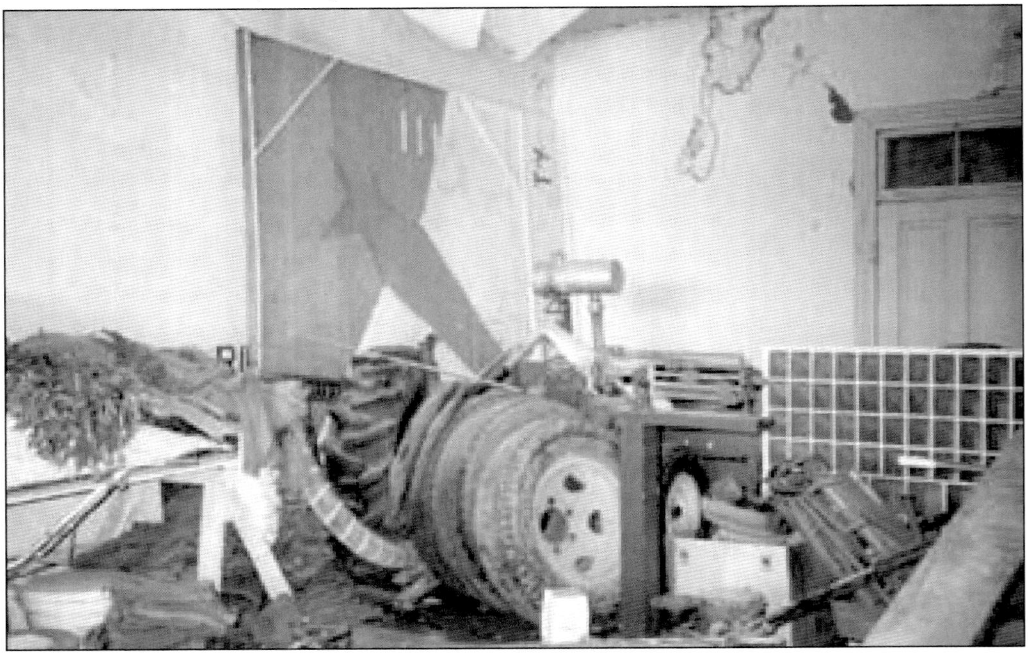

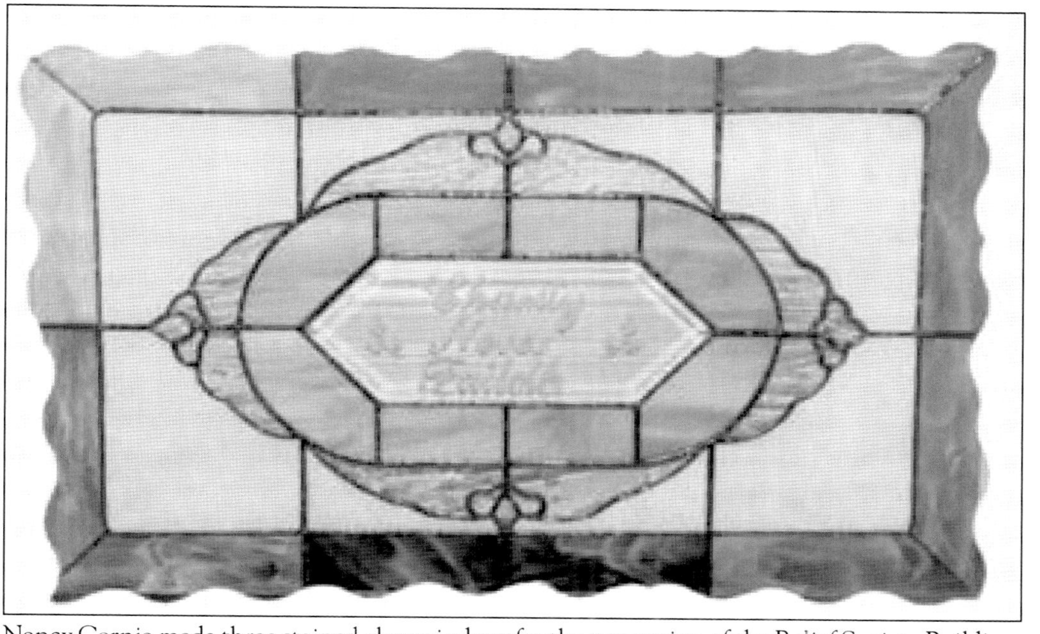

Nancy Cornia made three stained glass windows for the restoration of the Relief Society Building. She donated her time and charged only for the materials. Many people contributed donations of money or labor to bring about the restoration of this building. Many individuals and businesses from throughout the valley rallied together for the cause. The project would not have been possible without the quiet help of Mayor Kip Panter.

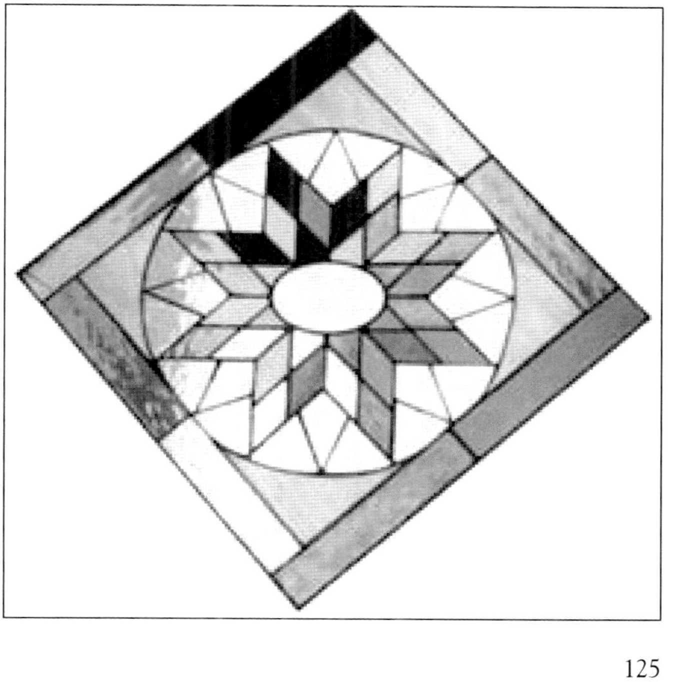

This window, located under the stairs in the back of the building, was designed by Kathy Jones, who used an old star quilt for a pattern. Star quilts were popular among the early settlers. It is very likely that many have been made during the quilting bees in the Relief Society Building.

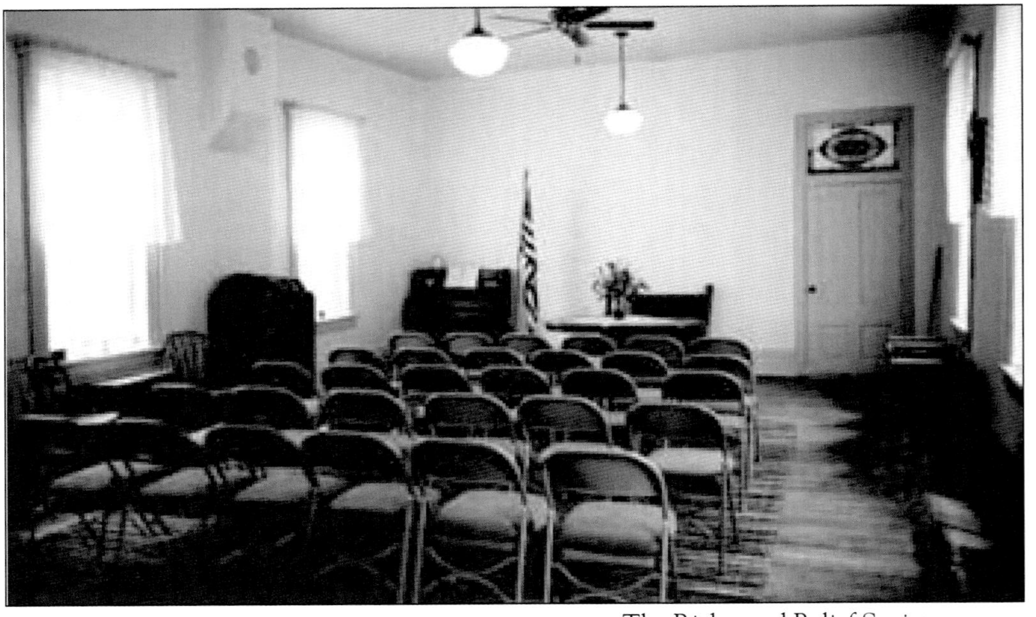

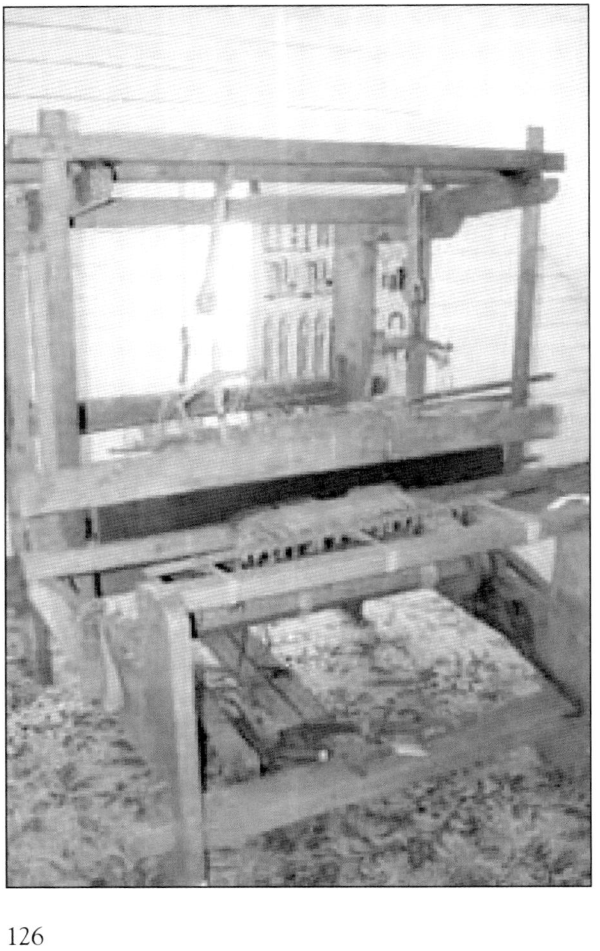

The Richmond Relief Society Building is city-owned. The Daughters of Utah Pioneers meet here monthly, and it is available to anyone else to rent. The upstairs houses a collection of North Cache memorabilia, including report cards dating back to 1921. The North Cache Bulldog also resides in the attic, along with old sports uniforms, prom dresses, and photograph albums. The interior of the main floor is pictured after restoration.

Found in the attic of the Relief Society Building, this loom dates back to a design from the 1700s. It was brought across the plains and reassembled. If the Relief Society Building had been demolished, this treasure would have gone down with the ship. It has its original shuttle, and with a little restringing, it would be in perfect working order. A partially woven piece of linen is still in place.

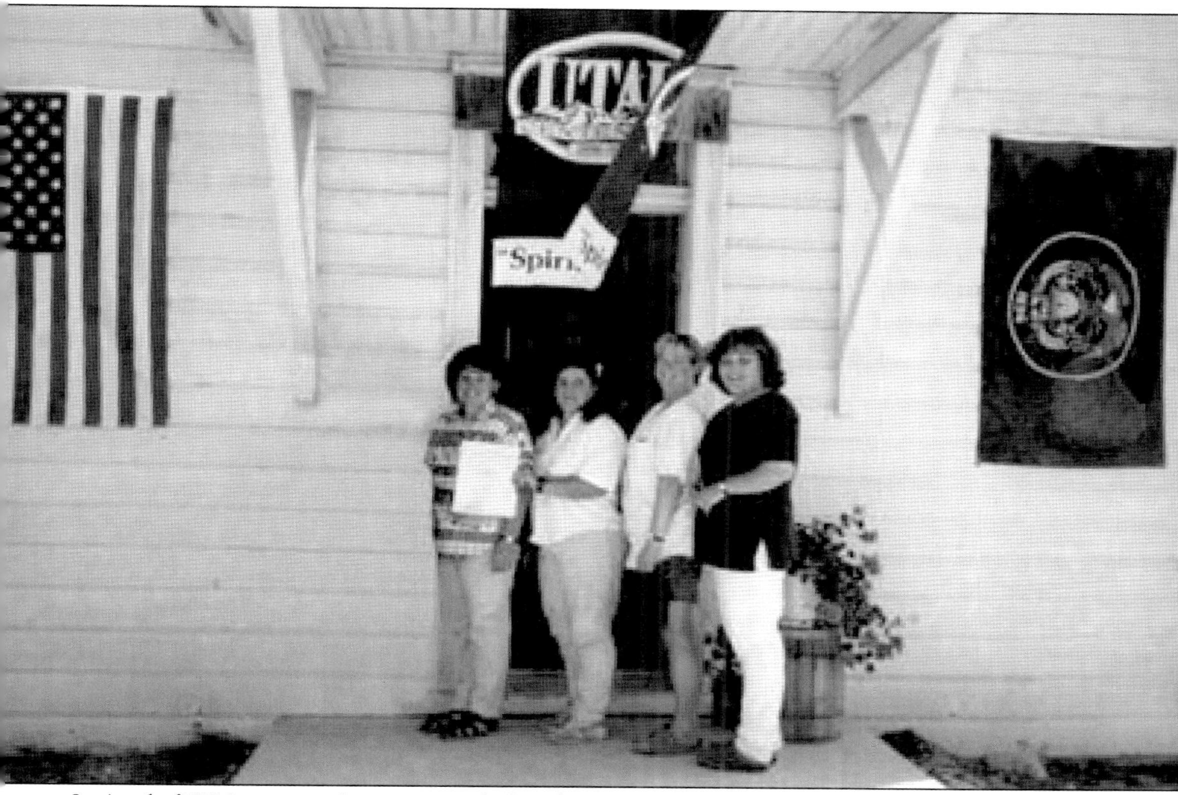

In April of 1996, a group of women went before the city council to offer an alternative to the proposed demolition of the old Relief Society Building. With the support of Mayor Kip Panter, permission was granted to the group to restore the building to its original design. Upon completion, it would be turned over to the city for use as a community meeting place. Restoration began in 1996, and it was placed in the National Register of Historic Places. Under the direction of (pictured from left to right) Marie Lundgreen, Marty Higham, Kathy Jones, and Cheri Housley, contributions of labor, money, and materials were amassed. Many people and organizations donated to the cause, and renovations were completed in 1998.